D0961578

WORDS OF FIRE

ANTHONY COLLINGS

WORDS OF FIRE

*Independent Journalists Who Challenge
Dictators, Druglords, and Other
Enemies of a Free Press*

New York University Press • *New York and London*

NEW YORK UNIVERSITY PRESS
New York and London

Library of Congress Cataloging-in-Publication Data
Collings, Anthony.
Words of fire : independent journalists who challenge dictators,
druglords, and other enemies of a free press / Anthony Collings.
p.   cm.
Includes bibliographical references and index.
ISBN 0-8147-1605-9 — ISBN 0-8147-1606-7 (pbk.)
1. Journalists—Biography. 2. Government and the press.
3. Journalism—Political aspects. I. Title.
PN4820.C65 2001
070'.92'2—dc21   2001000040
[B]

New York University Press books are printed on acid-free paper,
and their binding materials are chosen for strength and durability.

Manufactured in the United States of America

10 9 8 7 6 5 4 3 2 1

To the more than thirteen hundred journalists who have been killed since 1812 in the course of their professional work reporting the news

I am willing to sacrifice all I have for the country's modernization and journalism.

—Chinese journalist Gao Yu, during appeal
of her prison sentence

Contents

Acknowledgments   xi

Map: World Press Freedom   xii–xiii

Introduction   1

I   Looking for Trouble: The Behavior of Independent Journalists

1   "They Are the News": Facing Mexican Druglords   13

2   She Had to Be There: Taking Risks in Russia   26

3   Opening the Door: Courage in Asia   36

4   Guerrilla Journalists: Underground in Nigeria   44

5   A Precious Pen: Defiance around the World   53

II   Pushing the Envelope: Stories That Trigger Attack

6   The General's Mercedes: Crime and Corruption   65

7   A Veiled Woman: The Separatists   77

8   Brother against Brother: Civil War   89

9   In the Thick of It: Protests and Riots   99

10   Money at Stake: Economic Secrets   105

11   The President's Mistress: Exposés   113

12   We Are Not Amused: Satire   120

III   Shoot the Messenger: Types of Attacks on Journalists

13   We Have Ways: Violence and Imprisonment   135

14   We Have Other Ways: Legal and Economic Pressures   142

IV   The Messenger Reacts: Responding to Attacks

15   Chilled or Defiant: The Painful Choice   153

16   Cat and Computer Mouse: Using the Internet   167

17   The Great Firewall: China and the Internet   186

18   Send in Uncle Walter: Advocacy Groups   195

       Conclusion: Tomorrow's News: The Outlook   210

       Notes   225
       Bibliography   253
       Index   255
       About the Author   269

Acknowledgments

This book was made possible by support from the Department of Communication Studies at the University of Michigan, including travel grants from the Marsh Fund. I especially thank Department Chair Michael Traugott for so much help and encouragement over the years. Others in the department who have helped tremendously include Susan Douglas, Nick Valentino, and Derek Vaillant, as well as Victoria Green and the office support staff.

I also thank everyone at the Committee to Protect Journalists, including current and former staffers Bill Orme, Ann Cooper, Judy Leynse, Judy Blank, Joel Simon, Kavita Menon, and Lin Neumann. Special thanks go to Alan Knight at Queensland University, Ellen Mickiewicz at Duke University, and Kenneth Lieberthal at the University of Michigan.

Journalists around the world who have been kind enough to share their experiences and thoughts include Khaled Abu Aker, Liu Binyan, J. Jesús Blancornelas, Miguel Cervantes Sahagún, Ying Chan, Shieh Chung-Liang, Mike Chinoy, Mick Deane, Mark Feldstein, Li Hongkuan, Viktor Ivancic, Kin-ming Liu, Freedom Neruda, Zamir Niazi, Dapo Olorunyomi, and Yelena Masyuk.

I am deeply indebted to Niko Pfund at New York University Press for his editorial guidance.

Finally, I thank family and friends, the most important people of all, especially my sons Andrew, Daniel, and Matthew; my friend Jim Barnett; and my life companion Alesia.

CANADA

WESTERN
EUROPE

UNITED STATES

MEXICO

NIGE

FREE

United States, Canada, Western Europe, Estonia, Latvia, Lithuania, Poland, Czech Republic, Slovakia, Hunga
Bulgaria, South Africa, Botswana, Mali, Benin, Israel, India, Nepal, Bangladesh, Thailand, Japan, South Kore
Mongolia, Hong Kong, Taiwan, Philippines, Papua New Guinea, Australia, New Zealand

PARTLY FREE

Latin America (except Cuba), Albania, Bosnia, Macedonia, Croatia, Yugoslavia, Romania, Moldova, Ukraine,
Russia, Turkey, Georgia, Armenia, Jordan, Kuwait, Pakistan, Indonesia, Morocco, Senegal, Guinea Bissau,
Burkina Faso, Nigeria, Gabon, Central African Republic, Uganda, Tanzania, Malawi, Mozambique, Madagasca
Namibia, Lesotho

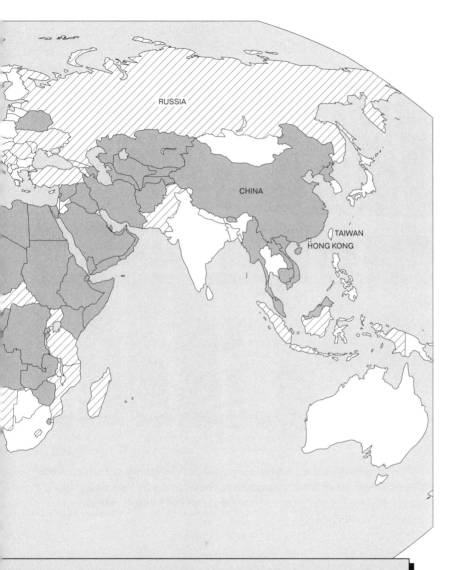

RUSSIA

CHINA

TAIWAN
HONG KONG

MAP OF WORLD PRESS FREEDOM

NOT FREE

Cuba, Belarus, Algeria, Libya, Egypt, Sudan, (and other African countries unless otherwise indicated),Syria, Iraq, Iran, Saudi Arabia, Afghanistan, China, Kazakhstan, (and other Central Asian countries), Myanmar, Laos, Cambodia, Vietnam, Malaysia, Singapore, North Korea

Source: This map is based on two online maps and one book. The online maps are "Freedom of the Press Worldwide in 2000," on the Web site of Reporters Sans Frontières, www.rsf.fr, accessed May 2000, and "Map of Press Freedom 2000," on the Web site of Freedom House, www.freedomhouse.org/pfs2000/pfsmap2k.pdf, accessed May 2000. The book is *Attacks on the Press in 1999* (New York: Committee to Protect Journalists, March 2000). Note: Political changes in Yugoslavia and Croatia in 2000 are also reflected in the map.

Waving to fellow journalists from behind his prison bars in Tekirdag, Turkey, editor Ocak Isik Yurtçu received an International Press Freedom Award on July 16, 1997. He was imprisoned for defying a ban on articles about the Kurdish minority. Credit: AP/Wide World Photos.

Introduction

FROM BEHIND THE bars of a prison window, Ocak Isik Yurtçu grinned as he held up his award, showing it off to one hundred fellow journalists cheering outside.

It was an extraordinary scene that day, July 16, 1997, at the remote prison in Tekirdag, Turkey. Yurtçu, a stocky, bearded editor, sentenced to more than fifteen years in prison for publishing stories about the Kurdish separatist rebellion, proudly displayed a plaque naming him as a recipient of the International Press Freedom Award of the Committee to Protect Journalists.

But the day before, in San Luis Río Colorado, Mexico, there was no public cheering. Benjamín Flores González was shot dead as he walked up the driveway to his newspaper office. The brash young publisher had defied warnings by drug traffickers to drop his crusading brand of journalism. Despite the publisher's assassination, his colleagues continued to report the drug story.

That same year in Abidjan, capital of the Ivory Coast, a journalist named Freedom Neruda was released from prison after serving twelve months for a satirical article that poked fun at the country's leader. Neruda had turned down a government offer of early release from prison if he dropped an appeal. For him, dropping the appeal would be tantamount to admitting wrongdoing—and as far as Freedom Neruda was concerned, he had done nothing wrong.

At a district court in Taipei that year, two journalists won acquittal of criminal libel charges brought by a powerful local politician they had implicated in an alleged secret plan to funnel $15 million in illegal donations to the Clinton reelection campaign. One of the journalists, a short, feisty Chinese American named Ying Chan, used the Internet to help mobilize international public opinion in her favor and win the lawsuit.

These journalists have one thing in common: defiance, a refusal to be censored, as they write and speak the words of fire that antagonize those in power. These journalists and many others around the world are fighting a daily battle on the front line of freedom of the press. It's a never-ending battle between independent-minded journalists and the dictators, druglords, and other powerful forces who want them silenced. This book is an overview of that battle—who is winning, who is losing, and how new technology, including the Internet, could affect the outcome.

For journalists it can be a brutal world. Since 1812, more than thirteen hundred have been killed while reporting the news. Twenty-four lost their lives in 2000, apparently because of their professional work, according to press-freedom advocacy groups. In previous years the death toll has ranged as high as seventy-two (in 1994). For the ten years of 1990–1999, the number of journalists reported killed in the line of duty totaled 458. As William A. Orme Jr., former executive director of the New York–based Committee to Protect Journalists (CPJ), put it: "Nearly every week, a journalist somewhere in the world is killed."

In addition to those killed in 2000, at least eighty-one journalists were in prison at the end of that year because of their work. Four years earlier, a record 181 journalists were behind bars. Each year scores of reporters are attacked in other ways, ranging from beatings to death threats and harassment. In its report titled *Press Freedom Survey 2000*, the New York–based freedom advocacy group Freedom House presented grim statistics for the years 1982 through 1999. During that eighteen-year period, a total of 892 journalists were killed; 448 were kidnapped or abducted or simply disappeared; and 4,450 were arrested or detained. The world's journalists also come under legal pressures. Almost one-fourth of 186 countries surveyed in one recent year were considering imposing tough new laws making it even more difficult for journalists to do their work.

And yet, despite all the attacks on independent journalists around the world, there is actually *more* freedom of the press today than a decade ago. The cold war is over. With it has gone much of the brutal suppression of press freedom by forces on both sides, right and left, ranging from virulent anticommunist military regimes in Latin America to communist dictatorships in what was once the Soviet sphere. The rise of the Internet has brought with it a powerful new medium that is difficult for governments to censor. There is more literacy than before, and with it a growing demand for news in the form of the written word.

Perhaps the most significant condition fostering greater press freedom is the fact that there are more and more democracies in the world. A separate survey by Freedom House found that by the beginning of the twenty-first century, nearly two-thirds of the world's countries were democracies—a record number. In population terms, this means three-fifths of all the people on this planet were living in countries with democratically elected governments as the new century began.

To understand the context for attacks on journalists, the world may be divided into three groups of countries, depending on the extent of press freedom (see the map on pp. xii–xiii). In one category of countries, the overwhelming consensus of the citizenry strongly supports a free press. There, independent journalists can go about their business with relatively little impediment. The prime example is the United States, with arguably the freest press in the world, a nation that exerts a great influence on other societies as the world's only superpower and as a dominant force in business, technology, and culture.

Other areas of the world with the freest conditions for their journalists include Canada, Western Europe, some parts of the former Soviet sphere (the Baltic republics, Poland, the Czech Republic, Slovakia, Hungary, and Bulgaria), South Africa, Israel, Thailand, Japan, South Korea, Hong Kong, Taiwan, the Philippines, Australia, and New Zealand. These are the nations deemed by Freedom House to have the least onerous conditions for the press, nations where 21 percent of the world's population lives. To their number I would add India, because even with some exceptions, including censorship and harassment in the border state of Kashmir, the press in India as a whole is a free institution, thriving as a pillar of a long-established democracy.

Most of these countries with the freest press are stable democracies where dissent is tolerated and where those in power are held accountable by a number of independent institutions, including a multiparty political system, an independent judiciary, and the press. Many, but not all, are advanced industrialized nations. Often they have a capitalist, free-market economy, although free enterprise does not always guarantee a free press—as seen in Singapore, a free-market economy where the press is government controlled. In these countries with the freest press, violent attacks on journalists are rare, although they do occur, as we will see in the tragic case of Veronica Guerin of Ireland.

At the other end of the press-freedom continuum are the nations where the only recognized journalists are state employed or state controlled, such as Singapore. *Press Freedom Survey 2000* found that 40 percent of the world's population lived in those countries, the ones with basically no press freedom. The prime example is China, with a population of more than 1 billion people—about a fifth of the world's total population. That one country alone accounts for more than half of all the people in the world whose press is not free. At the beginning of the year 2000, nineteen journalists were imprisoned in China, the highest number for any country. The Committee to Protect Journalists named Chinese president Jiang Zemin among the top ten enemies of freedom of the press in the world. In the 1990s, Freedom House ranked China at the top of the list of what it called the "worst of the worst"—nations where civil and political rights were nonexistent.

The other countries lacking substantial press freedoms include Iraq, Iran, Saudi Arabia, Syria, Libya, Afghanistan, North Korea, Myanmar, Vietnam, Singapore, Belarus, and Cuba. Within this category are varying degrees of repression, ranging from total dictatorships to slightly less onerous authoritarian regimes. In some of these countries, there are even a few cracks in the wall where journalists occasionally find a way to report the news in a manner that differs from the official version. That has happened in Iran. And China has the oddity of Hong Kong, a bastion of press independence whose 7 million people came under Beijing's control in 1997, when Britain handed over its colony. Many worried that Beijing might impose tight censorship of news in that vibrant, freewheeling city, but three years later there had been no major change. In addition to the reporters in Hong Kong are a handful of independent journalists even on the mainland of China—journalists such as Gao Yu—and their stories are part of this book too.

But it is the countries that lie somewhere between the extremes of repression and freedom that are the primary focus of this book. They are the battleground countries, where it is still an open question whether independent journalists will prevail. By Freedom House's calculation, 39 percent of the world's population lives in these countries with a partly free press. The most populous countries in this category of battleground nations with a partly free press are Indonesia (212 million), Brazil (168 million), Russia (147 million), Pakistan (147 million), Nigeria (114 million), and Mexico (100 million). Out of that group, this book focuses on trends and case histories in Mexico, Russia, Taiwan, and Nigeria, while noting important skirmishes between journalists and their antagonists in other partly free countries.

From year to year in these battleground countries the conditions fluctuate, growing better one year, deteriorating the next, then improving again the year after. Freedom House reported that in 1999 three countries made significant improvements in press freedom over 1998, while two suffered harsher conditions. Forty-eight countries improved slightly. The median ratings for all countries improved by 4 percent. It is the thesis of this book that, at least in the past decade, independent journalists have made significant gains in the battleground countries and have a fighting chance of prevailing against their antagonists. And, as will be seen in the concluding chapter, conditions are becoming increasingly favorable for independent journalists in the future.

While their cultures vary widely, the countries in this middle category have some features in common that help us understand the context in which independent journalists clash with those in power. By and large these are developing nations emerging from decades of one-party or military dictatorship. Often their independent journalists in the past have been associated with opposition parties or dissident groups. The reporters have suffered repression when the opposition was repressed and have enjoyed greater freedom when the opposition gained a freer rein.

Neither side—neither government nor independent press—enjoys unqualified support from all major sectors of society. In many cases, the government controls radio and television but not all the newspapers and magazines, while journalists command respect and support from some elements of the population—often those supporting opposition parties—but not enough to assure protection from attack. Kavita Menon of the Committee to Protect Journalists speaks of "the dangers that journalists face when the press is strong while other democratic institutions are weak." In Pakistan, Peru, Nigeria, Bangladesh, and Indonesia, Menon says, "the press has also outpaced the development of the judiciary, the legislature, and even political parties. The reason is that unlike other pillars of democratic government, the press can develop independently, without government support or an institutional bureaucracy." Being more independent, newspapers in these partly free nations can develop at their own vigorous pace, but being more independent also means they are left more exposed to attack, without the protection of other strong institutions.

Threats to press freedom vary from one country to another and from one region of the world to another. Some of the threats are physical and violent, such as the assassinations and beatings of journalists in

Mexico and other parts of Latin America. Some of the threats are non-violent but nevertheless insidious, taking the form of seditious libel lawsuits in such places as Taiwan and Singapore and economic pressures against independent journalists in countries such as those of the former Soviet Union.

What news stories, photographs, cartoons, headlines, or other items are most likely to trigger attacks on journalists by governments or criminal organizations? The answer varies widely by country and region, but there is a general pattern. The news stories that seem to anger these powerful entities the most are the ones that threaten to weaken their grip on power. These include exposés of criminal behavior, corruption, and violations of human rights—exposés that hurt the public image of the powerful or could lead to their criminal prosecution. Another topic that triggers attacks on journalists in some countries is independent reporting on ethnic separatist movements, such as that of the Kurds in Turkey.

One type of story that virtually assures attacks on journalists in all countries of the world, even the freest ones, is any attempt at independent-minded war coverage. Even in the strongholds of press freedom such as the United States, press restrictions are imposed for the duration of a war. (The most notable exception was the extraordinary freedom journalists enjoyed during the Vietnam War.) Usually journalists are severely limited in their access to the front and in their ability to file meaningful reports from war zones, free of propaganda and censorship. Sometimes press control is motivated by legitimate government concerns of national security. Other times it is motivated by more dubious concerns, such as boosting morale or covering up government mistakes. For whatever reason, journalists who violate censorship rules or eschew official propaganda in their news reports risk reprisals.

In the freest nations, wartime censorship and other controls are only temporary and are lifted as soon as the war is over. In the nations with the least freedom, press controls are permanent, war or no war. And in the countries that are the main focus of this book, the partly free nations, from time to time one finds either actual military conflict (including civil war, separatist uprisings, and ethnic strife) or the social equivalent of war, with tensions between competing interest groups rising to the level of crisis because demarcation lines that would indicate the limits of their power have not yet been agreed on. Journalists caught up in the middle of these warlike power struggles often face the greatest danger.

How to explain the apparent paradox that there is an overall trend toward more democracy, yet attacks against journalists, especially violent attacks, remain a serious threat to press freedom in the battleground countries?

In the stabler countries at either end of the continuum, both the freest nations and the dictatorships, there is less violence against journalists partly because there is less radical social change. Wars and upheavals in those countries are largely things of the past. But in the partly free countries, change is often the order of the day; conditions are still in flux; and the working environment, at least temporarily, becomes more dangerous for the press. The more movement toward open societies, the more journalists who try out their newfound freedom. CPJ's former executive director Orme said:

> The number of journalists in jail and the number of journalists assaulted and murdered because of their work is first and foremost a function of the number of journalists out there trying to do their job. That number has literally doubled [in the decade through 1997] because of political change.

This book gives examples of the published works of journalists who suffered attack, with commentary by the journalists themselves and others as to what it was about their reporting that angered their antagonists enough to provoke retaliation. Another theme is that independent journalists are developing more effective ways to fight back. Some do so in court. Russian television correspondent Yelena Masyuk, who angered the establishment by reporting from the rebel side in the first war in Chechnya, successfully sued right-wing newspapers that accused her of lying and corruption. Other journalists, including those of Mexico, are learning to put aside petty rivalries and form self-protective professional associations, although these efforts at solidarity do not always succeed.

Some benefit from international press-advocacy groups such as the Committee to Protect Journalists, based in New York, or Reporters Sans Frontières (Reporters Without Borders), based in Paris. The advocacy groups themselves are finding new, more effective ways to put pressure on those who attack journalists. The CPJ has won the freedom of some imprisoned reporters and helped shorten the sentences of others. CPJ persuaded the White House to add the plight of threatened journalists to the agenda for President Bill Clinton before he met in 1997 with Argentina's President Carlos Saúl Menem.

Other journalists are turning increasingly to cyberspace to try to outwit their antagonists, with varying degrees of success. A Belarussian publisher whose newspaper was shut down found a new home for his pages on a borrowed Web site. A Serbian radio station used E-mail and an Internet audio Web site to disseminate the news after the government prevented it from broadcasting. But when Nigerian reporters boasted that they were obtaining state-of-the-art computers so that they could enter cyberspace, police got word of their plan and torched their office, destroying their computers.

They're not all angels, these independent journalists. Some damage their own credibility by unprofessional conduct, in some cases letting themselves be bought off by the powerful figures whose misdeeds they should be exposing and in other cases even stooping so low as to blackmail the very persons they investigate—journalists silencing themselves to enrich themselves. Some back down in the face of threats and spike the stories they had been preparing for publication. That is one way of measuring the chilling effect of attacks on journalists. It takes enormous courage to publish and be damned, and not all reporters, editors, and publishers possess such courage. That makes it all the more remarkable when journalists do refuse to be bought off or scared off, when they do stand up to those in power.

This book focuses on the effects of the attacks: Do they chill or embolden their intended targets in the press? Why does the reaction by journalists vary from one culture to another? And what are some examples of stories that were suppressed—and others that were published—in the face of threats?

The behavior of these journalists is interesting in its own right, but it also sheds light on a broader theme: the viability of democracies around the world. To the extent that journalists are cowed, their would-be democracies are deprived of vital information needed for the successful functioning of a free society. To the extent that journalists are defiant, their countries benefit from a better understanding of powerful forces at work behind the scenes, forces whose interests may not always coincide with the best interests of the citizenry. A recent study based on research at Oxford University's Center for Socio-

Legal Studies emphasizes the importance of press freedom for emerging democracies:

> Moving towards a free and independent press early in the process of transition may provide a building block for the future stable set of democratic institutions. . . . One might argue that the emergence of democratic institutions in transition societies will come faster and with greater public support and involvement if there is a free and independent media to develop and inspire public opinion.

Americans have a stake in the success or failure of democracies around the world. This is not only because we are in sympathy with them ideologically but also because we believe that, in the long run, democracies are more efficient and stable than dictatorships, and a stable world is a safer world for all of us. Journalists play a key role in this process. The success or failure of democracies depends partly on the ability of their press to keep the citizenry informed.

With democratic development and the growth of a free press so strongly intertwined, much is at stake in these battles over press freedom. As Mexican author Jorge C. Castañeda put it: "When a journalist is murdered in Latin America, a bit of democracy dies with him."

PART I

LOOKING FOR TROUBLE

The Behavior of Independent Journalists

Four months after being shot during an assassination attempt, Mexican publisher-editor J. Jesús Blancornelas chats at his home in Tijuana, Mexico, with author Anthony Collings. Blancornelas named the names of drug traffickers and their henchmen in his newspaper. Credit: Courtesy of Anthony Collings.

I

"They Are the News"

Facing Mexican Druglords

AT 9:30 A.M. on Thursday, November 27, 1997, J. Jesús Blancornelas stepped out of his house, opened the door on the passenger side of his red Ford Explorer, and sat in the front seat. He and his personal body-guard-chauffeur began driving through a quiet, middle-class, residential neighborhood of Tijuana toward his office, six blocks away.

Blancornelas was sixty-one years old, a short, feisty newspaper editor and publisher with a trim gray beard. He had made a name for himself as a muckraker. His specialty: exposing details of corrupt Mexican officials and drug traffickers. For years, friends and associates—and even a former police chief—had warned him that this was dangerous. That morning he had no way of knowing just how dangerous it was. A few blocks away, ten gunmen were waiting to kill him.

Bodyguards normally provided to him by the Mexican state of Baja California had been suddenly and inexplicably removed a month earlier. Blancornelas still had his own personal bodyguard and driver, a thirty-eight-year-old bespectacled, mustachioed man named Luis Lauro Valero Elizaldi, and Blancornelas himself carried a small pistol in a fanny pack strapped to his stomach, but there was no guarantee that this protection would be enough.

Blancornelas had challenged the powerful Arellano brothers, Ramón Arellano Félix and Benjamín Arellano Félix, alleged leaders of the dominant crime family of Tijuana. According to U.S. and Mexican officials, the Arellanos controlled the cocaine trade in the northern border city and its flow into nearby San Diego and elsewhere in California. The Arellanos were believed to be typical *narcos*—Mexican drug traffickers whose power has grown with their enormous riches and their ability to buy off or terrify Mexican government officials. U.S. authorities estimated that up to 70 percent of all the cocaine snorted in the United States entered the country from Mexico. They identified the Arellano family as one of the main suppliers—and said the Arellanos would kill anyone who threatened their ability to control the drug trade.

In recent weeks Blancornelas had escalated his attacks on the Arellano brothers. Only a month earlier his weekly tabloid, *Zeta*, had published a letter from the mother of two men. She said her sons ("my kings") had worked for the Arellanos and had been executed by the crime organization. In the letter she revealed intimate details of the family and accused one of the Arellanos of cowardice: "Why did you do this to my kings? Ramón, are you afraid of them?"

In the latest issue of *Zeta*, editor and publisher Blancornelas had coauthored a report revealing that a man believed to be the gang's top assassin—known only by his nickname, "C.H."—was involved in another crime, the November 14 shooting of two soldiers outside a courthouse. Authorities later revealed that "C.H." was the nickname of David Barrón Corona, a Mexican who had grown up in San Diego. His body exhibited tattoos that included sixteen skulls—one skull, apparently, for each of his victims. The publisher of *Zeta* could not know it at the time, but on that morning, November 27, 1997, as Blancornelas rode to work, David Barrón Corona was among the gunmen waiting to kill him.

Blancornelas was not the only journalist to take risks. Nine years earlier, his friend and business partner Héctor Félix Miranda had been just as defiant, and had paid for that defiance with his life. Nicknamed "El Gato" (The Cat), Félix Miranda wrote columns accusing local figures of corruption, drug trafficking, and other crimes. One of his targets was a racetrack owner whose father was a federal cabinet minister and former mayor of Mexico City. Félix Miranda's sassy, provocative style earned him popularity with many readers in Tijuana—but not all. On April 20, 1988, while driving to work, Héctor Félix Miranda was killed by an assassin with a shotgun.

Ever since that murder, Blancornelas had continued to list his friend Félix Miranda as copublisher, as if he were still alive, and in each issue he published words from Félix Miranda as if they had been written from the grave—words accusing the racetrack owner of ordering his murder. By 1997, two bodyguards for that businessman were serving prison sentences for the crime, but authorities had never announced who ordered the kill, and as was often the case in Mexico, the investigation had petered out.

Now Félix Miranda's surviving partner, Blancornelas, was continuing their aggressive brand of journalism—publishing far more about the drug cartel than many other Mexican newspapers. His defiance of the *narcos* had won him renown. In 1996, the U.S.-based Committee to Protect Journalists gave him its International Press Freedom Award. But along with renown came danger. A former police chief cautioned that accepting this award would be tantamount to signing his own death warrant. Blancornelas dismissed the warning and went to the award ceremony. In 1987 his newspaper office was ripped by gunfire, and over the years he received numerous death threats. Some of Blancornelas's many supporters among the rising middle class felt he was taking too many risks going up against the Arellano brothers.

These same drug traffickers had claimed many victims, even a Roman Catholic cardinal killed accidentally during a shootout at Guadalajara Airport in 1993. One of the gang leaders, Ramón Arellano Félix, was on the FBI's Ten Most Wanted list. The gang was part of a violent culture in Tijuana that made the city dangerous for any public figure. Only one year after the cardinal's death, a presidential nominee who had been considered certain to win the national election was gunned down in Tijuana. That crime was Mexico's equivalent of the assassination of President John F. Kennedy.

Tijuana was not the only dangerous border city. San Luis Río Colorado, only a three-hour drive to the east of Tijuana, was where a gunman had killed Benjamín Flores González, another publisher who had crusaded against drugs. That was in July 1997—only four months before gunmen laid the ambush for Blancornelas. And elsewhere in Mexico that same year, two other journalists were killed and at least twenty others kidnapped or assaulted because of their work.

For years Mexico has been Latin America's second deadliest country for reporters, after Colombia. The most notorious case was the 1984 assassination in Mexico City of the country's best-known muckraking columnist, Manuel Buendía. He had been investigating links between senior police officials and drug traffickers. Buendía was shot in the back as he walked to his car. The director of Mexico's equivalent of the FBI headed up the investigation—until he himself came under suspicion. Eventually this senior police official was convicted of ordering

Buendía's murder. (For more details, see chapter 6, "The General's Mercedes: Crime and Corruption.") For Buendía, as for other Mexican journalists, there was great risk in reporting the drug trade and its violent enforcers. As one reporter put it: "The most dangerous thing is to name the killers and their ties to the police who protect them."

Attacks on Mexican journalists range from assassination to assault and economic and legal pressures. The attacks have become one way of measuring the extent to which the drug culture is eroding Mexican institutions. As John Ross in the *Nation* put it:

> Journalists working in Mexico these days have become like canaries in the coal mine. Their daily travails measure the poisonous gas seeping to the nation's surface.

Reporters trying to pursue the drug story have been assaulted by a wide range of people, even by some Roman Catholic church officials, according to Mexican newspapers. In September 1997, during a fracas in Mexico City, one of the aides to an archbishop reportedly whacked a reporter on the head with a crosier (a bishop's staff of office). Other aides to the archbishop allegedly kicked journalists and smashed a reporter's tape recorder. All this because the reporters wanted to ask about a priest who had praised a druglord for his charitable contributions. The priest's comment reinforced the suspicions of critics of the church that it, too, like so many other Mexican institutions, had received drug money. And in fact, that suspicion was not allayed when the former papal nuncio to Mexico, Archbishop Geronimo Prigione, admitted that he had met privately with Tijuana's Arellano druglords.

By early November 1997, there had been so many attacks over the years on reporters, editors and publishers that Blancornelas joined about thirty leading Mexican and American journalists at a conference in Mexico City to discuss self-defense. On November 27, less than three weeks after Blancornelas attended that self-defense conference, gunmen gathered on Chula Vista Street to kill him.

The sky was overcast that morning, the streets still wet from rain that had stopped earlier. Traffic was light. Blancornelas and his driver chatted quietly. It was a Thursday, the weekly deadline day for his newspaper. Across the border in the United States, Americans were celebrating Thanksgiving.

A group of known drug dealers rode in a car behind them. Blancornelas asked his driver what the hoodlums were doing in this neighborhood. The driver said that perhaps they were selling drugs.

On Chula Vista Street a white Nissan suddenly pulled in front of the car Blancornelas and his driver were riding in and cut them off. A gunman jumped out and began firing a pistol. Luis Valero, Blancornelas's driver, quickly turned right down San Francisco Street, but another car, a green Pontiac, pulled alongside. Four men inside opened fire with automatic rifles. David Barrón Corona, the tattooed man, advanced on foot directly in front of Valero, firing an automatic rifle. Valero pushed the publisher to the floor to try to protect him and returned fire, at the same time putting the car into reverse in hopes of escaping the ambush. The car mounted the sidewalk and crashed into an iron fence.

In all, 127 bullets were fired in the exchange. A bullet entered Blancornelas's right side, fractured a rib, and broke into two fragments. One fragment of that bullet entered his stomach and intestines. The other stopped just short of his spinal column. A second bullet grazed the back of his right hand. Two more bullets narrowly missed his face.

Blancornelas was too surprised to pull the pistol out of his fanny pack, but he did use a CB (citizens band) radio to simultaneously call his home and his office. "We've been shot!" he said and gave the location on Chula Vista Street.

At the end of the gun battle, Blancornelas's bodyguard-driver, Luis Lauro Valero Elizaldi, hit by thirty-eight bullets, lay dead in the car. On the street David Barrón Corona also lay dead, shot in the eye, apparently hit by accident by one of his fellow gunmen during the crossfire. The other gunmen escaped. Blancornelas was rushed to the Hospital del Prado and underwent two operations in the next forty-eight hours. To the relief of his family, friends, and associates at *Zeta*, the doctors said he would survive.

Four months later I interviewed Blancornelas in the living room of his home (now heavily guarded outside by elite federal government troops in full battle gear) as he recuperated from the gunshot wounds and underwent rehabilitation. His voice quavered at times and he had trouble walking, but he said he was determined to continue as before: "We are journalists. We have the right and the duty to let people know the things that endanger society."

And as if to prove that the attempt on his life had not silenced him, Blancornelas pointed to the front page of the latest issue of *Zeta* on his

Front page of November 28, 1997, issue of Blancornelas's weekly newspaper, *Zeta*, reports on the attempt on his life. Photo shows, on left, body of David Barrón Corona, one of the attackers, and, on right, Blancornelas's bullet-riddled car. Headline above the *Zeta* logo says: "Blancornelas: Stable." Below it says: "Corrupt Law Enforcement." (*Narcojudiciales* is an invented word implying drug-corrupted law enforcement officials.) Smaller headlines say: "'C.H.' One of the Assassins" and "Terán's Responsibility." (The last headline refers to the state governor, Terán, who allegedly had withdrawn Blancornelas's bodyguards before the attack.)

coffee table. Displayed under the *Zeta* logo, just under the newspaper's motto ("In Baja California, free as the wind"), was a banner headline. It told of a prominent businessman who had been named by an inform-ant as being involved with the Arellano gang. "Today information was published that goes beyond the official information," Blancornelas said,

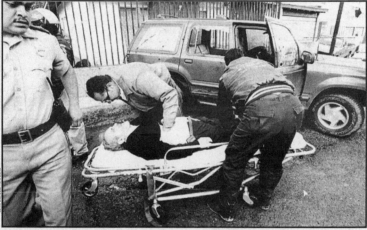

DEL 28 DE NOVIEMBRE AL 4 DE DICIEMBRE DE 1997   ZETA   PÁGINA 13 A

"NARCOJUDICIALES"
LOS ASESINOS

El Co-Director de ZETA, Jesús Blancornelas, recibe los primeros auxilios por socorristas de la Cruz Roja, después de que él mismo solicitó ayuda

El 28 de octubre ZETA publicó en su primera plana *"Carta a Ramón Arellano"*. Ese día, sospechosamente, la escolta asignada por el Gobierno del Estado para la protección de J.Jesús Blancornelas, desapareció sin que mediara explicación.

Tres semanas les dieron, con esta acción, a los asesinos para seguir y vigilar los movimientos de Jesús Blancornelas, elaborar un plan para el atentado y finalmente emboscarlo.

La retirada de los judiciales asignados por el Gobernador *"por órde-nes superiores"*, como algunos de ellos lo afirmaron, tiene por lo menos cuatro lecturas:

1.- Un acuerdo entre narcojudiciales o narcofuncionarios estatales para dejar el camino libre a los sicarios.

2.- Miedo a un atentado como consecuencia de la publicación de ZETA.

3.- Quien ordenó el retiro de la escolta se enteró de que se planeaba o que ya se había decidido asesinar a Blancornelas.

4.- Negligencia o ineptitud del Gobierno del Estado, al no prever un posible atentado contra el periodista.

El ambiente para un atentado contra el Co-director de ZETA, comen-zó a generarlo el Gobierno del Estado por conducto del Procurador de Justicia José Luis Anaya Bautista a partir del asesinato, en abril del pre-sente año, de Héctor Navarro Terríquez y Carlos Estrada García.

Abrazándose al hecho de que Blancornelas, en representación de Choix Editores, S. de R.L., sostenía un litigio en tribunales de California con

Inside page of same issue of *Zeta* shows Blancornelas on stretcher after being shot. His car is in the background. Headline says: "Corrupt Law Enforce-ment—The Assassins."

switching from Spanish to English. He added, in an apparent attempt to answer criticism that he was overdoing the drug story: "People need to understand that our job is [the] newspaperman's [job]—journalism—not a war against narco-traffic."

The attempt on his life elevated Blancornelas's prominence well beyond Tijuana. In contrast to the many other violent attacks on journalists in Mexico, attacks that made few headlines outside their hometowns, this one became national and even international news. Such major Mexico City dailies as *Reforma*, the state-controlled national television, and the independent, privately owned TV network Televisión Azteca provided extensive coverage. The high-profile news coverage put pressure on the federal government to intervene. In response, President Ernesto Zedillo Ponce de León assigned elite federal protection forces, similar to the U.S. Secret Service, to provide twenty-four-hour protection not only for Blancornelas but also for his wife and three grown sons. Blancornelas's sons all work at *Zeta*, and each time one of them goes out to report on a story, two federal bodyguards armed with assault rifles and bulletproof vests accompany him.

In addition, the investigation into the attack on Blancornelas was assigned to a federal prosecutor. This is important, because federal criminal investigators have better resources than those at the local level, similar to the difference between the FBI and local police in the United States. Also, federal investigators in Mexico enjoy more public trust than the state and local authorities. "The federal prosecutor's office is working well in Tijuana," Blancornelas says. "But there's corruption in the state prosecutor's office." And local police cannot be counted on for help. As one of *Zeta*'s editors, Francisco Ortiz Franco, put it: "A good number of the police help the drug traffickers."

That raised a serious question of whether the attack on Blancornelas would ever be fully investigated, even with help at the federal level. Some political analysts felt corruption was too widespread for the federal government to fully investigate any drug-related crime. They noted that one drug trafficker, Amado Carrillo Fuentes, reputedly spent more on bribes every year than the entire Mexican Justice Department spent on its annual budget (which was $425 million in 1998). Although the government reportedly uncovered links between Carrillo Fuentes and several top officials, it took no action. "One explanation," said Raymundo Riva Palacio, a prominent Mexico City columnist, "could be that the penetration of narcos in the government and society is so great that the regime couldn't handle unveiling it."

If so, that would make it all the more important that Mexican journalists such as Blancornelas do the job the government cannot do—expose drug corruption and other social ills.

Blancornelas is typical of a new breed: gutsy, aggressive journalists around the world who push the envelope of press freedom in newly opened societies. In some ways they are similar to the reporters and editors who fought for press freedom in the early days of U.S. history, and some of them are paying the same price. John Peter Zenger was arrested and charged with libel in 1734 for publishing attacks on British colonial policy in his *New York Weekly Journal*. He fought back in court and won. A century later, Elijah Lovejoy, editor of the Alton, Illinois, *Observer*, was killed by a mob for opposing slavery. Today, having won the battle for press freedom, American journalists rarely face arrest or murder in the United States, but the outcome of that same battle in other countries has not yet been decided.

One of the conditions that these battleground countries have in common is an imbalance among institutions, with the press corps vigorous and aggressive but other democratic institutions weak. This is typically the case not only in Mexico but in such other partly free nations as Peru, Nigeria, and Pakistan. Noting the situation in Pakistan, where the former premier threatened and harassed journalists, CPJ's Kavita Menon says:

> In a more fully developed democracy, journalists who expose government corruption can count on other institutions to step in and take up the cause. An independent attorney general could open an investigation; a congressional committee could hold hearings; political parties could use the allegations to force a leader from power.

Another condition that many of these battleground countries have in common is that they are going through a period of rapid social change, often taking the form of a transition toward a more open, pluralistic society. Mexico is typical of that trend. The conflict in Mexico between independent journalists and those who would silence them comes at a time of greater political freedom for the nation's 100 million citizens. After nearly seven decades of dominance by the PRI (Institutional Revolutionary Party), the country is opening up, and for the first time the possibility exists for a viable opposition. In elections in 1997, the PRI lost control of Mexico City and the national congress, and in a national election in July 2000, the PRI lost the presidency for the first time since 1929.

With that political opening has come a greater openness in the news media. State-controlled national television no longer suppresses all mention of opposition candidates. Compared to a decade ago, there are more provincial newspapers willing to take on officials of the government, army, and police who have been corrupted by the drug gangs. "There's more pressure from society on the media to be independent," says *Zeta's* Ortiz Franco. "That's because society is more participatory, due to political change, now that the opposition is a fact." "The PRI no longer controls things as it once did," says Joel Simon of the Committee to Protect Journalists. "The Mexican press is liberated. Some are aggressive for professional reasons and some are getting back at people who once controlled them. . . . So these journalists are now aggressive out of pride and self-respect."

All of this makes for greater tension between reporters and politicians. As journalist Jorge Zepada of the Mexico City daily *El Universal* put it:

> Those who hold political power have lost the traditional mechanisms for controlling the press, and the shift toward a freer press has translated into growing hostility toward journalists.

To be sure, the liberation of the Mexican press has its limits. As before, the government pays many newspapers to run advertising disguised as news stories (called *gacetillas*)—and this gives the government the power to coerce publications into providing favorable coverage. As William Orme writes in *A Culture of Collusion*: "For many publications, reliant as they are on government cash, a declaration of independence would be tantamount to a declaration of bankruptcy."

Still, the trend is toward the kind of freedom that Blancornelas has espoused for years. Born in San Luis Potosí in central Mexico, he refused to follow in his father's footsteps as a car dealer and instead, because he loved bicycle races, landed a job as a sports reporter. He had no formal training as a journalist and learned on the job. He moved to Tijuana to work on another newspaper but was frustrated when many of his stories didn't make it into print. "There was a group of us reporters who couldn't publish what we wrote," he said. "We were censored very much." What types of stories got spiked? "Election results, debates in the chamber of deputies, the death of a governor who was in a hotel room with a woman. They didn't want to let us publish it."

In 1977, Blancornelas, his friend Héctor Félix Miranda, and two other journalists founded a small evening newspaper so that they could publish what they considered to be news, not the kind of bland pro-government pap published in other papers. Their new paper was called *ABC*. Blancornelas and Félix Miranda wrote columns filled with aggressive investigative stories exposing corruption. And in a break with traditional journalistic practice in Mexico, Blancornelas forbade his staff to accept any bribes from government officials. Poorly paid Mexican journalists for years had received such favors as the monthly *embute*, an envelope stuffed with amounts of cash ranging from $20 to $2,000. Other bribes included free nights at nightclubs, the services of prostitutes, and gifts of new-model cars and European vacations. Reporter Raymundo Riva Palacio said a former governor of Chiapas state once paid an editor $40,000 not to write a negative article about him.

In later years many other publishers banned bribes, but back in 1977, Blancornelas was one of the few to impose high professional standards. "It was an exciting time," recalled Miguel Cervantes Sahagún, who was a police reporter for *ABC* in the 1970s. "I was working for a paper that created an uproar in Tijuana and I was part of an editorial team that was in conflict with the local government. It was unusual. Most journalists in Baja California had a modus vivendi with the government. They were not professional journalists, at least as far as Americans or Europeans see it. They practiced bureaucratic journalism. The agenda of the local government was the story. Blancornelas wanted to do something different."

A little too different for some, apparently. The state governor of Baja California demanded that Blancornelas fire copublisher Félix Miranda for writing columns that revealed the governor's nepotism. (He had put his son, cousin, uncles, and brother-in-law on the state payroll, Félix Miranda claimed.) Blancornelas refused to fire his partner. On November 2, 1979, the governor used a state-controlled labor union to close down *ABC*. But six months later Blancornelas and his colleagues were back in business, this time publishing a new weekly newspaper called *Zeta* (the letter *z* in Spanish, at the other end of the alphabet from *ABC*). Why did they defy a powerful state government that was determined to silence them? "Because we were a team of journalists who had been censored," Blancornelas said, "and we wanted to still publish no matter what."

The newsprint he depended on was controlled by the government, so Blancornelas at first had to print *Zeta* in San Diego and smuggle it across the border. "The police were looking for us," editor Ortiz Franco recalled. "They wanted to confiscate it. We avoided them by using a decoy. Héctor [Félix Miranda] would first cross the border in his car and the police would go after him. Then the car with the real copies of the paper in the trunk would follow." Initial circulation was only five to ten thousand, but by 1998 it had grown to sixty thousand.

Eventually, as part of nationwide reforms, the government got out of the newsprint business. *Zeta* was able to publish in Tijuana and struggled along for a few years, publishing the stories that other papers could not or would not. (Blancornelas finally managed to publish that story about the indiscreet governor who died in the hotel room.)

More important, *Zeta* aggressively exposed wrongdoing by the dominant PRI in Baja California. Some observers believe this helped pave the way for the state's voters in 1989 to do something unheard-of: they elected a governor from the opposition PAN (National Action Party). It was the first time in decades that an opposition party had won any Mexican state election. The winning candidate was Ernesto Ruffo Appel, mayor of Ensenada. "*Zeta* had an important role in giving people information on how Ruffo was doing as mayor and the fact that he was being harassed by the [PRI] governor," says former Tijuana mayor Héctor Osuna Jaime, who credits *Zeta* with helping the opposition win, although he feels that the rise of the middle class also played a role.

To be sure, Blancornelas has his detractors. Some say he is a publicity seeker who plays up his own scoops and tries to discredit those of others. Some critics claim he has lost his edge, that he compromised himself by getting too close to his sources in the federal government in Mexico City, and that he no longer is as critical of the powerful PRI as he once was. And former mayor Osuna Jaime, while an admirer of Blancornelas's attacks on corruption, says he's overdoing the drug story:

> I think he is not accomplishing anything by naming the names of the drug traffickers. . . . I respect him but he is taking too much of a risk. . . . He should focus on the problem but not on the details.

Still, even his critics concede that Blancornelas blazed a trail in Tijuana that a number of other journalists are following. "Now when investigators give press conferences on drug traffickers," reporter Cervantes Sahagún said, "more journalists attend than before, because there is a new generation of journalists more conscientious about their work. They take it seriously." That new generation tends to be better paid and better educated than journalists of Blancornelas's generation. In some cases, that education now includes professional journalism training in college.

Blancornelas said he saw no going back to the days of the tame, pro-government newspapers that provided only superficial coverage of the news. He said the public now demands in-depth reporting: "Mexican journalism that does not follow these changes will disappear."

Mexico is one of the world's battleground countries of press freedom, and its journalists bear the scars of that battle—some of them literally. During his recovery, Blancornelas showed me a scar on the back of his right hand from one of the bullets, and he said he had no feeling in his right leg. Clearly, with the loss of his friend Félix Miranda and his companion Valero Elizaldi and his own gunshot wounds, Blancornelas has paid a price for his brand of journalism. But if he had it to do over, he said, he would not do anything differently in his coverage of the drug traffickers. As he put it: "I was doing my job. . . . They are the news. I am a journalist."

2

She Had to Be There

Taking Risks in Russia

YELENA MASYUK, A tall, tough, businesslike television correspondent, was no stranger to danger. Masyuk and her camera operator Ilya Mordyukov and her sound engineer Dmitri Ulchev had risked their lives time and again as they covered the rebel side in the first round of fighting in Chechnya between Russia and separatists.

Now, on May 10, 1997, they were driving west on a road from the Chechen capital, Grozny, to the neighboring Russian republic of Ingushetia. In their car were videotapes of that day's news coverage: a public rally and an interview with Salman Raduyev, leader of the rebels who were fighting Russian troops. Masyuk and her crew wanted to get the tapes to a location where they could transmit her report to NTV, Russia's only independent national television network. But that report was never seen by viewers.

Six masked gunmen ambushed the car and forced Masyuk and her crew into another car. They took them from one location to another. Masyuk, thirty-one years old, was beaten. Her captors seized her personal possessions, including an icon she wore around her neck. At last, apparently out for ransom money, they took Masyuk and her crew to a cold, wet cave thirteen hundred feet up in the Caucasus Mountains. It was a bear's cubbyhole, seven feet by seven feet in area, in rugged terrain where nineteenth-century Chechens once hid to avoid deportation by czarist Russians. So small was the opening to the cave that Masyuk had to enter feet first.

For 101 days they were held there, fed one piece of sausage, one piece of bread, and one cup of tea a day. It was so damp that several nights in a row they could not sleep because there was no dry spot in the cave. They had to use a makeshift toilet just outside the entrance to the cave because the slope was so steep that they could not wander far-

With flak jacket and microphone, Russian TV war correspondent Yelena
Masyuk reports from a bunker on the Chechen side during the first round of
fighting between Russia and Chechen rebels in the mid-1990s. While reporting,
she and her crew were captured and held hostage for 101 days. Credit: Andrew
Collings, from videotape provided by Committee to Protect Journalists.

ther away. I asked Masyuk if she had feared for her life, and she told me,
in blunt, matter-of-fact Russian, that daily life was such a struggle there
was no time for fear: "Death was not what we thought about."

Having been held at gunpoint myself in Lebanon as a CNN correspondent, I know what she meant. But my own capture lasted only a
few hours. Hers lasted 101 days and was infinitely more terrifying. Her
employer, NTV (Nyezavisimaya Televidenya—Independent Television), a privately owned network, says it paid $2 million in ransom, and
at last, on August 18, 1997, just hours before a summit between Russian
and Chechen leaders, she and her crew were released. It is still unclear
why they were captured by the very Chechens from whose side of the
war they had reported, but what is clear is that their release was good
news for supporters of press freedom. They were greeted as heroes on
their return to Moscow.

Being held hostage was only the latest of many threats to Yelena

Masyuk. Whenever she went back to Chechnya she knew the risk. In fact, only two weeks before she was captured, a Russian colonel used the pages of *Zavtra* (Tomorrow), a right-wing Russian newspaper, to threaten her with physical harm. He, like many other ultranationalists, resented her reports on the casualties inflicted on Chechen civilians by Russian troops. They saw her as unpatriotic ("being fed from a stranger's hand," as one article put it in August 1996). They considered her a traitor. They wanted her silenced.

So did the regime of President Boris Yeltsin. On July 13, 1995, the Russian General Prosecutor's office opened a criminal investigation of her under Article 189 of the Criminal Code (harboring a criminal) and Article 190 (failure to report a crime). Masyuk told me she was concerned: "I could have got a sentence of up to eight years in prison." Why? Because she had refused to reveal to the Russian government the location where she had interviewed Shamil Basayev, a Chechen field commander. Other Russian journalists had interviewed him as well, but she was the only one to face a criminal investigation.

It was partly a question of timing. Her interview came shortly after Basayev raided a hospital in the southern Russian city of Budennovsk in June 1995. He took more than a thousand Russian civilians hostage and later managed to escape capture by the Russian army and return to his safe haven in nearby Chechnya—something that infuriated Moscow. Coming right after this daring raid, Masyuk's interview with Basayev on Chechen territory added fuel to the fire. "They couldn't understand," she told me, "because they couldn't get onto the territory of Chechnya. We showed something from Chechen territory. It was a revealing interview. It showed the weakness of the Russian forces."

Masyuk says she had not expected to face prison just for refusing to tell Russian officials the location of her interview with Basayev. "It was a surprise. They immediately told us they were treating us not as journalists but as Russian citizens and that this changed my personal duty and responsibility, so that now I was obligated to give Russia certain information." As she recounted this investigation, I asked her which was more important, being a Russian citizen or being a journalist, and her reply indicates her priorities: "The more important law is the one governing the press."

NTV had come under earlier pressure from the Kremlin to stop showing the carnage in Chechnya in this first of two wars that would ultimately take tens of thousands of civilian lives. On December 15, 1994, as the fighting escalated, Deputy Prime Minister Oleg Soskovets announced that the Russian government was considering revoking NTV's license to broadcast on channel 4, a government channel. According to the Committee to Protect Journalists, a public outcry forced the government to abandon that idea, but NTV remained a thorn in its side, and the Kremlin's next step was to threaten NTV's war correspondent with prison.

Despite the threat, Masyuk, backed up by her network, refused to divulge the information. As it turned out, the prosecutor did not press charges (he later resigned amid allegations of corruption), but Masyuk was on notice: powerful forces in the Russian establishment saw her as an enemy. Those same forces continued to suspect all journalists later, during Russia's second war in Chechnya, and in that second round of fighting, at the end of the 1990s and on into the year 2000, the Kremlin permitted far less independent reporting. Its ability to tighten censorship was enhanced by public revulsion at what was seen as Chechen responsibility for terrorist bombings in Russia.

But during the first round of fighting in the mid-1990s, when it was somewhat easier to report from the rebel side, Yelena Masyuk went to Chechnya again and again. She had to resort to subterfuges to escape detection. As she put it:

> It's become common in Chechnya to threaten journalists, to deprive them of their accreditation, their documents and their tapes, and that's why very often journalists who want to get true information by any means dress as the native Chechens and avoid the Russian checkpoints. I have been in Chechnya several times, and I myself have been subjected to these refusals to be allowed to [go] where the Chechens are. Sometimes I had to dress up as a Chechen, as well as my camera operator, and the Chechens would help me get past the Russian military checkpoints. The Chechen women would bring our equipment through in a truck, and they put the camera underneath one of their skirts.
>
> When we tried to get into this village called Bamut, which has been famous for its tenacity, to avoid the Russian checkpoints—because we had been three times refused when we tried to get through in a car— we took horses and rode twenty kilometers [twelve miles] over the mountains.

Why take so many risks to cover the Chechen war? "To show the Chechen side of the story, to give them a chance to tell their point of view, to show how terrible the war was for civilians and even Russian soldiers," she said at one point, and later added: "There were things happening there that were important for Russian history. I figured I should be there." And because she was there, despite all the efforts to silence her, details of civilian suffering were brought home to Russians through the powerful imagery of television. That was not the story the Russian government wanted told. Masyuk says the official version of the war was intended to deceive the public, and many journalists simply rewrote what she calls "the bare official reports that the Defense Ministry hands out." She adds:

> It is these reports that say how many times federal [Russian] positions were put under fire by the Chechens, how many were killed, how many wounded. Of course, the number of Chechens wounded and killed are not reported. Now, the reason that journalists are just using these dry military communiques is that the Russian military has forbidden journalists to get into areas where they are carrying out what they call cleansing operations. Basically, in more informal language, it is that the Russians are just shooting up and robbing the Chechen villages.

No wonder the Kremlin wanted her muzzled. It seems clear that her detailed reports played a role in helping focus public opinion on the fiasco in Chechnya. In a detailed study of the role of Russian television, Duke University professor Ellen Mickiewicz reports:

> It would be inaccurate to say that television "caused" Russians to turn away from the war in Chechnya. The process was much more complex, as it had been in the United States during the Vietnam war. . . . It did not take television, uniquely and solely, to make the case to ordinary Russians that things were not as they should be. . . . But the insistent drumbeat on television provided little letup from unwelcome news.

Amid increasing public pressure at home and abroad to end the war, Moscow did so in 1997, only to resume the fighting two years later.

Yelena Masyuk was on the front line of the Chechen war, and also on the front line of the war over censorship. The censorship struggle in Russia began in earnest in the late 1980s. After almost seventy years of Communist dictatorship, Soviet leader Mikhail Gorbachev loosened government control of the press as part of his policy of *glasnost*. In 1989 the Berlin Wall came down. Two years later the Soviet Union collapsed. Having endured czars and Communists, with only a brief democratic interval in 1917, some 147 million Russians were now able to receive un-censored Russian news for the first time. During this period, as more and more of the old walls restricting freedom came down, Russian jour-nalists moved quickly to expand their field of action and see how far they could go. They discovered that they could go fairly far, but free-dom came at a price. In the decade of the 1990s, at least thirty-four jour-nalists were killed in Russia. Some of them were caught in wartime crossfire or otherwise killed by accident, such as young American pho-tographer Cynthia Elbaum, who was decapitated by shrapnel during a Russian bombing raid on Grozny. But others were deliberately targeted and murdered because of their professional activity.

The body of Nadezhda Chaikova, a correspondent for the newspa-per *Obschchaya Gazeta*, was found near a sewage pipe outside the Chechen village of Gekhi in March 1996. There were signs she had been murdered execution-style: blindfolded, forced to kneel, shot in the back of the head, and then dumped on the outskirts of town. No one has been charged, but press advocacy groups suspect Russian involvement, ei-ther directly or indirectly. "Russian Federal troops, angered at Chaikova's videotaping of Samashki, a village they had demolished, were suspects," reported Catherine Fitzpatrick of the Committee to Pro-tect Journalists. Correspondent Chaikova, like Yelena Masyuk, had had close contacts with the Chechen rebels and had made a name for herself exposing Russian military atrocities.

Eight journalists who covered that first round of fighting in Chech-nya disappeared and were presumed dead, including Andrew Shu-mack, an idealistic American freelance photojournalist from Warren County, Pennsylvania. He was last seen alive in Grozny, the Chechen capital, on July 24, 1995. More journalists disappeared in the second round of fighting (1999–2000). Many others have been beaten up, phys-ically intimidated, and threatened in other ways.

Russian reporters are finding it more difficult now to continue the kind of aggressive, hard-hitting exposés of the misdeeds of the power-ful that they published in the late 1980s—in the first heady days of

Gorbachev's *glasnost* and in the early post-Soviet period after decades of censorship. One reason for the greater difficulties today concerns personal safety. There are increasing threats to the lives of investigative reporters, and not just from criminal organizations. Some assassinations have been linked to current or former government officials. For example, a retired military intelligence officer was arrested in early 1998 and charged with organizing the 1994 killing of a young investigative reporter named Dmitri Kholodov, who had accused top officers of black-marketeering and arms smuggling. (For more details on the Kholodov case, see chapter 6, "The General's Mercedes: Crime and Corruption.")

While it is reassuring that investigators finally indicted someone in the Kholodov case after four years, all too often the attacks on journalists are barely investigated. Usually the government's response is sluggish or nonexistent. Cases are often left unsolved, amid suspicions that higher-ups are obstructing justice. All this is bound to have a chilling effect on some would-be investigative reporters. "If you do journalism that deals with certain sensitive issues," said Yevgenia Albats, a former reporter for the Russian newspaper *Izvestia*, "you can easily get killed." Albats herself was fired by *Izvestia* after she published a book and a series of exposés on the FSB security police, the successor to the KGB.

The other main reason for the greater difficulty in telling the truth is economic pressure. Banks, oil companies, and other business enterprises closely linked to the government have been buying up media organizations.

Gazprom, the 40 percent state-owned natural gas monopoly that was once run by Yeltsin's prime minister Viktor Chernomyrdin, bought almost a third of the shares of the NTV network in 1996. (And some observers saw a softening of NTV's anti-Yeltsin rhetoric after NTV chairman Igor Malashenko joined Yeltsin's election campaign as media adviser.) In 1997, Uneximbank, a private bank, bought 20 percent of *Komsomolskaya Pravda*, the country's most popular daily with a circulation of 1.25 million. That same bank and LUKoil, Russia's biggest oil company, divided up ownership of *Izvestia*, the most respected national daily. LUKoil had already owned 41 percent and increased its share—and control—after *Izvestia*'s editor angered the company by reprinting a French newspaper report alleging that Chernomyrdin had amassed a $5 billion fortune from his cut of oil and gas exports. After LUKoil increased its holdings, editor-in-chief Igor Golembiovsky was fired. "The newspaper will now be a loyal supporter of the government," Golembiovsky lamented.

Writing in the *Columbia Journalism Review* in 1997, Neela Banerjee, a freelance writer in Moscow, concluded that "much of the independent media has moved back under the control of the state and of business interests close to it. Tough coverage of anything is a rarity." Before losing his job as foreign editor of *Izvestia*, Sergei Agafonov wrote in April 1997: "In such circumstances, a free independent press is doomed."

That remains to be seen. Despite all the difficulties, there are still a few defiant voices, and Yelena Masyuk's is one of them. It is all the more remarkable that she works for television and not print, as the independent journalists in most countries tend to be newspaper reporters, not broadcast correspondents. Television often is government controlled. NTV, the network she worked for during the first Chechen war, is independent but also has had many ties to the government. That made it all the more surprising that NTV would play up negative coverage of the war waged by that government.

Millions of Russian viewers saw Yelena Masyuk report from the other side in the Chechen rebellion. In typical scenes from her coverage, she is crouched down behind a wall, dark hair pulled back, speaking into her microphone, while next to her a Chechen soldier is firing an automatic rifle at Russian troops. Or she is seated, cross-legged, on the ground with a circle of Chechen soldiers around her, and she is holding out her microphone for them to give their side. Or she is looking out at the camera from inside a bunker, grim-faced, speaking into her microphone of the latest skirmish.

Masyuk says she saw terrible things and was so caught up in the story that she took too many chances with her own life. "In January 1995 at the time of the [Russian] storming of the headquarters [of the rebels in Grozny]," she told me, "we took pictures of wounded Chechen civilians. There were snipers. It was horrible. Now I realize I should not have gone there. There was a bridge. It was too open. You could get shot. We ran zigzag."

She took the chances and defiantly showed the other side of the war, but there were some things she chose not to show. "For example," she said, "a long close-up of a dead soldier, lasting several seconds or entire minutes: you should not do it, because it is too offensive. It is not a question of the correspondent's right to show the horror of war. It is a question of respect. This dead person has relatives."

Still, she covered the stories that many Russian television correspondents did not. "In war," she said, "many Russian journalists take
the side of the federal troops who do things that are wrong, and for a
journalist to show the wounded, the peaceful civilians—it evoked a
negative reaction [from the Russian government]."

To get some idea how shocking it was for the Russian establishment
to see her on the television screen reporting from the enemy side, you
would have to go back to the Vietnam War and the reporting by Harrison Salisbury of the *New York Times* on the bombing of Hanoi—and the
angry charges of "traitor" by the Johnson administration and its supporters. More recently, Peter Arnett's reporting for CNN from the
Baghdad side in the Gulf War provoked similar accusations by some in
Washington, including then-senator Alan Simpson, a Wyoming Republican, and by some ordinary citizens. Based on my own experience as a
journalist in Russia, first for the Associated Press (AP) and later for
Cable News Network (CNN), I know that during the Soviet period it
would have been unthinkable for a Russian national television correspondent to interview the enemy during a war or give any viewpoint
other than the official line. The closest I ever heard a Russian criticize
military policy was when my AP translator said that "the situation is
very complicated" during the 1968 Warsaw Pact invasion to crush
Czech democratization. Fearing microphones in our office, that was his
coded way of saying, "We shouldn't be doing this."

Masyuk's reporting from behind enemy lines provoked anger and
threats, but it also won her a Teffi Award, the top television award in
Russia, as well as honors from the Moscow Union of Journalists and
praise from former U.S. president Jimmy Carter, who said: "I have been
impressed with her professionalism and heroic dedication to reporting
news from Chechnya despite difficult conditions there."

When Carter met Masyuk in 1995, she was a media fellow at Duke
University's DeWitt Wallace Center for Communications and Journalism, having earlier been a journalism graduate of Moscow State University. At the beginning of the *perestroika* period, Gorbachev's effort to
reform the Communist regime, she worked for "Vzglyad" (View), one
of the first controversial political shows. After becoming a special correspondent for NTV, she covered fighting between ethnic groups in
Afghanistan and Tajikistan and ethnic tensions in Pakistan and Iran.
But it was her reporting from Chechnya that made her a household
name, the Christiane Amanpour of Russia.

For a while her network pulled her out of Chechnya because of the threats against her. On a visit to Washington in May 1996, she told a congressional panel that many Russian journalists were suppressing the truth about the bloody war in Chechnya out of fear that the truth would cost Yeltsin the presidential election and put Communists back in power:

> In the Russian media true information may constitute about twenty percent. With the elections coming up, any sort of information that might harm Yeltsin's chances is either edited or is just not put out. This particularly relates to Chechnya, because the war was unleashed by Boris Yeltsin and the Chechen war represents a huge loss for him.

A year later she was back behind enemy lines, and it was then that she was captured and held in the cave and finally released. Later that same year, worlds away from Chechnya, she attended a gala dinner of the Committee to Protect Journalists. At a black-tie ceremony under the chandeliers of the grand ballroom at the Waldorf-Astoria Hotel in New York, a ceremony attended by prominent American media figures including network anchors and Disney chairman Michael Eisner, she was presented with an International Press Freedom Award.

I asked her how to explain the phenomenon of independent journalists such as herself in a country that until recently has had no tradition of democracy or a free press. She replied: "The Russian people have always wanted to be free. It is the spirit of the Russian person to be free."

3

Opening the Door

Courage in Asia

IN RECENT YEARS a growing number of countries in Asia have begun to liberalize their social and political systems. From South Korea to Taiwan and Indonesia, societies have become more open, and as part of this historic evolution, journalists in these countries have tested the limits of their new freedom.

One of those journalists was Ying Chan. In 1996 she faced the prospect of imprisonment in Taiwan because of a story involving President Clinton. From her base in New York, the Chinese American journalist collaborated with a colleague in Taiwan to expose what looked like an illegal Asian connection to the Clinton reelection campaign, a huge fund-raising connection "made in Taiwan." At the time, in October 1996, she had no way of knowing how much trouble this story would cause her—or how much it would test her courage.

Smart and tough, with big glasses and a wide smile, Chan was born in Hong Kong but is an American citizen. She came to the United States in 1972 and did graduate work in sociology at the University of Michigan at Ann Arbor. Chan got a job in New York as a reporter for the *New York Daily News* and also as a producer for *NBC News*. In addition, she was a New York correspondent for *Yazhou Zhoukan* (Asia Week), a Chinese-language Hong Kong weekly newsmagazine distributed in that city and abroad. It is influential among the tens of millions of ethnic Chinese scattered widely throughout Asia and the rest of the world and is read in mainland China as well.

In New York in 1996, before the first U.S. news stories appeared indicating a Democratic Party fund-raising scandal involving illegal foreign donations, Chan was contacted by a source. He had a tip that the top money man for Taiwan's then-ruling Kuomintang (KMT—the nationalist party) had offered President Clinton's reelection campaign a staggering $15 million. "The story sounded wild," Chan told me. "I never expected it to explode. Remember, that was four or five months before the campaign finance story broke."

She worked on the story at her end, contacting sources in the United States, while her Taiwanese-born colleague Shieh Chung-liang, a bespectacled young senior editor at the magazine, contacted his sources in Taipei, the capital of Taiwan. At last they had confirmation. A source said he had been in the room in Taipei when the alleged offer was made by the Taiwan money man to a Clinton campaign intermediary. "It felt great," Chan said. "We did have something."

By the time they had the story nailed down, Indonesian and other allegedly illegal Asian fund-raising connections had emerged in stories in American newspapers about the Democratic presidential campaign. But none of these stories involved the amount of money claimed in the story reported by Chan and Shieh.

Their scoop was splashed on the cover of the October 25 issue of *Yazhou Zhoukan*, illustrated by a picture of the White House superimposed on a U.S. dollar bill. The following excerpt is an English-language translation of part of their article:

> SPECIAL REPORT—AN EXCLUSIVE INSIDE STORY
> Taiwan Involved in America's Election—A Disputed Case
> of Political Contribution
> . . . *Yazhou Zhoukan* has learned that a Clinton confidant and member of his fund-raising team has . . . established multiple relationships with Kuomingtang authorities in Taiwan. The size of the alleged contributions from Taiwan may dwarf those from Indonesia and may have helped to set up a secret unofficial diplomatic channel between Taipei and the White House.
>
> Yazhou Zhoukan has learned that during his visit to Taiwan on August 1st last year, Mark E. Middleton . . . , Clinton's confidant and former White House aide, met with Mr. Liu Tai-ying, chairman of KMT's Business Management Committee. Liu, who controls about US $2 billion in KMT assets, told Middleton that he is willing to contribute US $15 million to Clinton's re-election campaign.

The article carefully noted that both Middleton and Liu denied the alleged $15 million offer. But the article also noted that its source for the story was "an informed senior KMT official."

The story made headlines in the United States and around the world, but nowhere did it arouse more of a frenzy than on the troubled island of Taiwan. It is an island with an identity problem. Best known in the world as a major exporter of goods "made in Taiwan," it was once recognized by the United States as a sovereign nation, ruled by the KMT, the political arm of the army that lost to the Communists in China's civil war and fled to the island in 1949. Calling itself the Republic of China, for a while its government was deemed by Washington to be the legitimate government of all of China, even though it ruled only some 22 million people and not the 1 billion of the mainland. After President Richard Nixon's détente with Beijing, in 1979 the United States recognized the People's Republic of China—not Taiwan—as the real China. The final status of Taiwan itself was left unclear. Beijing claimed the island was a province of China. Taiwan claimed it was a sovereign state, although it had virtually no diplomatic recognition.

In the 1980s, Taiwan underwent a radical political change, from autocratic rule by the KMT to a pluralistic democracy. Martial law was lifted. Political opposition was permitted. With that change to a more open society came a more open press, but that did not mean the kind of neutral, objective reporting that American readers expect. Most Taiwanese journalists were partisan, supporting either the then-ruling KMT or the main opposition party, the Democratic Progressive Party, which later came to power in the year 2000. Nonpartisan investigative reporting of the type done by Chan and Shieh was unusual.

As a result of its uncertain international status, Taiwan was heavily dependent on the goodwill of the United States for protection against any encroachment by mainland China. And for that reason, politicians of Taiwan's ruling KMT were extremely sensitive to any bad publicity about them in the United States—such as the story by Chan and Shieh. Liu Tai-ying, the money man for the KMT named in their story, was so sensitive, in fact, that he sued the reporters for criminal libel and the magazine for damages of $15 million. The threat of having to pay enormous damages worried the publishers, Chan said. She and Shieh had their own reasons to worry. If convicted of criminal libel, they faced up to two years in prison.

This was an example of the kind of repression that comes not from threats of physical violence but from a lawsuit intended to achieve the same result: stopping journalists from revealing damaging information about the powerful. The broader issue in this case was which model of press law Taiwan would follow: that of Singapore or that of Hong Kong. Singapore, an odd city-state that combines a free-market economy with political repression, has used criminal libel lawsuits to great effect to prevent the rise of independent journalism. In contrast, Hong Kong, both as a British colony and even after the 1997 takeover by China, has remained a stronghold of press freedom. Chan and Shieh provided a test case for the limits of that freedom in the newly open society of Taiwan, once a virtual dictatorship of the KMT, currently a battleground country for journalistic free speech. Their kind of reporting would have been unthinkable ten years earlier. Now a court had to decide if that kind of reporting was still unthinkable in 1997.

The journalists' chances were not good. Liu was a powerful figure. His lawsuit was officially supported by the leadership of the ruling KMT. Pro-KMT journalists "began a smear campaign," Shieh said, "calling us fellow travelers of the Chinese communists." As Chan put it: "Shieh was under tremendous pressure: accused of being a Communist spy. Serious charges . . . There was talk about closing down the Taiwan edition of the magazine." Faced with that pressure, Chan and Shieh had to make some important decisions. Should they go along with those in the management of their magazine who were considering the possibility of an out-of-court settlement and apology? "There was constant tension," Chan said. "It's always a tendency, the corporate interest, to settle. They had lawyers' fees, you know?"

But for the journalists, a settlement and an apology were out of the question. "I did nothing wrong," Chan said. "Credibility is the only asset I have. There is no way I could back off from that." She decided to take a tough stance and stiffen the resolve of her bosses. "I needed to give confidence to the magazine, the management, the editor, that we are okay, we have to defend the story, so they don't cave in."

She took her fight worldwide, speaking out in her defense at every occasion she could find. At a dinner for visiting American journalists in Taipei in April 1997, she stood up and asked for support in her defense against Liu's lawsuit. Furthermore, to reach a truly worldwide audience, and to do it quickly and cheaply, she turned to the Internet. Using skills she had learned as a Nieman fellow at Harvard in 1995, Chan created her own Web site (www.yingchan.com), dedicated to her legal battle against the lawsuit. She sent E-mail messages and set up E-mail listservs aimed at press-freedom advocacy groups. (For more details, see chapter 16, "Cat and Computer Mouse: Using the Internet.")

Her strategy was to put every development out in the open, in hopes that this would create so much bad publicity for Taiwanese leaders that they would back down. She said the leaders would have preferred that all this be kept secret, that dirty linen not be aired in public. "There's a Chinese saying, 'Close the door and beat the dog,'" she said. Her strategy was to keep that door open.

Chan had to make another important decision. Living in New York, she could have avoided going to the trial in Taiwan and fought an extradition battle instead. But in an act of courage, she insisted on going to Taiwan and standing side by side with her colleague Shieh. Thanks partly to her extraordinary campaign, she and Shieh and their magazine won the support of ten heavyweight U.S. media companies, including the *New York Times*. These companies filed a legal brief with the court in Taipei noting, among other things:

> Freedom of the press is internationally recognized as a core democratic value that defamation actions can destroy. . . . This case presents an opportunity for the Republic of China to join the international community in rejecting the idea that journalists may be criminally punished for publishing allegedly false statements that may offend persons in power.

On Tuesday, April 22, 1997, Judge Lee Wei-shin of the Sixteenth Criminal Tribunal Court of Taipei announced his decision: not guilty. He found that Chan and Shieh had no malicious intent, that they had believed in the truth of their story, that they had carefully noted the denials by Liu and Middleton, and—perhaps most important of all—that campaign contributions were a legitimate subject for news reporting. As the judge put it, "political contribution is a matter of public interest and therefore should be subjected to public comment."

In New York, Chan posted the news on her Web site: "Victory!!!" Her codefendant Shieh was in Prague on vacation at the time. How did he get the good news? "My travel agent in Taipei saw the news story and faxed it to my hotel in Czechoslovakia," Shieh said. "I ran out to drink lots of beer!" To be sure, they still faced a possible appeal by Liu, but the lower-court victory for Chan and Shieh was an important development for press freedom in the newly democratic society of Taiwan. Among other effects, it emboldened local journalists in Taiwan to push for reforms in the libel law. "Our case has pushed the issue into the public limelight and sparked a debate," Chan said.

Chinese American journalist Ying Chan (right) and Taiwanese reporter Shieh Chung-liang were threatened with imprisonment in Taiwan for criminal libel because of their story on alleged campaign funding violations. After acquittal, they received International Press Freedom Awards at a ceremony in New York on October 23, 1997. Credit: Committee to Protect Journalists.

Not that Taiwan had suddenly become a hotbed of fiercely independent reporting. In fact, some analysts said, how Chan and Shieh's scoop got published pointed out the difference between Taiwanese journalism and the more freewheeling style of reporting in Hong Kong. "It was no accident that it had been a Hong Kong magazine that published [it]," said William Orme, former executive director of the Committee to Protect Journalists. "Few Taiwanese publications would have been bold enough to print the story."

The boldness of Hong Kong publications had been well known for decades, and after Britain handed over the colony to China on July 1, 1997, many observers wondered whether Beijing would let journalists at the sixteen major Hong Kong dailies continue on their merry way. There was evidence on both sides of the debate.

Fears that Hong Kong would lose its vaunted press freedom were heightened after a number of Beijing officials warned there would be limits on what journalists could report. Lu Ping, director of China's Hong Kong and Macao office, said well before the handover that Hong Kong journalists wouldn't be able to advocate Taiwanese independence. With unintended irony, he said: "Freedom of the press has to be regulated by laws, you see."

The *Asian Wall Street Journal* reported that one of the leading Hong Kong dailies, *Ming Pao*, began pulling its punches and toning down anti-Beijing commentary even before the handover:

> Staff opinion columns, once fiery, now often support China's line. Political news about China comes from official sources. When China was promoting shipping tycoon Tung Chee-Hwa to lead Hong Kong after July, *Ming Pao* devoted a full page to him for five days, with headlines like "Tung Impresses One Most by His Character."

"It's not as aggressive and feisty as it once was, especially in its coverage of China," said A. Lin Neumann, Asia program coordinator for the Committee to Protect Journalists, although he noted that this could be due to a change in ownership at *Ming Pao* rather than any political changes in Hong Kong.

In the months preceding the handover, a *Ming Pao* reporter in Beijing was arrested and convicted of stealing state secrets. That set off alarm bells among those fearing the worst from Beijing after it assumed control of Hong Kong. Those concerns abated somewhat—although not completely—after he was released. (See chapter 10, "Money at Stake: Economic Secrets.")

Kin-ming Liu, vice chairman of the Hong Kong Journalists Association (HKJA) in 1998, believed there was widespread self-censorship by the local press and that it began before the handover. Some local news media, he noted, had stopped using the word *massacre* to describe the June 4, 1989, crackdown by Beijing on pro-democracy demonstrators in Tiananmen Square. A 1994 poll conducted by the University of Hong Kong's Social Sciences Research Center on behalf of the HKJA showed that 33.6 percent of the journalists they contacted admitted to self-censorship.

Yet even Kin-ming Liu conceded that more than a year after the handover there had been no drastic curtailing of press freedom. Dr.

Alan Knight, a 1997 journalism research fellow at Hong Kong University, created a Web site to document any impact on press freedom caused by the handover. He saw the Hong Kong press as basically unchanged well after the transfer of power. "Material is published on Tibet, Taiwan and dissents," he told me. "Dissidents get wide coverage here." For example, he said, on November 22, 1997, Hong Kong's *South China Morning Post* led its front page with coverage of a press conference by Wei Jingsheng, a leading dissident who had been freed by China. "Two months after the handover, the Hong Kong press sees no problem of political interference," said L. P. Yau, editor-in-chief of *Yazhou Zhoukan*, the same Hong Kong weekly newsmagazine that broke the Taiwan money story. "There is no commissar to tell any publications how to run the newsroom, nor do the readers feel any deprivation of information. There are still all kinds of criticisms of China in the media."

Trying to reassure those who feared China would take away Hong Kong's press freedom, Chief Executive Tung Chee-hwa, the city's new leader, said in a speech one hundred days after the handover: "I can assure everyone that this government will remain an open government, respecting the freedom of the press and of the media." But not everyone was reassured. The CPJ's A. Lin Neumann noted that in the past Tung had expressed admiration for Lee Kwan Yew, the autocratic leader of Singapore, who had put a high priority on free enterprise but not on freedom of the press. Neumann said Tung's admiration of Lee "may signal more than just disinterest in free expression, presaging harsh treatment of independent journalists."

Among the millions of ethnic Chinese in Hong Kong, Taiwan, Singapore, and other parts of East Asia, the outcome of the conflict over freedom of the press remains far from clear. Pitted against the courage of journalists such as Ying Chan are powerful political and economic interests. As Chan noted after she and Shieh Chung-liang won their lower-court battle:

> Even as we celebrate our little victory tonight, we remember those who are still sitting in Asian jails or those who are being silenced by physical assault, by bombing, and by criminal libel statutes—a kind of legal terrorism.

4

Guerrilla Journalists

Underground in Nigeria

CHRISTINE ANYANWU STOOD up to the dictator.

In 1995 she was the publisher and editor-in-chief of the Nigerian newsweekly the *Sunday Magazine*. The dictator was Nigeria's General Sani Abacha. The issue between them: his spurious allegation that twenty-nine junior military officers and civilians had conspired to oust him—a claim his regime was using as a pretext for arresting opposition figures. All journalists were told to get in line and agree with the imaginary "coup plot," but Christine Anyanwu refused to bow to his will. In effect, she was saying the emperor had no clothes—that there was no plot and no justification for the arrests. She refused to publish a lie.

Agents of the State Security Service (SSS) arrested her on May 31, 1995. It was a dramatic day in the life of an extraordinary woman.

Christine Anyanwu was born in 1950 at Mbaise in Nigeria's Imo state. She studied journalism in Nigeria and later in the United States, first at the University of Missouri and later at Florida State University, where she received a master's degree in mass communication. Upon her return to Nigeria she became well known as energy correspondent for the television program *Energy and Education* on the state-owned National Television Authority (NTA), an important beat in a country whose economy depends on its oil riches. She worked as a *Newsweek* correspondent based in Nigeria; wrote a book, *The Legislators*; served as a foreign and diplomatic correspondent for NTA; and produced its current affairs program *Newsline* from 1986 to 1989. She became state commissioner of information for Nigeria's Imo state but returned to journalism in 1990, founding the *Sunday Magazine* at a time when newsmagazines were mounting a spirited attack on Nigeria's military dictatorships. Her magazine had a circulation of about ten thousand.

The early 1990s were heady times for Nigerian journalists. Pushy and persistent, they were continuing a tradition of vibrant independent reporting that dated back more than a hundred years in this, Africa's most populous nation with 114 million citizens. In those early years of the 1990s there was another military ruler, General Ibrahim Babangida. On June 12, 1993, a presidential election was held—and the apparent winner was a millionaire oilman and press baron named Moshood K. O. Abiola, candidate of the Social Democratic Party. But before the winner could take over the government, General Babangida simply annulled the election results. Five months later, in the chaos that followed, Babangida himself was ousted in a military coup. Next year Abiola, the millionaire who had won the election, tried to have himself declared Nigeria's legitimate president but was arrested and charged with treason. His newspapers and any others that supported him were shut down. His wife was later assassinated. All of this was intended to consolidate the grip on power by Nigeria's new dictator, the leader of the military junta, General Sani Abacha.

Abacha's opponents repeatedly challenged the annulment of the 1993 elections. Seeing these opponents as a threat to his regime, Abacha had them arrested in early 1995—on the pretext that they were plotting a "coup." It was in this context that Christine Anyanwu, one of the nation's leading journalists, published reports in her weekly *Sunday Magazine* expressing doubt that there ever was any plot.

One article was published in early March 1995 under the sarcastic headline "Yes, There Was a Coup Plan." The article, written by reporter Comfort Obi, noted that journalists waited more than two hours for one of Abacha's generals to show up at a press conference he had called amid expectations that he would finally offer some kind of proof for the claim of a coup plot. Instead, Obi reported, when Major General Abdulsalam Abubakar finally appeared, he failed to name the alleged coup plotters. In the published article, Obi added:

> By not revealing names, Abubakar seemed to have given room to more speculations. Who really are those arrested?

This was not the kind of unquestioning support that the regime expected of journalists. To make it worse, Anyanwu published a list of nineteen persons believed to have been arrested—despite a veiled

Nigerian publisher Christine Anyanwu was sentenced to fifteen years in prison in 1995 for defying military dictator Sani Abacha and publishing stories casting doubt on his claims of a coup plot. After serving three years of her sentence, Anyanwu was freed upon Abacha's death. Credit: Committee to Protect Journalists.

warning by Abubakar that journalists "be careful about mentioning" any names.

Christine Anyanwu proceeded to publish more articles doubting the existence of any coup plot, again with sarcastic headlines—"Coup Update: Bloodbath Soon" and "Echoes of Coup Rock the Nation."

On March 15 the SSS police came looking for reporter Obi, but he had gone into hiding, so instead they arrested his publisher, Anyanwu. She was held for a week on charges of conspiracy and publishing false news designed to cause fear and alarm to disturb the public peace. She was released on $610 bond. On May 31 she was arrested again. This time she and three other journalists were charged with being accessories to "treasonable felony." In July they were tried before a secret military tribunal. Her trial lasted two hours. She had no legal counsel and no right of appeal.

On July 4, 1995, Christine Anyanwu and the three others were convicted and sentenced to life in prison. She was forty-four years old.

Anyanwu was sent to the notorious Gombe Prison in Bauchi state, northern Nigeria. After international protests, her sentence was reduced to fifteen years, but her conditions remained onerous: solitary confinement; no visitors, not even her two children; and no medication to treat malaria and an eye condition that could lead to blindness. Her *Sunday Magazine* was forced to close. For her courage she won awards abroad, including that of the Independent Women's Media Foundation and the Paris-based Reporters Sans Frontières (Reporters Without Borders), whose prize was received on her behalf by Nigeria's Nobel literature laureate Wole Soyinka on December 9, 1995.

She was released from prison in 1998 after the death of the dictator Abacha. She had served three years of her fifteen-year sentence. As she put it afterward: "Nigerian prisons are a hell where one should thank her god if one eventually comes out alive."

The story of Christine Anyanwu is just one example of the suffering inflicted on professional journalists for doing their job. By some accounts, forty-four Nigerian newspapers and magazines were shut down by government decree in the eight years from 1990 through 1997. By the end of 1997, seventeen journalists were behind bars—the largest number for any African country—and two dozen other journalists had been driven into exile.

In May 1998 the Committee to Protect Journalists named Abacha as the world's number-one enemy of freedom of the press:

Five years into his dictatorship, Abacha has escalated his outrageous assault on the country's once-thriving independent press and reneged on his promise to return the country to democracy. His brutal tactics keep 21 Nigerian journalists behind bars: Nigeria now holds more journalists in prison than any other African nation. The February murder of *Guardian* editor Tunde Oladepo, in front of his wife and children, and the April life sentence meted out to *Diet* editor Niran Malaolu were warnings to journalists not to criticize Abacha's stage-managed referendum to secure his succession unopposed.

"Nowhere in Africa," said exiled journalist Dapo Olorunyomi, "is the press assailed and persecuted as in Nigeria."

The journalists not in prison faced almost daily harassment and the threat of violence. It was not an empty threat. In 1986 a flamboyant editor named Dele Giwa was killed by a parcel bomb that he opened at his breakfast table—a bomb his colleagues believe was sent by government security agents. In 1996, Kudirat Abiola, the wife of publisher and winning presidential candidate Moshood K. O. Abiola, was assassinated, and that same year Alex Ibru, publisher of Nigeria's *Guardian*, escaped an attempt on his life. (Candidate Abiola himself died later in prison.)

For Nigerian journalists, violence was a way of life. In one month alone—October 1997—"five Nigerian journalists were verbally abused, five imprisoned, eight beaten and one tortured," said Reporters Sans Frontières. The military regime went after the press in other ways too, some of them bizarre. On June 25, 1993, it arrested four men in Minna, Nigeria, merely for reading an underground photocopy of the *News*, a popular newsmagazine. In 1995 it arrested a news vendor at Lagos Airport for shipping five thousand copies each of the *News*, *Tempo*, and *Tell* magazines, which had been legally permitted to publish. According to exiled journalist Olorunyomi, even the judge in the case was at a loss to understand why the vendor had been arrested. At a court hearing the perplexed jurist asked the prosecutor: "Are these publications banned or proscribed?" To which the prosecutor replied: "Your Worship, they are simply not patriotic."

Perhaps most bizarre of all, in September 1997 armed police and troops broke up a farewell reception given by political dissidents for U.S. Ambassador Walter Carrington at the end of his four-year tour. "This is a regime," said Bill Orme of the Committee to Protect Journalists, "that actually sent goons to beat up journalists covering the good-bye party for the American ambassador."

Despite such brutality, a number of Nigerian journalists kept up the fight. In March 1996, faced with constant intimidation, the country's most popular newsmagazine, *Tell*, accused Abacha of rigging local elections in a story headlined "Gunpoint Democracy: The Junta Arm-Twists Nigerians at the Polls." As one journalist put it: "We are trying to show it's impossible to ban us."

Why couldn't the dictator silence all independent journalists in Nigeria? For one thing, he didn't have enough control over his own forces. "Some members of the security forces sympathize with the opposition and, occasionally, tip off journalists when a raid is imminent," said Cindy Shiner, Lagos correspondent of the London *Guardian*. Not only in Nigeria but in many other battleground countries, control, or the lack of it, by government officials is an important factor for explaining the ability of independent journalists to withstand efforts at repression. As CPJ's Kavita Menon notes, the printed press in a country usually does not need government support to develop, and "because it is decentralized, the press is often extremely difficult to control."

In Nigeria, the regime also put more emphasis on broadcast than on print media in its effort to control the news. It had a monopoly hold on radio and television, the main source of news for the largely illiterate rural population, while newspapers and magazines were privately held. Some press-freedom advocates also believe that the Nigerian regime tolerated some independent reporting in publications read by literate urban professionals as a way for opponents to let off steam.

More important, aggressive journalism is a part of Nigerian culture that goes back even before British colonial rule. (Nigeria was a British colony from 1903 to 1960.) The country's first independent newspaper was published in 1893. As journalist Dapo Olorunyomi puts it:

> If Nigerians continue to invest an abiding faith in the press, it is partly because the press has always represented a vital matrix for their civil society, going back to the 19th century when Lagos newspapers argued for democracy and independence.

Starting in the late 1980s, Olorunyomi says, a new generation of well-educated and politically engaged journalists became a sort of "surrogate parliament." This development, along with Nigeria's tradition of independent journalism, "dovetailed perfectly with the needs of the already troubled Nigerian middle class, the major consumers of the printed word, who demanded a new information and analytical compass to grapple with an increasingly complex global experience."

Helping provide them that compass was Babafemi Ojudu, a young editor who for years played a cat-and-mouse game with police. His story is a study in persistence and defiance against great odds—a story that provides evidence that Nigeria is still a battleground country for press freedom even during periods of repression.

In rural Ekiti in western Nigeria, Ojudu's father screamed when his teenaged son told him he wanted to be a journalist, but there was no stopping the youth. In college, without telling his father, Ojudu plunged into active campus journalism. By his senior year he was contributing to national newspapers. He left the university in 1984 and worked for two years as a city reporter for the *Guardian*, the nation's leading daily. Then he moved into magazine journalism, where the real action was. For two years he reported for *African Concord*, one of the magazines published by millionaire politician Abiola, who later became an opposition leader. Ojudu rose to become assistant editor. "As young men managing the affairs of the magazine," Ojudu later told students at Howard University in Washington, D.C., "we thought there was no limit to the expression of our journalistic freedom. We were soon to find out that we were wrong."

Back in those days, Ojudu said, his publisher Abiola was still friends with the ruling military regime—and the publisher was appalled in 1992 when editor Ojudu and his young colleagues ran an unflattering story on then-ruler Babangida. "It was," Ojudu said, "a revealing psychoanalysis of his person and of course an account of the depth to which he has taken the country." Babangida sent soldiers in combat gear to close down the publishing house and demand an apology. The publisher did apologize, but that still wasn't good enough. The dictator wanted another apology—from Ojudu and his four fellow editors. "We insisted he was not going to get one," Ojudu said.

The insubordinate young editors resigned, raised money, set up a publishing company, and six months later came out with their own magazine, the *News*, which published freely for three months. Then another attack on the ruler—headlined "Babangida's Method and Tactics"—led to their offices being shut down. They published clandestinely while police hunted for them. "We were declared wanted on network news," Ojudu said. They dumped their magazine and replaced it with another, *Tempo*. "We helped mobilize public opinion against the dictator and he was pushed out," Ojudu claimed, although it is hard to prove just what role his magazine played in Babangida's downfall. In any case, Ojudu and his friends felt confident enough to revive the *News* and add two newspapers: *PM News*, a local daily for the metropolitan area of Lagos, the nation's largest city, and *AM News*, a national daily.

Abacha, the new dictator, gave them a breathing space of a few months, then sent his police after them. And that is when the cat-and-mouse game began.

Ojudu practiced what he called "guerrilla journalism." He kept on the move, a toothbrush in his briefcase, his bags always packed, rarely living in his own apartment or seeing his wife and young son, often staying with friends, moving at least once a week, and occasionally wearing a disguise. As editor of *AM News*, he met with his staff inconspicuously at soccer games and movie theaters and constantly moved printing presses to new locations under cover of darkness. When police raided one printing base, he simply set up another. As he told the London *Guardian*: "Every time they ban one of our publications we come up with another."

To escape detection, the 350 men and women reporting for Ojudu's publishing group wrote their stories in longhand and delivered them using "dead drops"—secretly prearranged drop-off locations, from roadside piles of trash to a cemetery grave. Editors collected the stories and took them to hideouts to prepare them for publication and then smuggled the finished stories to printing presses.

What kind of stories did they do? "I did a report on the oil minister that the government did not like and was arrested and thrown in jail for ten days," Ojudu said. "Then I did a profile of Mrs. Abacha. She went with 350 Nigerian women to the United Nations Conference on Women in Beijing and she spent millions of dollars." General Abacha didn't appreciate the exposé on his wife's spending habits. Police broke into Ojudu's office and arrested him. This time he was "stripped and tortured from 8 o'clock until 2 in the morning. I passed out. They then dumped me in front of a medical clinic."

Ojudu's band of guerrilla journalists suffered many setbacks. Kunle Ajibade, editor-in-chief of the *News* magazine, was sentenced along with Christine Anyanwu and two other journalists to fifteen years for reporting the wrongful arrests of alleged "coup" plotters.

When another of Ojudu's band, journalist Dapo Olorunyomi, nar-rowly escaped arrest, police seized his wife. Olorunyomi went into exile in Maryland and eventually, in 1998, his wife and children joined him. And another of Ojudu's guerrillas "called it quits follow-ing intense pressure from family," Ojudu said.

That left two leaders of the publishing group still active. "In 1996 I and my colleague were arrested, tortured and jailed three times each," Ojudu reported. They were released but banned from travel—a ban that Ojudu managed to evade in 1997, when he went to Washington and later to a press-freedom conference in Nairobi, where he boasted of using mobile phones and laptop computers to elude police and keep his publishing enterprise going. To get to the Nairobi conference Ojudu rode a motorbike, slipped past a security detail, secretly crossed the border into neighboring Benin, and caught a flight to Kenya. If he had tried to fly from Lagos, he said, he would have been arrested on the spot and his passport would have been impounded.

Having just told the Nairobi conference of his ability to elude po-lice, Ojudu left Nairobi and, on November 17, 1997, while trying to slip back unnoticed into Nigeria, was caught and arrested. He was put in the Ikoyi Prison near Lagos and managed to smuggle a letter out de-scribing conditions in a "dungeon . . . I am in solitary confinement and food is passed to me like a caged lion." Later, friends said in early 1998, he was transferred to the better conditions of the Inter-Center Prison Hospital in Lagos with an undisclosed ailment. Ojudu was released in July 1998 after the death of the dictator Abacha.

By 1999, Nigeria had a civilian government, but questions re-mained about the prospects for democracy. What would finally happen to Nigeria's guerrilla journalists was anybody's guess, but there was no question what their readers thought of them. "We rely on the bravery of journalists like Ojudu to get the real story of what is happening to this country," lawyer Gani Fawelhinmi told London's *Sunday Times*. "No-body else will tell us."

5

A Precious Pen

Defiance around the World

MOST OF THE attacks on journalists take place in the battleground countries where the press is partly free. In those countries, such as Mexico, Russia, and Nigeria, independent journalists are officially permitted to exist but must struggle against repressive forces. In other countries, the ones at the extremes of the press-freedom continuum, attacks and pressures on journalists are far less likely to occur, for totally different reasons. At one end, in the totalitarian dictatorships where the only officially tolerated journalists are government controlled, there are virtually no independent local journalists apart from those in prison, and therefore no one is at large to be attacked. At the other end, in the freest countries, independent journalists usually enjoy popular support and the protection of strong, stable institutions such as an independent judiciary, and would-be attackers are deprived of the impunity that is an important precondition for violence against reporters. At both ends of the spectrum, harsh reprisals against journalists are rare—but they do exist, as we see in this chapter.

For journalists who step out of line in the most repressive countries, the punishment can be death. A foreign journalist suffered that fate in Iraq.

It was September 1989 in Baghdad. British citizen Farzad Bazoft, a newly arrived correspondent, learned of an explosion at a missile plant at Qaqa, south of the Iraqi capital. It seemed a good candidate for a story for his London newspaper, the *Observer*, so Bazoft decided to investigate. He went to the site and collected samples of soil to analyze for his story, but before he could complete his reporting he was arrested. Bazoft, thirty-one years old, was taken to Abu Khareb Prison twenty miles east of Baghdad. There, Iraqi officials say, the Iranian-born British journalist confessed to spying for Israel. Some Western journalists

Chinese journalist Gao Yu (left) with her son Zhao Meng in Beijing in 1990. She served all but seven months of a six-year prison sentence for leaking state secrets in articles published in Hong Kong. She was released in 1999. Earlier she had been held for fourteen months without charge after taking part in the 1989 Tiananmen Square pro-democracy demonstrations. Credit: AP/Wide World Photos.

believe he was tortured into signing a false confession. From Western capitals came demands for his release, but the dictatorship of Iraqi leader Saddam Hussein ignored them.

On March 15, 1990, Farzad Bazoft was hanged.

Months after his execution, he was still being referred to ominously by Iraqi officials who sought to intimidate other foreign correspondents. With chilling sarcasm the officials would ask a newly arrived journalist if he were grooming himself to be "the new Mr. Bazoft."

In China, Gao Yu also learned a hard lesson.

She was a respected writer and journalist. In 1977 she wrote the screenplay for *Spring*, a film about artists who had been rehabilitated after their persecution during the ten years of the Cultural Revolution.

The end of the repressive Cultural Revolution was a time of hope for her: "As the open-door reforms brought intellectuals into a splendid part of the century, I commenced my journalistic career." She specialized in economic reporting during the reform period of the 1980s and allied herself with the pro-democracy movement.

Gao wrote investigative pieces on economic matters and interviewed leading supporters of reform. She worked in Beijing for the semi-official *China News Service* and later became deputy editor-in-chief of *Economics Weekly*, run by an independent research institute that supported reform. Leaders of that institute were later arrested and convicted of fomenting student protests at Tiananmen Square.

Gao Yu herself was arrested twice. The first time was during the height of the tumultuous 1989 pro-democracy demonstrations at Tiananmen Square. On May 19, 1989, according to human rights advocates, Gao negotiated a deal between the protesting students and Chinese authorities. Under the deal, the students would withdraw from the square in exchange for a meeting between student leaders and a group of Chinese officials. The deal fell through when Beijing proclaimed martial law.

Gao was taken into custody at noon on June 3, 1989, only hours before troops attacked the student demonstrators. No one outside the Chinese government knows the precise death toll. Beijing officially claims that no more than three hundred students and troops were killed. Western intelligence agencies put the figure at upward of one thousand. What is not in dispute is that the bloody repression of the pro-democracy demonstrations dominated the news about China for years afterward.

Gao Yu was held for fourteen months without charge. A former mayor of Beijing, writing a report on the Tiananmen clashes, accused her of being a major "conspirator" behind the protest movement. He claimed that an article she had written the year before—an interview with two reformist scholars in *Economics Weekly*—was a "political program for the turmoil and rebellion." But no formal charges were ever brought against her on those grounds, and after showing symptoms of a heart condition, she was released from detention on August 28, 1990.

Gao continued to work as an economics reporter. She did freelance work under a pen name for the Hong Kong magazine *Mirror Monthly*, a pro-Beijing publication owned by Xu Simin, a leader of mainland China's National People's Congress. In March and April

1993 the magazine published two four-page articles by her (under the name Liu Jiang) about preparations for key meetings of senior Communist Party officials. She also wrote two other articles on the same subject in *Overseas Chinese Daily*, another Hong Kong publication that was pro-Beijing, under a different pen name. Those articles resulted in much harsher punishment for her than before.

In the articles she made two main points. One was that the party had abandoned an earlier commitment to separate itself from government policy. The other was that former leader Deng Xiaoping, although he had retired from all official positions, remained influential. She revealed that a few casual comments by Deng had caused officials to drop plans to cool down an economy that they had felt was overheating.

Later in 1993, after writing the articles, Gao was offered and accepted a fellowship as visiting scholar at the Columbia University Graduate School of Journalism in New York. She was to fly from Beijing to New York on October 4, but as she was preparing for her trip, only two days before her scheduled departure, she was arrested and taken to the new Beijing State Security Bureau Detention Center in the southern part of the capital. Eventually she was tried in secret before the Beijing Intermediate People's Court and convicted of "illegally providing state secrets to institutions outside [China's] borders." Her articles had consisted mostly of dry economic details, hardly the basis for serious criminal charges—except that her information came from official Chinese Communist Party documents marked *juemi* (top secret). Her court proceedings dragged on for more than a year.

Finally, on November 10, 1994, at the age of forty-nine, Gao Yu was sentenced to six years in prison. She appealed, arguing that she was being victimized for her liberal political views, that some of the information in her articles had already been reported in the Hong Kong press, and that in any case her articles had caused no harm to China. Her lawyers told the court she had been merely doing her job as a reporter. She lost the appeal and began serving her sentence in Yanquing Prison, in a Beijing suburb. Human rights advocates reported that she shared a cell with common criminals and suffered from a variety of medical ailments, including vertigo, heart disease, and edema (swelling) in her legs. They said she received no specialist medical attention. Gao herself wrote in December 1994: "Every day I have to take large doses of medicine. . . . My calves are blue and swollen."

Gao's arrest came the same year that another Chinese journalist was released from prison—and some saw a connection between the two events. Wang Juntao, a prominent dissident intellectual who had run *Economics Weekly*, had been sentenced to thirteen years after the crackdown in Tiananmen Square. He was released in early 1994 "apparently as part of China's efforts to secure American renewal of its most-favored-nation trading status," according to Hong Kong journalist Daisy Li Yuet-wah. She added:

> Many people see Gao's case as an example of China's "revolving door" system: When one prominent dissident is released, another is detained. This ensures that there is another victim for the next round of trade concessions.

Whether in fact she was being held as a bargaining chip for trade talks is impossible to say, but Gao herself felt she was being punished for her political views in general rather than the specifics of her articles. "The judgment of the [lower court] was a political judgment," she told the appeals court.

> It is about me, but also about the June 4 [pro-democracy] movement. . . . It is evident that to sentence me to jail is simply to substitute me for the man you labelled "the principal criminal of the June 4 movement," Wang Juntao, who . . . is currently in the United States.

Gao's case became a *cause célèbre* among human rights activists. Protesters in Hong Kong demanded she be released. A Hong Kong television reporter in Paris asked visiting Chinese premier Zhu Rongji to comment on the protests; the reporter later was reprimanded by a Chinese official for asking such a question. Even the United Nations became involved. On May 3, 1997, UNESCO—the United Nations Educational, Scientific, and Cultural Organization—gave Gao a $25,000 press freedom award at a conference in Bilbao sponsored by the International Federation of Journalists. It was accepted on Gao's behalf by Timothy Balding, head of the World Association of Newspapers, who said Gao's husband had told him the prize money would be spent on medicine for her.

In China, Gao had learned of the prize from family members visiting her in prison. She sent a message to the Bilbao Conference: "This exciting piece of news was all we talked about during my monthly thirty-minute meeting with them." She expressed thanks to her parents, to all Chinese intellectuals, and to the world press and added: "I feel tremendously proud. I ardently love the journalistic undertaking that I am devoted to. . . . The pen is the most precious thing I own in my life."

On Monday, February 15, 1999, in a gesture timed to improve the atmosphere for a visit by the U.S. secretary of state to discuss trade and other matters, China released Gao from prison "for medical reasons" after she had served all but nine months of her six-year sentence. Her family said she had been told not to talk to foreign media or she would go back to jail, and she was ordered to abstain from political activity and not to leave her Beijing neighborhood without government permission. Just over a year later she was reported to be still under virtual house arrest in China and was unable to travel to Boston to receive a press freedom award from the International Press Institute.

While independent journalists such as Gao Yu rarely exist in the most repressive nations, they are commonplace at the opposite end of the spectrum, in the countries with the maximum amount of freedom of the press, primarily the United States, Canada, Japan, Australia, and the nations of Western Europe. Most of the battles over press freedom have already been fought and won by independent journalists in these countries, yet even here reporters sometimes face threats to their lives for reporting the news. One such journalist was Veronica Guerin.

The married mother of a small boy, she was Ireland's leading investigative journalist as a reporter for the widely read *Sunday Independent*. Her specialty was Dublin's criminal underworld and what she called its "violence, money and evil." Her friends described her as a lively, energetic person, "always on the phone," stubborn, persistent, persuasive, able to obtain the interview that no other reporter could get.

Guerin was determined to name names despite repeated threats to her safety. "And once on to a story, she was so meticulous and so determined. She just wouldn't give up," wrote fellow journalist Alan Byrne. "Others would avoid making difficult calls, say that the story just wasn't working, give up and head home. Not Veronica. She would keep going until she had the story—whatever the personal risks and dangers."

In 1994 she wrote a series of articles about the assassination of Irish gangster Martin Cahill, known as "The General." After it was published, two shots were fired at her home. Three months later, in January 1995, she published a critical profile of the suspected mastermind of the

Investigative reporter Veronica Guerin (shown in this undated photo with her son, Cathal) won renown for her stories about Ireland's drug-trafficking underworld. After numerous threats from druglords, she was shot dead in 1996. Credit: AP/Wide World Photos.

largest robbery in Irish history. The next day a masked man entered her home, pointed a gun at her head, and then shot her in the thigh.

In both incidents, no arrests were made. Despite the fact that her assailants remained at large and that the second shooting was believed to be a warning from organized crime, Guerin persisted in her reporting. "I am letting the public know exactly how this society operates," she wrote.

Guerin had developed such good contacts in the Dublin underworld that, after she was shot, "some of those criminals got in touch to sympathize with her," Byrne said. "Veronica, though, just wanted to find out who had ordered her to be shot. And when she found out, she went, on crutches, to see the person to let them know she wasn't scared."

In September 1995 she met with an Irish businessman to seek an interview for one of her investigative stories. He slammed her head against her car and threatened to kill her if she wrote anything about him. For her courage in the face of these many threats, Guerin was honored with a Press Freedom Award of the Committee to Protect Journalists. The award was presented to her in December 1995 by Lesley Stahl of CBS's *60 Minutes*, who said: "Her commitment to defending the public's right to read the truth is impregnable."

But Guerin's story did not end there.

Next year she was onto a story about drug dealers. Byrne recalled her mood:

> She was on the phone, very excited, saying that her paper was going to name the three biggest heroin dealers in Dublin. Lacking her bravery, I urged her to be careful, said how dangerous it sounded. But her response was simple: "Somebody's got to do it."

On June 26, 1996, in the middle of a bright summer day, Guerin was in her red Opel sedan in south Dublin, waiting at a traffic light. Two men on a motorcycle drove up. One of them smashed her driver's-side window and shot her in the face and chest six times with a .357 Magnum pistol. Guerin, thirty-seven years old, died almost instantly. She left behind her husband, Graham, and six-year-old son, Cathal.

The assassination of Veronica Guerin caused an uproar. One press-freedom advocacy group said it "shocked the whole country."

Letters of outrage poured in to Irish newspapers, such as this one from Eoin Neeson:

A brilliant and revealing star of truth is no more, but the indomitable light she turned on what corrupts and desecrates our society survives, even in her death. She has done this state much service in a short life. *Ar dheis Dé go raibh a anam dilis*. (May your soul be on the right-hand side of God.)

Her funeral was attended by Ireland's president, prime minister, and head of the armed forces, as well as the Catholic archbishop of Dublin. Prime Minister John Bruton called the assassination of Guerin an "attack on democracy" and vowed a thorough investigation. More than one hundred people were taken in for questioning. Three men were charged in connection with the crime. By mid-1999, two of them had been sentenced to life in prison and the third was awaiting trial.

Leading Irish and British journalists promised to carry on Guerin's brand of investigative reporting. In a joint statement they said:

We view this assassination as a fundamental attack on the free press which is essential to the democratic process. Journalists will not be intimidated. We hereby commit our news organizations to continue the investigation of the stories which cost Veronica Guerin her life.

Agreed and signed by

—Ireland:

Aengus Fanning, editor, *The Sunday Independent*; Vincent Doyle, editor, *The Irish Independent*; Conor Brady, editor, *The Irish Times*; Gerry O'Regan, editor, *The Star*; Tom Collins, *The Sunday World*; Martin Lindsay, editor, *Sunday Life*; Joe Mulholland, director of news, RTE.

—Britain:

Alan Rusbridger, editor, *The Guardian*; Peter Stothard, editor, *The Times*; Charles Moore, editor, *The Daily Telegraph*; Andrew Marr, editor, *The Independent*; Paul Dacre, editor, *The Daily Mail*; Will Hutton, editor, *The Observer*; John Witherow, editor, *The Sunday Times*; Peter Wilby, editor, *The Independent on Sunday*.

The same type of solidarity and collective vow to continue a reporter's investigative work came after a rare murder of a journalist in the United States: the 1976 car-bombing in Phoenix of crime reporter Don Bolles of the *Arizona Republic*. Bolles was lured into a trap by a man posing as an informant. Authorities never established a motive, despite suspicions by some journalists that organized crime was involved. Bolles had done investigative reports on state officials.

After Bolles's murder, American journalists formed a group known as Independent Reporters and Editors (IRE). It completed his investigation of organized crime, pressed for punishment of his killers (a process that took seventeen years), and created a permanent organization to protect the rights of investigative reporters. In this case, and that of Denver radio commentator Alan Berg, killed in 1992 by white supremacists, "a firm response from the news media and from law enforcement left the indelible mark that reporters' lives were not fair game," investigative reporter Ana Arana concluded.

That's hardly the case in the most repressive countries of the world, where those who attack journalists enjoy impunity. There, at the other end of the press-freedom spectrum, the rights of independent journalists carry little weight. That makes it all the more remarkable when a few defiant individuals risk their safety, their freedom, and their lives. As Gao Yu of China told the court: "I have consistently, now and in the past, upheld the country's best interests with my pen. . . . For the past fifteen years I have done my duty for journalism. Who does not have feelings? Who does not have parents? Who does not have sons and daughters? Who does not have brothers and sisters? But I am willing to sacrifice all I have for the country's modernization and journalism."

PART II

PUSHING THE ENVELOPE

Stories That Trigger Attack

6

The General's Mercedes

Crime and Corruption

ON A MONDAY in October, a young journalist named Dmitri Kholodov went to the Kazan Railway Station in Moscow to pick up a briefcase.

It was where his informant had told him it would be, in a luggage locker. The informant, speaking by phone from Russia's domestic intelligence agency, had told Kholodov the briefcase contained incriminating evidence of army corruption—just what the reporter needed to complete his investigation. What the informant did not tell him was that the briefcase contained not incriminating evidence but a bomb.

Kholodov, twenty-seven, brought the briefcase back to his office at *Moskovsky Komsomolets*, Moscow's most popular daily newspaper. He shouted to a colleague, deputy editor Vadim Poegli: "Vadim, I think I've got something."

Then he sat down and opened the briefcase.

It was October 17, 1994. Kholodov was scheduled to testify in a few days to a committee of the Duma (lower house of parliament) on his investigations. He was one of the brightest stars on the newspaper and had made a name for himself as an investigative reporter. His newspaper was aggressively probing allegations of corruption by senior military officers, including Defense Minister Pavel Grachev.

The young reporter investigated the theft, smuggling, and black market sales of Russian military property in the former East Germany—everything from food, cigarettes, and liquor to oil, electronics, synthetic drugs, armored vehicles, and even MIG warplanes. "The scope of operations over there in Germany," he had reported that summer, "can be illustrated by the disappearance of two trains supposed to take military property . . . from the Western Army Group to Russia." All of this was happening as Russian troops withdrew from Germany in the aftermath of the cold war.

Kholodov reported that senior Russian officers were enriching themselves by thefts and illegal sales and the bribes that facilitated them. He told of one colonel who had ordered that fourteen Volvos be flown by military plane from Germany to Moscow for delivery to his headquarters. "He was never arrested," the reporter wrote. There were even suspicions that Defense Minister Grachev himself had taken a bribe in the form of a luxury car. As Kholodov reported:

> In 1992, the leadership of the Western Army Group [of the Russian military in Germany] bought through front-men in Berlin a Mercedes worth 150,000 DM [German marks—about $235,000] and sent it to Moscow. Soon they saw the car in Moscow and inside it sat the Defense Minister, Pavel Grachev.

The reporter said the gift apparently came from a Russian airborne division general who was later arrested for taking bribes. Kholodov's newspaper gave Defense Minister Grachev a nickname that stuck: "Pasha Mercedes."

The Mercedes-500 was one of two allegedly bought illegally with the proceeds of sales of Russian military property, including five thousand Jeeps and half a million gas masks to a Spanish company. Other stories in this scandal included accounts of massive looting of government property by senior officers. One secret report by the government's top anticorruption official was leaked to Kholodov's newspaper. It told of Russian officers in Germany selling off more than $50 million worth of military goods—but giving the government only $13.5 million in proceeds. "When people say there is a whole army of mafiosi in Russia," Kholodov wrote, "they do not realize how close they are to the truth. Our Russian army is sliding down into the world of organized crime."

Anyone who tried to shine a light down into that dark world was taking a risk. But taking risks was nothing new for Dmitri Kholodov. During his four years at his newspaper, he had taken on dangerous assignments covering civil wars in Tajikistan, Georgia, and Chechnya and had received several death threats since he had begun his investigation of the Russian military.

For Dmitri Kholodov, as for other independent journalists in the battleground countries of press freedom, crime and corruption stories were among those most likely to trigger reprisal. Powerful figures who break the law and enrich themselves at the cost of the public will take extreme measures to keep their malfeasance secret. Their ability to silence investigative reporters is limited only by the extent to which they risk getting caught. In certain countries it is more dangerous than in others for reporters to delve deeply into crime and corruption, because the targets of their investigations enjoy protection from punishment for any attacks they inflict on journalists. The greater their corruption of law enforcement institutions, the greater the impunity they enjoy.

This was especially true in Russia. With the collapse of communism, Russian society was more open. There was more freedom to *report* on crime—but also more freedom to *commit* crime. According to some accounts, Russia had an estimated five thousand criminal gangs, and Moscow's murder rate exceeded that of New York City. Organized crime controlled or received extortion payments from nearly all legitimate private business. With crime went corruption. When reform-minded General Anatoly Kulikov, the new boss of the Interior Ministry, tested police honesty, he found that only two out of twenty-four officers refused a proffered bribe.

Journalists investigating the underworld found plenty of material to report—but at a price. Six of the seven murders of journalists in Russia in 1993–1995 bore the marks of contract killings. In the decade of the 1990s, according to press advocacy groups, thirty-nine journalists were killed in Russia or the Soviet Union, many of them while investigating crime and corruption. Most of the murder cases remained unsolved, a cause for serious concern by independent journalists who wanted to expose the power of the Russian mafia. "We are being shot or bought off so that we stop being an obstacle to a new dictatorship," said Shod Muladjanov, editor of the daily Moscow newspaper *Moskovskaya Pravda*, "and no law enforcement body in the country protects our rights."

On that Monday in Moscow in October 1994, Dmitri Kholodov opened the briefcase. The bomb exploded. It tore through the lower part of his body, leaving him mortally wounded, and slightly injured another journalist.

After the murder of the crusading journalist, thousands of mourners—some reports claimed up to ten thousand—filed past his coffin in the Palace of Youth. Weeping women piled flowers around the casket. A brass band played the "Funeral March." At his funeral, the nation's most prominent democratic leaders expressed horror at the crime. President Boris Yeltsin said he would personally supervise the investigation. Public pressure on the government to punish those responsible was formidable. Defense Minister Grachev, who denied any involve-ment in the crime, at first offered the lame explanation that Kholodov might have accidentally killed himself. Grachev later blamed the mafia and said he doubted the murderer would ever be found. Many of Kholodov's colleagues suspected military officers, for the obvious rea-son that it was their crimes that were being uncovered by the reporter. Yet weeks, months, and years went by with no arrests.

It was a crime that Russians could not forget. Three years later a film called *Schizophrenia*, a fictional story of high-level corruption and mafia connections, used as its opening sequence actual footage from Kholodov's funeral. As one journalist for a British newspaper put it, the film director's message was that "murders in Russia are not solved be-cause the authorities themselves order them."

Finally, in 1998, almost three and a half years after the murder, in-vestigators said they had solved the crime. The first arrest was that of a retired colonel, Pavel Popovskikh, former head of intelligence for the army's paratroopers. He was charged with organizing the murder. Five days later Vladimir Morozov, an active-duty major in the paratroops, was also charged with involvement. And two months later an unnamed civilian suspected of being an accomplice was also charged. But many Russians suspected that those three weren't the only ones responsible, that the guilty included people higher up on the chain of command—higher up and untouchable. As one headline put it: "The Person Who Ordered the Hit Still Remains to Be Found." The case remains open.

Most attacks on Russian crime reporters remain unsolved. Take these examples from 1994 to 1997:

Yuri Soltis of the Interfax News Agency was found beaten to death at a train station near Moscow.

Viatcheslav Rudnev, a freelance reporter who did stories on crime and corruption for newspapers in the city of Kaluga, southwest of Moscow, died of a fractured skull. (Police investigated briefly and ruled it an accident—but made no effort to follow up on the death threats he had received.)

Vadim Alferyev in the Siberian city of Krasnoyarsk was found beaten to death.

Not only in Russia but elsewhere, it is the impunity afforded those who attack journalists that raises serious questions about the willingness or ability of authorities to protect journalists who expose crime and corruption. The impunity the criminals enjoy suggests that in some cases the authorities themselves are behind the very attacks they should be punishing. A good example is the case in Mexico of Manuel Buendía Tellezgirón.

He was Mexico's equivalent of Walter Cronkite. At the age of fifty-eight, Manuel Buendía Tellezgirón was the most trusted and respected journalist in the nation, winner of two prestigious awards. He had spent his working life as a muckraking reporter and columnist, most recently for *Excelsior*, Mexico City's most influential newspaper. In his column, "Private Network," published on the front page of *Excelsior* and syndicated in two hundred other newspapers, he exposed corruption. By the spring of 1984 he was focusing more and more on suspected links between powerful drug traffickers and high-ranking government officials.

On May 4, he wrote that the drug trade was creating "an extremely grave situation." He quoted Catholic bishops in southern Mexico who said that farm workers were forced to grow marijuana and that "he who denounces, dies." On May 14, Buendía Tellezgirón quoted unnamed sources who complained of "the complicity, direct or indirect, of high public officials on the state and federal level" in the drug trade.

Just over two weeks later, on Wednesday, May 30, at 6:30 P.M., Buendía Tellezgirón finished his work for the day, walked down the six flights of stairs from his office, and headed along Insurgentes Avenue toward his gray 1982 Ford Mustang in a parking lot in the busy Zona Rosa district of Mexico City. According to witnesses, a tall young man in jeans, a black jacket, and a baseball cap approached him from behind, grabbed his overcoat, and fired four bullets from a .38 Super into the columnist's back, then ran away. Buendía Tellezgirón carried a revolver at his waist but never had a chance to draw it. (His widow said later: "He used to say, 'To kill me, they will have to shoot me in the back.' They must have prepared well.")

The first senior investigator to arrive on the scene was José Antonio Zorrilla Pérez, head of Mexico's equivalent of the FBI, the DFS (Dirección Federal de Seguridad). Zorrilla Pérez had been one of Buendía Tellezgirón's main sources. The investigation dragged on for five years with much bungling, including lost evidence, and no major breakthrough until June 11, 1989—when senior investigator Zorrilla Pérez himself was charged with masterminding the murder. He and another former DFS officer were convicted and sentenced to thirty-five years in prison. Three former federal police officers were also convicted as co-conspirators and sentenced to twenty-five years.

The fact that the first senior investigator on the case turned out to be the man who ordered the murder raises a serious question: When the police are the criminals, how can there be justice? How can there be any assurance that those who attack reporters and editors will be punished for their crimes? That is one reason why it is so dangerous for journalists to cover stories that link crime and corruption. Often there are vast amounts of money at stake. Exposés threaten to deprive criminals and corrupt officials of the secrecy they need in order to continue to make enormous illicit profits. Threatened by the truth, protected by impunity, they have every reason in the world to silence journalists—and nothing to fear. As Mexican author Jorge C. Castañeda put it: "The impunity is blinding and shameful."

In many parts of the world, corruption stories have replaced political ones as the most dangerous to cover. Former CPJ head William Orme Jr. told me:

> The grave dangers to journalists 20 years ago were largely ideological. If they were going to be murdered they were murdered by people murdering them because they felt they were leftists, largely, but sometimes rightists. . . . These were politically motivated attacks that took place in the context of the cold war and this huge global battle between the left and the right. Now most of the deaths are caused by people writing about corruption.

Of all the stories linking crime and corruption, probably none is more dangerous for journalists to cover than the drug story—especially in the Latin American nation of Colombia. So violent have been the attacks on the press that, according to one tally, throughout the decade of the 1990s, Colombia was second only to Algeria as the most dangerous place in the world for journalists. One of the victims was Colombia's leading editor and publisher.

Guillermo Cano Isaza began his career at the age of seventeen covering bullfights for the national daily newspaper *El Espectador* (The Spectator) of Colombia. In the next forty-four years he worked his way up to foreign correspondent in Europe and finally to editor and publisher. As his democratic country fell more and more under the sway of the Medellín cocaine cartel, Cano Isaza campaigned for a hard line against illicit drugs and in favor of extraditing drug criminals to the United States—criminals who included druglord Pablo Escobar Gaviria. Cano Isaza called Escobar "The Godfather." Soon Cano Isaza and his newspaper moved to the top of Escobar's enemies list.

Despite the growing power of Escobar and his killing and bribing of judges to undermine democratic institutions, white-haired, bespectacled publisher Cano Isaza remained hopeful. He wrote in his column, "Notebook":

> While there are events that lead to discouragement and despair, I do not hesitate to say that Colombians are capable of advancing toward a more egalitarian, more just, more honest and more prosperous society.

That idealistic belief clashed with the reality of Escobar and the lengths he was willing to go to protect his drug wealth. On December 17, 1986, shortly after 7 P.M., Cano Isaza was driving his red Subaru station wagon through the pre-Christmas traffic of Bogotá's El Espectador Avenue. As he slowed to make a U-turn in front of his office building, a young man sidled up, opened a black case, and fired eight bullets from a MAC 10 submachine gun into Cano Isaza's chest, then sped off with another man on a motorcycle. Guillermo Cano Isaza died of his wounds. He was sixty-one.

Colombia's president led the funeral procession, but not everyone mourned the death of the crusading publisher. Druglord Escobar held a victory party in his stronghold of Medellín. For the next nine years he did everything in his power to thwart the murder investigation. Despite judicial reforms intended to keep the identities of judges secret in some cases to protect them from criminals, Escobar managed to find out the names of the judges involved. Some judges were forced to take payoffs. Those who did not were killed or saw members of their families killed.

Escobar also struck again at the newspaper after its editors refused to give up their campaign against him. Escobar's men issued death threats to the paper's reporters and editors, including Cano Isaza's two sons, Juan Guillermo and Fernando. The paper shut down its office in the city of Medellín after two executives were killed. For two years copies of the newspaper had to be delivered in that city under military escort. Escobar's thugs bombed the newspaper's headquarters, burned down the Cano family summer home, and shot dead the Cano family lawyer who had overseen the murder investigation. The judicial proceedings dragged on for years, disrupted by bribed judges, deaths, threats, and appeals. Escobar himself was among those charged as masterminds of the murder, but a corrupt judge threw out the charges. The actual hitman was found dead. His mother was identified as an accomplice, one of four people finally convicted of direct involvement in carrying out Cano Isaza's murder. Three later were acquitted on appeal. The fourth, who had been allowed by police to escape from detention, remained at large until his capture in 1997, two years after his conviction.

Although Escobar himself was never convicted of masterminding the crime, he did face justice of a sort. Charges against him were reinstated. He surrendered to police, then escaped, then in 1993 was tracked down and shot dead by special teams of Colombian antinarcotics police, helped by U.S. intelligence agents. As for Cano Isaza, his memory is enshrined in the annual international award for courageous journalism, the UNESCO/Guillermo Cano World Press Freedom Prize. That was the prize won by Gao Yu while she was imprisoned in China.

It is not just in Colombia that the drug story spells trouble for reporters and editors. In 1996, Vinicio Pacheco, a court reporter for Radio Sonora in Guatemala City, reported a crime wave including drug trafficking, car thefts, and kidnappings. He himself was kidnapped in the center of the city, blindfolded, beaten, and burned with cigarettes. His captors held a gun to his head and slashed his feet while the thugs played recordings of his radio reports. After several hours of torture, he was released outside the city. More threats were directed at him, and eventually he moved to Costa Rica.

In Peru, the newsweekly *Sí* was harassed in 1994 for reporting alleged links between the army and drug traffickers. Henchmen for a local druglord called "El Barón" burned copies of the magazine. The army accused the publication and three others of tarnishing the military's image. The news director for a radio station was threatened with death although he said he was not a source for the story in *Sí*; he was forced to flee his home and move to another town. Also in Peru, a TV reporter working on drug stories revealed the existence of a clandestine airstrip used by Colombian planes. Five days later, gunmen sprayed his house with bullets.

In Paraguay, a newspaper reporter who identified local drug traffickers in the border region with Brazil received death threats—one of them phoned in during a live radio interview. Next day a TV reporter covering the same story got an anonymous phone call warning him to drop the story or he would be "permanently silenced."

In the southern African country of Zambia, *Crime News* accused President Frederick Chiluba and his wife, Vera, of involvement in drug trafficking. Managing Editor Stewart Mwila and his deputy were arrested and held for several days. In the West African country of Ghana, the *Free Press* and the *Ghanaian Chronicle* landed in trouble for linking the president with drugs. In 1996 they reprinted an article from the New York–based biweekly the *African Observer* that reported the arrest in Switzerland of a Ghanaian diplomat on charges of selling drugs and alleged that Ghana's president, Jerry Rawlings, bought arms with the proceeds from illicit drug deals. The editors of the two publications and the publisher of the *Free Press* were arrested, released, rearrested, and finally rereleased after being charged with "publishing false news with the intent of injuring the reputation of the State."

Crime and corruption stories often go hand in hand. And when it comes to corruption, few countries could beat Indonesia. Until he was forced by bloody riots and international pressures to abdicate in 1998, longtime dictator Suharto developed the art of nepotism to a fine degree, lining his pockets and those of his family and friends with billions of dollars from the national treasury and lucrative business contracts. It was no surprise that he did not look kindly upon journalists who tried to reveal the extent of his corruption. Newspapers were shut down and editors packed off to prison for daring to raise questions.

Suharto's attacks on journalists were made easier by the laws he imposed. For example, it was a crime for any journalist to insult the great leader. Under that law, one editor was sentenced to two years in prison for merely writing a headline: "This Country Has Been Messed Up by a Man Called Suharto." In a bizarre interpretation of what press freedom is all about, Dr. Ramlan Surbakti of Airlangga University in Surabaya, East Java, explained the policy: "The Press in Indonesia can freely express itself as long as its articles won't question the people in power and their family businesses."

Journalist Ahmad Taufik refused to go along with that strange notion. Born in Jakarta, he began as a reporter in 1986 at the age of twenty-one. He worked in the Bandung bureau of *Tempo*, the nation's largest-circulation newsmagazine (190,000 copies, 1.4 million readers), known for its daring and independence. Four years after Taufik joined the staff, *Tempo* tested the limits of a brief 1990 experiment by Suharto to relax censorship, a policy called *keterbukaan* ("openness," in the nation's Bahasa Indonesia language). Taufik was among a new generation of independent journalists who took advantage of this opening to do stories that normally were taboo. "We have a lot of problems with corruption and nepotism," he said.

His magazine infuriated Suharto and other officials by exposing their wrongdoing as well as publishing stories about labor and ethnic unrest. *Tempo* covered government scandals including the exorbitant $1.1 billion purchase of thirty-nine secondhand East German warships. It revealed a mass killing in Jakarta, the mysterious murder of a labor activist, and the imprisonment of twenty-one students who criticized Suharto.

As far as Suharto was concerned, the openness policy was causing a little too much openness. In June 1994 his regime banned *Tempo* and two other weeklies. Thousands of Indonesians across the archipelago took to the streets in protest, and many were beaten by troops and police. To try to fill the void left by the banned publications, two Suharto cronies were given permission to create two new magazines, filled with pro-government pap.

The state-sponsored—and largely government-controlled—Indonesian Journalists' Association, the PWI, said it "understood" the reasons the government had shut down *Tempo* and the other two independent newsmagazines. Angered by PWI's lack of solidarity with the reporters and editors thrown out of work, Taufik and more than fifty other journalists met in the West Java town of Sirnagalih, issued a defiant declaration of independence ("We reject any form of interference"), and formed a new press union free of government control. They called it the Alliance of Independent Journalists (AJI)—and elected Taufik president. In effect, Ahmad Taufik was now the leader of the movement for freedom of the press in Indonesia.

Led by him, the AJI free press union defied a law that required all publications to be government licensed. Instead, without any permission, it published eleven editions of a new monthly magazine called *Independen*. It claimed a circulation of ten thousand. More stories about nepotism and corruption filled the pages—stories that were sure to further infuriate Suharto and his wealthy cronies. Taufik was taking chances but indicated he saw no acceptable alternative. "You have the choice," he said, "of either being a courageous man or a coward."

One of Suharto's cronies, a man named Harmoko, was the information minister. Taufik in *Independen* alleged that Harmoko was demanding that publishing companies give him lucrative shares of their stock if they wanted his permission to publish. In effect, Harmoko was allegedly using the repressive press-control laws to enrich himself. For Harmoko, this was the last straw.

One evening in March 1995, Taufik and other AJI members and a number of opposition politicians were dining at a downtown Jakarta hotel to celebrate the end of the Muslim month of fasting known as Ramadan. Copies of *Independen* were on display. Thirty police officers, apparently at the behest of the Bakin security police, raided the hotel and arrested thirty-year-old Taufik. Taufik's wife said later that he was held in an interrogation room at police headquarters, released at 3 A.M., then rearrested at home three hours later as he was sleeping. Taufik and two others were charged under Article 19 of the press law (unlicensed publishing) and Article 154 of the Criminal Code (expressing "feelings of hostility, hatred or contempt toward the government"). Taufik said he was treated like an enemy: "They put a gun to my head to frighten me. They kept me in inhuman cells with criminals."

At his trial, attended by cheering supporters, Taufik remained defiant: "Journalists should tell the truth and only the truth. I'm prepared to be jailed just for the truth." And he was. Taufik received a thirty-two-month sentence. He appealed—and got an even longer sentence, thirty-six months. He began serving that sentence in Jakarta's Cipinang Prison, where he continued to work on corruption stories that he smuggled out to underground publications. AJI's magazine *Independen* was shut down, but supporters bounced back with a successor, *Suara Independen* (Independent Voice). He interviewed a fellow prisoner who was a leader of East Timoran separatists, and as punishment for that article, Taufik was transferred 130 miles southeast to Cirebon Prison, where it was more difficult for family and friends to visit.

Taufik and his fellow independent journalists refused to give up. They continued to smuggle stories out to underground publications and also made use of the Internet to outwit censors. (See chapter 16, "Cat and Computer Mouse: Using the Internet.") In July 1997, after worldwide protests by press-freedom advocacy groups, Taufik was released—having served two years of his three-year sentence. Although on probation, he remained defiant, digging up exposés on military links to the underworld and publishing them in a newsweekly called *D&R*. As the public learned more of the truth about Suharto's corrupt and bloody three decades of power from journalists such as Taufik, Suharto's support eroded. That gradual erosion accelerated in 1997 and 1998 with a financial crisis, an 85 percent drop in the value of the currency, international pressures for reform, riots over price increases, and brutal police attacks on student demonstrators. The dictator finally fell from power. As for Taufik, his persistent pursuit of the corruption story in Indonesia won him an International Press Freedom Award.

7

A Veiled Woman
The Separatists

IT'S NOT ONLY stories of crime and corruption that are dangerous for journalists. Covering separatist movements can also be deadly. At stake is not money but national identity. Ethnic minorities risk their lives to break free of subjugation. Nation-states fight desperately not to be torn apart. They see separatists as a fundamental threat to their territorial integrity, so much so that the states take extraordinary measures to try to crush them.

Even a government committed to liberal democratic principles including a free press—for example, the government of India—will suspend those freedoms if it fears they could play into the hands of the separatists. This means that independent journalists cannot expect protection from the government. And even if they could get such protection, they might not want it. Being seen in the company of government troops would only deepen the suspicion in the minds of some separatists that journalists are agents of the state and therefore suitable targets for kidnapping, assault, and murder.

Threats to press freedom accompany separatist uprisings everywhere in the world, from East Timor in Indonesia to Chiapas in Mexico, from the Tamils of Sri Lanka to the Kurds of Turkey and the Serbs, Croats, Bosnian Muslims, Albanians, and other ethnic groups in the former Yugoslavia. While war coverage is always dangerous, separatist coverage in all these countries is especially risky for journalists. The conflicts are often bitter and protracted, with no clear front line and no clear breakthrough by either side. Propaganda becomes especially important as each side tries to end what often are stalemates, and any reporter who casts doubt on the truth of propaganda statements risks retaliation. Not only do journalists face the usual danger of becoming accidental casualties from shelling or

gunfire, but they also risk being deliberately targeted for assassination because of their work as journalists.

Take the case of Mushtaq Ali.

In September 1995, Srinagar, the summer capital of the northwest-
ern Indian state of Kashmir, tucked away in an obscure corner of the
world high in the Himalayas, appeared to visitors from the outside to
be an occupied city, filled with military convoys and bunkers every few
blocks. At that time some four hundred thousand Indian troops and police were in the Valley of Kashmir, deployed there in an unsuccessful effort to put down a Muslim separatist uprising supported by neighboring Pakistan. India and Pakistan had fought two wars over Kashmir,
and now, in 1995, there was more fighting, this time between Indian
troops and the Kashmiri separatists.

The Muslim separatists were fighting for *azadi* (freedom) from
India, either in the form of an independent state or a merger with the
fellow Muslims of Pakistan. Whatever form their intended political status took, whether an independent state or union with Pakistan, it would
mean separation from India and its largely Hindu population.

Tensions with India were especially high after a clash earlier that
year that had ended in the burning of a fifteenth-century shrine to Kashmir's patron saint, Sheikh Nuruddin Wali. Adding to the tension was
the emergence of shadowy local militias that worked closely with Indian troops in opposing the separatists. Since the separatist uprising
had begun in 1989, more than twenty thousand people had died.
Among innocent victims were visitors from the outside world, one of
them an unfortunate Norwegian tourist who was beheaded.

Independent journalists who refused demands to take sides risked
attack themselves, sometimes from *both* sides. An editor saw his office
raided by Indian troops, on the one hand, and his home burned down
by separatists, on the other. A photographer had shrapnel embedded in
his temple by a separatist grenade and his leg broken by Indian security
forces. "We are all trapped between two sides here," he said.

It was in that dangerous context that the case of Mushtaq Ali took
place.

In Srinagar at 3 P.M. on Thursday, September 7, 1995, a woman covered from head to toe in a black *burkha* (veil) entered a building on Res-
idency Road. It was the office and home in Kashmir of Yusuf Jameel, a
well-known correspondent for two respected, independent British
news organizations: the British Broadcasting Corporation (BBC) and

Reuter News Agency (Reuters). He was also a correspondent for the *Asian Age* newspaper. The woman, whose veil indicated she was an orthodox Muslim, did not identify herself but delivered a small parcel in an envelope and left.

By its size and shape it appeared to be a thin paperback book, identified by a label as a review copy. The BBC correspondent took the package out of the envelope and was about to open it when the telephone rang. He turned to answer it. While he was on the phone his colleague, a news photographer named Mushtaq Ali who happened to be in the office with him, took the package from him. Mushtaq Ali was twenty-six years old, a photographer for the Paris-based international news agency Agence France-Presse. He also worked as a camera operator for Asian News International, which provides TV news footage for Reuters.

Ali opened the package. Hidden inside the book was a bomb. It exploded. The blast ripped open his abdomen, severely injured his right hand, disfigured his face, and cut off his left hand. Two other journalists were also injured, but less seriously. All three were rushed to SMHS Hospital. The other two were treated and later released, but Ali was put on life support. Doctors said his brain and heart were functioning, and his blood pressure improved slightly overnight, but he had suffered massive injuries to internal organs. Leaders of two separatist groups came to the hospital to pay their respects. For three days doctors tried to save his life. On Sunday, September 10, the young photographer died.

His death stirred strong reactions. Hundreds of people gathered outside the hospital. Shops in the neighborhood of the BBC office closed to protest the parcel bombing. Ali's funeral was attended by separatist leaders and Indian government officials, as well as Ali's fellow journalists. The Hurriyat (Freedom) group of separatists called a three-day protest strike throughout the Valley of Kashmir.

No group claimed responsibility for the bombing and no culprit was ever found. Local journalists believed the intended victim was not Ali but Yusuf Jameel, the BBC correspondent he had helped. (Two weeks earlier another BBC office, across the border in the Pakistani capital of Islamabad, had been attacked by a militant Islamic group whose members beat two correspondents, smashed equipment, and set fires.) Jameel, well known for his Urdu-language reports on the BBC, had been repeatedly attacked by both sides. Grenades were thrown at his home; separatists threatened him because of his impartial reporting; and Indian security forces clubbed him on the head and threatened him at gunpoint. As Jameel put it: "It is a dangerous place to live for people like us."

That was an understatement. Among previous attacks:

Indian security officers seized Mukhtar Ahmed Baba, twenty-five, a reporter for *Greater Kashmir*, in 1993 and questioned him about separatists who had visited the newspaper office. He says he was beaten, ordered to strip, and suffered electric shocks to his genitals.

In 1994, one week after an Indian army major threatened to kill reporter Ghulam Mohammad Lone if he did any more stories about troop movements and alleged human rights abuses, masked gunmen entered Lone's home and killed him and his seven-year-old son.

In 1996 unidentified gunmen kidnapped thirty-eight-year-old editor Ghulam Rasool Sheikh after he had denounced killings and arson near his hometown of Pampur. Weeks later his body was found floating in the Jhelum River.

In other incidents, a TV engineer died in a rocket attack and a Radio Kashmir newscaster was shot dead at his home. (The newscaster had worked under a pseudonym in the vain hope that this would protect him.) Broadcast journalists were seen by separatists as being extensions of their enemy, the Indian government, because of state ownership of radio and television stations. But print journalists were targeted by the other side, the pro-Indian forces, because local newspapers were seen as favoring the separatists. Regardless of which news medium employed them, Kashmiri journalists trying to report events impartially faced an uphill battle. Not only were they regularly subjected to death threats, but reporters occasionally were kidnapped by separatists, while Indian security forces had the power to jail journalists for up to two years without a warrant under draconian security laws. After a three-week fact-finding trip to Kashmir in March 1995, Vikram Parekh of the Committee to Protect Journalists concluded: "Put simply, there is no freedom of the press in Kashmir today."

As a result, India, for all its renown as Asia's largest democracy and its generally strong tradition of a free press, was a risky place to work for a number of journalists. The twenty-two killed there in the 1990s—including those in the Kashmir region—made India the sixth most dangerous country for reporters. Of the five countries that exceeded India in the number of journalists killed—Algeria, Colombia, Russia, Croatia, and Tajikistan—all were countries where governments also fought bloody battles with ethnic separatists or other rebels. (Clashes involving groups who are not ethnic separatists—for example, the Islamic fundamentalists of Algeria—are covered in chapter 8, "Brother against Brother: Civil War.")

Wars between central governments and ethnic separatists are often brutal, and the brutality carries over into the methods used against journalists. From 1991, when the Chechen parliament declared independence from Russia, the barbaric slaughter in that part of the world made Chechnya one of the most dangerous and terrifying places for journalists to work. Four journalists were assassinated in 1996, all of them killed apparently in connection with their work. For example, in two separate but suspiciously similar incidents, reporters Natalya Alyakina (of dual Russian and German citizenship) and Ramzan Khadzhiev (an ethnic Chechen) were waved through Russian checkpoints—then shot dead. At yet another Russian checkpoint, four CNN journalists got out of their armored Land Rover—clearly marked "TV" on the roof—and came under gunfire from a Russian helicopter. Producer-correspondent Steve Harrigan and his crew managed to scramble to safety. During the second round of fighting in Chechnya, in 1999 three Russian journalists were killed during Russian air attacks, and in February 2000 a photographer was shot dead by Chechen militants who had taken him hostage.

In Spain, sixty-two-year-old columnist Jose Luis Lopez de la Calle provoked death threats for his articles attacking Basque separatists known as ETA. ("ETA" stands for "Basque Homeland and Freedom" in the Basque language.) Lopez de la Calle accused the ETA guerrillas of the same fascist tactics used during the Franco era, when the journalist himself was jailed for five years for leftist activities. After a long campaign against the separatists, the end came in the year 2000. In February, his house in the town of Andoain was firebombed. Then, on Sunday, May 8, Lopez de la Calle went out to buy newspapers and have a coffee and croissant at a local café. On his walk home, he was shot four times in the head and throat by two gunmen. Officials blamed ETA for his death.

For journalists in other parts of the world, the separatist story carries other dangers. Instead of death, they may face long years behind
bars. One of the worst countries on that score has been Turkey, which
likes to think of itself as an enlightened European state. In each year
between 1993 and 1998 no country in the world imprisoned more
journalists. At the end of 1994, seventy-four reporters, editors, and
publishers were locked up in Turkish prisons, and most of them were
there for reporting news about the Kurdish separatists. Those seventy-four constituted more than a third of all the imprisoned journalists in the world (a global total of 173). In 1995, Turkey had 51 of the
182 held in prison worldwide. In 1996 the number rose to 74 of 181.
By the end of 1997 the number had dropped to 29 out of 129—an improvement but still the highest number of any country. Two years
later, eighteen Turkish journalists were behind bars, putting Turkey
in second place behind China.

At first glance, Turkey seems to have a thriving free press. Except
for one main taboo subject, journalists in Turkey can cover virtually any
story they want. They aggressively go after politicians, criminals, corrupt officials, and other targets. Article 28 of the Turkish constitution
backs them up: "The press is free and shall not be censored."

The press is free—except for this main taboo.

Unless they toe the government line, journalists may not publish
one word about Turkey's single biggest problem: the Kurdish minority
and its separatist movement in the southeastern region bordering Iraq
and Iran, a rebellion that began in 1984 and has cost more than twenty-
seven thousand lives.

Journalists can get into trouble just for noting that there *is* a Kurdish
minority (estimated at some 10 to 12 million people, or about 20 percent
of Turkey's population). TV stations are warned not to air interviews
with Kurds who answer questions in the Kurdish language. Even articles about Kurdish cooking can be cited by prosecutors as terrorist
propaganda. As press-freedom advocate William Orme put it: "Political
columnists dispassionately saying the Kurds have a point—they go
straight to jail."

Editor Ocak Isik Yurtçu was one of those journalists.

Yurtçu was widely respected, a quiet, introverted man, affection-
ately nicknamed "Isik Baba" (Uncle Isik). He was born in Adana, southern Turkey, the son of a correspondent for the leftist daily newspaper
Cumhuriyet. Yurtçu left law school to work full time for left-wing oppo-

sition papers in Ankara and Istanbul, eventually reporting, editing, or writing columns for nine different newspapers.

His specialty was dissident journalism. After a 1971 coup, he published accounts by political prisoners who said they had been tortured in military jails. This and other investigative pieces earned him a distinction rarely accorded to journalists: honorary membership in the National Writers' Union of Turkey. The stories also earned him a different kind of distinction: arrests, fines, and other reprisals. In the 1980s he was arrested again, this time for protesting another coup and for being a leftist union official.

But it was his defiance of the ban on Kurdish stories that brought him the most trouble. In 1991 he was among a group of journalists who lost their jobs when a mainstream daily went bankrupt. Looking for something to do, they joined the *Özgür Gündem*, a new left-wing daily that was launched as a way to keep the Kurdish story in the spotlight. Although not a Kurd himself, Yurtçu agreed to be "responsible editor" of the pro-Kurdish paper. In Turkey, being "responsible editor" means not only managing the editorial staff but also being legally responsible—risking libel lawsuits and criminal prosecution—for any articles that do not carry a byline. "He was perfectly aware of the risk he was taking," a former editor-in-chief said. "But for him that was an integral part of what being a journalist in Turkey meant."

The name of the new paper, *Özgür Gündem*, translated as "Free News." Yurtçu soon discovered the limits of that freedom. In a brief, eight-month stint as editor, he helped the paper gain a circulation of one hundred thousand and a reputation for balanced reporting. But because of its articles on the outlawed Kurdish separatist party—the PKK (the Kurdistan Workers' Party)—as well as articles on security operations by Turkish troops against the PKK and alleged Turkish human rights violations against the Kurds, the newspaper came under attack. Police raided offices and arrested staff reporters in the cities of Diyarbakir, Van, and Agri. Contributing writers were arrested. The paper's Ankara bureau was bombed.

As responsible editor, Yurtçu himself was a prime target. The only question was: What form would the attack take? He had known that the Kurdish story would be dangerous for him. "They can use laws to put you in prison just for mentioning the word 'PKK' in your news story," he said. "They take this as 'praising the terrorist organization.' How can you write about the Southeast without mentioning the PKK?"

Yurtçu was not the only one to take risks by defying the ban on independent coverage of the Kurdish story. At various times, other journalists suffered these attacks:

Two journalists were sentenced to twenty months for merely quoting a legislator who said, among other things, the Kurds were "in the process of forming a nation."
In one year alone, nineteen journalists were assaulted by police, and one of the journalists was beaten to death.
A correspondent said he was interrogated for twenty-seven days and forced, while blindfolded, to sign a document he couldn't see.

American Aliza Marcus, a Reuters correspondent, also defied the ban. In a November 25, 1994, dispatch from Diyarbakir, she reported what sounded like human rights violations by the Turkish army:

TURKISH ARMY TARGETS KURDISH VILLAGES
By Aliza Marcus
DIYARBAKIR, Turkey—Forcibly evacuating and torching Kurdish villages in southeastern Turkey is now a central part of the military's 10-year battle against Kurdish rebels, villagers and human rights activists say.

Local human rights officials say nearly 1,900 villages in the southeast—or 16 percent of the area's 12,000 settlements—have been partly or fully emptied, often under military pressure.

More than 500 settlements were evacuated and many burned down in the first 10 months of this year.

"Nothing has changed here, just the pressure is getting worse and things are being done more openly," said Halit Temli, head of Turkey's Human Rights Association's Diyarbakir office.

Such reports were backed up by a 21-year-old member of the security forces in an interview with Reuters Thursday near Diyarbakir, the administrative center of the region.

"What else can we do? These people are supporting the terrorists. (The guerrillas) will only be finished off when all the villages in the region have been burned and destroyed," the man said.

Marcus's English-language wire-service report was picked up, translated, and published in the Turkish newspaper *Özgür Ülke*, which was later shut down by authorities. Marcus herself was charged in Istanbul's State Security Court with violating Article 312 of the Turkish Penal Code, which made it a crime to incite racial hatred—a law frequently used to punish journalists who reported the atrocities committed against the Kurds. Eventually, foreign press-freedom advocacy groups pressured the government to drop the case.

But the campaign of repression went on. Even a Nobel nominee was not immune from attack. Yasar Kemal, a Turkish author of Kurdish origin, was convicted at the age of seventy-two under Article 312. His offense lay in two articles in a collection of essays titled, ironically enough, *Turkey and Freedom of Expression*. One of the articles, also published in the mainstream German newsweekly *Der Spiegel*, described what Kemal called a "campaign of lies" to cover up oppression of the Kurds. He accused the Turkish government of imposing "a system of unbearable repression and atrocity" and called for "an end to this dirty war." He referred to the PKK fighting force as "guerrillas" rather than using the government's official term for them: *separatist terrorists*. And he denounced as "a crime against humanity" the government's efforts to suppress the Kurdish language and culture.

Kemal received a suspended two-year sentence, but the message was clear: no one, not even the country's most prominent writer, would be allowed to comment on the Kurds without paying a price. To be sure, it was not only the government that tried to suppress the truth. The separatists also took harsh measures against independent journalists. Two Turkish TV documentary journalists were imprisoned for three months by the PKK after defying a virtual death threat by the Kurdish guerrillas against anyone who reported *any* news from the southeastern region.

Against this backdrop of continued attacks on journalists, Ocak Isik Yurtçu was charged with offenses that included "separatist propaganda" (Article 8 of the Anti-Terror Law) and "insulting the government." Fellow journalists urged him to emigrate and escape what was sure to be a harsh prison sentence, but Yurtçu chose to stay and face trial. While he was awaiting trial, other editors replaced him—until they, too, were arrested. One editor lasted only twelve days. In April 1994, faced with some two hundred legal actions, including court orders temporarily shutting it down, the paper went out of business.

In 1993, Yurtçu was tried and convicted, and on December 28, 1994, he lost his appeal. At the age of forty-nine, he began serving a sentence

of fifteen years and ten months at Adapazari Prison in Sakarya. The ordeal was worsened by his medical conditions that included acute
asthma, rheumatism, and heart problems. Loneliness was another ordeal. Shouting to one visitor so that he could be heard through thick
panes of steel-enforced glass at the prison, while soldiers stood against
the wall listening, Yurtçu welcomed the opportunity to speak to someone from the outside. "I just want people to know that I am here," he
said, "because it seems like everybody has forgotten me."

But not everybody had forgotten him. Colleagues abroad organized a campaign to free him. Yurtçu became a *cause célèbre*. Press-freedom advocacy groups in Paris and New York gave him awards for
courage. One of the awards included enough money—almost $10,000—
to pay his court fines. Marie-Guy Baron, a senior French journalist at the
daily *Le Figaro*, was among those who campaigned on his behalf. Baron
told one interviewer:

> I attempted to meet Isik in Sakarya Prison, but I was unable to get per-
> mission from the Turkish Ministry of Justice. I could send him a box of
> chocolates. And I will continue campaigning for his release.

At one point as the campaign gathered steam, Yurtçu was offered a
presidential pardon—and turned it down. "I see no reason why I
should plead for a pardon," he said, "for I am not guilty."

A change of government in Turkey provided a rare opportunity for
the campaigners for Yurtçu's release. A more moderate government
took power and sought improved relations with the West, partly in
hopes of improved economic ties to Europe.

In July 1997 the New York–based Committee to Protect Journalists sought to take advantage of that opening. It sent a high-powered
delegation to Ankara led by CPJ vice chairman Terry Anderson, a
man who could not be accused by Turkey of being soft on terrorism:
he himself had spent seven years as a hostage held by terrorists in
nearby Lebanon. Also in the delegation was well-known CNN war
correspondent Peter Arnett, as well as CPJ executive director William
Orme and leaders of Paris's Reporters Without Borders and Vienna's
International Press Institute.

They were met by Turkey's top leaders. Deputy Prime Minister Bulent Ecevit, himself a journalist who once had been imprisoned, told
them: "I am personally disturbed by the number of journalists in jail in

Turkey." Prime Minister Mesut Yilmaz denounced the fact that restrictions on press freedom in his country had been explained away in the past as part of the fight against terrorism: "That was unacceptable then, and it is unacceptable now."

As if those comments were not surprising enough, the government then promised a limited amnesty for imprisoned editors and efforts to ease the harsh censorship laws. And it let the delegation visit Yurtçu in prison—an event that was covered live on Turkish television. Yurtçu was moved from a prison hospital to another location to receive the delegation.

And so, on July 16, 1997, at Saray Prison in the remote town of Tekirdag, seventy-five miles west of Istanbul in an area near the Greek border, Yurtçu met with the delegation in the prison library and belatedly received the CPJ's 1996 International Press Freedom Award. He went to the barred window and waved the plaque to the cheering crowd below. "I hope," Yurtçu said, "that not only journalists but everyone imprisoned for their thoughts can win their freedom."

Among those visiting him that day were Nobel nominee Yasar Kemal, who had been tried for the *Der Spiegel* article and who had once worked on a newspaper with Yurtçu's father. Also on hand for the visit was Yurtçu's stepdaughter, herself a journalist. Arnett told Turkish reporters it was "one of the most important and joyful days of my journalistic career." A month later, after two and a half years behind bars, Yurtçu was freed—one of six editors amnestied. But there was a catch. They had to refrain for three years from the kind of journalism that had landed them in prison. And the government reneged on its other promise, legal reform. Eventually repressions against journalists resumed. The war against the separatists remained the top priority.

Anticipating even at the time that the government might not keep all its promises, CPJ delegation chief Anderson wrote:

> That would be unfortunate indeed. This is not just a matter of tossing a few journalists into jail. Assaults on press freedom are directly linked to other widespread violations of human rights in Turkey. They are both a result of the simmering, unwinnable and horribly expensive war in the southeast and a method for keeping that war going without allowing the Turkish public to understand its cost, economically or in human lives.

As Orme told me: "They have 150,000 NATO ground troops fighting in open battle, occupying something like 25 to 30 percent of the country's terrain with huge losses in life, the largest single drain on the budget. . . . If you can't write about that, overwhelmingly the most important single fact about the country—" He shrugged as if to say: "then you can't write about anything that counts." And one Turkish journalist, hiding behind the pseudonym "Ahmet Emin" to avoid reprisal, lamented the continuing censorship: "The loser, as usual, has been the public. On important issues, neither the Turks nor the Kurds are informed about what is happening within their own country."

The same could be said about all the places in the world torn by violence over separatism. In Srinagar, Kashmir, two years after Mushtaq Ali was killed by the bomb in the BBC office, journalists gathered for their second annual Mushtaq Memorial Lecture to honor his memory. They heard foreign correspondent Mark Tully, former South Asia chief of the BBC, praise reporters, photographers, and editors as watchdogs of the truth who perform a vital role, especially in places such as Kashmir. Tully told them: "Mushtaq's death is not defeat but victory for free and fearless journalism."

Perhaps. But it's difficult to see his death as a victory, other than in a moral sense. The constant threats to independent journalists have taken their toll. Truthful reports from Kashmir are few and far between. The separatist story there is especially important now that India and Pakistan have exploded atomic devices and could unleash a regional nuclear war over Kashmir. With so much at stake, it is all the more important for the public in India and Pakistan and the rest of the world to have the truth about what is happening there.

In Kashmir, as in all the other places torn by separatism, the truth is unlikely to come from government or separatist propaganda. The truth is likely to come, if at all, from only one source—independent journalists.

8

Brother against Brother

Civil War

ON A SUNDAY evening in July 1994, Yasmina Drici was driving with a friend near her home in Rouiba, a suburb of Algiers. Drici was a proofreader at *Le Soir d'Algérie*, an independent evening newspaper. A group of unidentified men in police uniforms stopped the car, searched through Drici's pocketbook, found her press ID—and slit her throat. She bled to death.

She was not the only journalist to fall victim to the carnage in Algeria. During one three-year period occurred incidents such as these:

On a Friday, the Muslim day of worship, reporter Djamel Ziater was shot to death while visiting his mother's grave.
Unidentified men beheaded three reporters.
After investigative reporter Zineddine Aliou Salah's name appeared on a death list posted at mosques in Blida, south of Algiers, unidentified men approached him as he was leaving his home and shot him dead.

And so it went, day after day, year after year, in what was, for a while, the world's most dangerous country for journalists. Between 1993 and 1996, fifty-eight reporters and editors were murdered. The reason for such a high death rate: Algeria's civil war.

Of all the types of stories that trigger attack on journalists, few are more dangerous than civil wars, because of the fratricidal intensity of the fighting. A civil war has all the malignant power of a family feud carried to extremes. Journalists risk their safety if they take sides—or refuse to take sides. Sometimes they are even singled out for attack. In the civil war in the African nation of Sierra Leone, where ten journalists were killed in 1999, rebels reportedly drew up death lists of journalists believed to be sympathetic to the government. As the CPJ's Orme put it, "the belligerent factions themselves see the press as part of the enemy, except it's a much more vulnerable part of the enemy."

No one knows how many people altogether have been killed since the fighting in Algeria began in 1992. After five years of slaughter, Amnesty International estimated the toll at eighty thousand dead. Independent-minded Algerian editor Salima Ghezali decided to come up with her own estimate of the death toll—and in doing so put herself at risk.

Ghezali went to a cemetery every day and counted the new, unmarked graves. Using that and other information, she came up with an estimate of one hundred thousand dead. She went ahead with plans to publish that figure despite threats by both sides against anyone revealing the truth.

It was an act of defiance against the two sides in the civil war: a government that brutally censored the press, and Islamic fundamentalist terrorists who marked all journalists for death—terrorists so ruthless that in 1996 and again in 1997, rebel leader Antar Zouabri was named by the Committee to Protect Journalists as the world's worst enemy of the press.

"To be a journalist," Salima Ghezali said, "to be an editor-in-chief, particularly when we condemn violence on both sides, it needs some strength, and I think I've got it."

She gained that strength as she grew up, the daughter of a stonemason of modest means in Bouira, fifty-five miles southeast of Algiers, on the other side of the Atlas Mountains from the Mediterranean coast. She had nine brothers and sisters. In a country where few women had a chance to advance, she obtained a degree in literature and taught French at the Khemis el-Khechna High School, then became active in the General Union of Algerian Workers. In the 1980s she helped found Algeria's feminist movement and rose to become president of the Women's Association of Europe and North Africa.

During that period, Algeria's one-party state was shaken by demonstrators demanding a more open society. The regime bowed to pressure and liberalized. It permitted press freedom and multiparty elections—but after a first round of voting that indicated Islamic fundamentalists were about to take power, the government cancelled the second round and imposed a state of emergency. Eventually this led to civil war.

Against this background of turmoil, in November 1994, Salima Ghezali joined with ten journalists to take over a forty-thousand-circulation French-language weekly newspaper called *La Nation*. She became Algeria's only woman editor, set the paper on an independent course— and soon got in trouble with the government.

La Nation advocated a peaceful political solution, rather than taking sides in the civil war. "Choosing sides," Ghezali said, "simply means choosing victims." As if that were not defiant enough, she then published a letter that had been written in prison by Ali Benhadj—the second highest figure in the banned fundamentalist party, the Islamic Salvation Front. The government responded with a faxed order to the printers of *La Nation* suspending her newspaper for a week.

Ghezali backed the fundamentalist party's call for a demonstration—and again her paper was suspended. Later the same year, just before presidential elections, she was ordered to appear before a government prosecutor without any official reason given, in a clear act of harassment. What happened after that? "The authorities closed our newspaper for the three weeks just before the elections."

There was worse to come, but meanwhile Ghezali traveled to New York and told human rights advocates, journalists, and educators about the grave dangers for journalists from both sides: the government permitted newspapers to publish stories about rebel assassinations of editors and reporters because this made the rebels look bad, and the rebels knew that killing anyone in the press was a way to get publicity. "Due to the government's censorship of any news related to security issues," she said, "rebel attacks on army or police forces are not reported, and no Islamists are allowed to publicly express themselves. Killing journalists, then, becomes a way for the terrorists to tell you they are there."

In fact, the militant Armed Islamic Group issued a communique threatening death to any journalist working for the state-controlled radio and television, saying they all propped up "the rotten apostate regime." It indicated the same went for print journalists and warned: "Those who fight with the pen shall die by the sword."

To make matters worse, Ghezali said, Algerian journalists, weakened by a lack of legal protections and professional solidarity, faced not only assault by the rebels but arrest by the government. She cited the case of Djamel Fahassi. Although he worked for a state radio station, the French-language Alger Chaîne III, and therefore should have enjoyed protection by the government, Fahassi earlier had written for Islamist newspapers. She said he was abducted by government security forces—but the government said it didn't know anything about it. "His family," she said, "and my newspaper, *La Nation*, tried to get some support for him. But after *La Nation* published several articles on his case, the pro-government newspaper *Horizons* ran a story claiming that Fahassi was well and vacationing abroad." She added ominously: "He is still missing."

Ghezali expressed the frustration of journalists who could not do their job because of the "scandalous" silence imposed on them:

> We can witness a murder, a police operation or an arrest but are not allowed to write about it. . . . For the last six months in Algiers, we have heard loud explosions every evening. There's gunfire, and there are mass arrests. But we don't see these things in the newspaper. So people know the press is unable to report what is happening.

Ghezali returned from New York to Algiers and continued her defiance of the threats by both sides, greatly increasing the danger for her. "Of course," she said, "I am always afraid, but sometimes the anger is stronger than fear." She had good reason to be afraid. Journalists were increasingly marked for death. As one of them put it: "I was afraid to take my son to school, afraid to visit my wife in her office, and wary of the people around me on the street."

Some tried to joke about it. An Algerian journalist named Saïd Mekbel, director of the morning paper *Le Matin*, survived two terrorist attempts on his life in the same day, then, incredibly enough, found a way to write humorously about it. "At this rate," he wrote, "they'll succeed in killing me. . . . Do you suppose that they know that they're causing problems between me and my wife? . . . I have not managed to convince my better half that if, on certain nights, I fail to return to my conjugal abode, it is simply out of prudence." He added:

> Sometimes I have to do acrobatics to elude the eyes of the moles who study my habits on the terrorists' behalf. . . . I cover my tracks by walking backwards toward my house to make it look like I've gone out. . . . I don't know whether or not this ruse has successfully thrown off the enemy, but at least my bizarre behavior has attracted the attention of the neighbors who have recommended to my wife that she get me examined by a psychiatrist.

His humorous approach pleased his readers—but not the terrorists. On Saturday, December 3, 1994, as he was dining in a downtown Algiers restaurant near his newspaper office, Saïd Mekbel was shot in the head. He died the next morning in Ain-Naadja Hospital. The Armed Islamic Group claimed responsibility.

Despite such dangers, in early 1996, Salima Ghezali decided to go to a cemetery every evening and count the new graves. This information went into a special report on human rights violations in Algeria. The plan was to publish the special report in the March 6 issue of *La Nation*, timing it to simultaneous publication of the same report in Paris in the respected French monthly newspaper *Le Monde Diplomatique*. But the Algerian Ministry of the Interior banned the March 6 issue of *La Nation* with the report on human rights violations. Then authorities seized the March 19–25 issue of *La Nation* at the state printing house, Société d'Impression d'Alger, as well as the March 25–April 1 edition and the newspaper's Arab-language sister publication, *Al-Hourria*.

At the end of 1996, authorities tightened the screws. The state-owned printing press refused to print either paper, citing outstanding debts—even though it continued to print other newspapers that owed money. In March 1997, *La Nation* and *Al-Hourria* paid off their debts—but still the state-owned printing press refused to print either of them. It soon became clear what was really happening: Ghezali's independent voice was being choked into silence.

After her newspaper had been closed for almost a year, Ghezali gave an eloquent speech before the European Parliament in Strasbourg, France, where she was awarded the Sakharov Prize for democracy, one of her many awards. She said:

> My country is burning: At this very moment men, women and children of flesh and blood are suffering in their flesh and losing their blood, because a double-edged terror denies them of the first of all liberties, that of living free.

After detailing the horrors of atrocities on both sides in the civil war, she focused on the efforts to get rid of independent journalists such as herself: "What is taking place in Algeria today is shocking, but the accompanying silence is just as much so."

Trying to break that silence while her newspaper remained shut down, Ghezali wrote for a Belgian newspaper and made use of the

Internet. She contributed articles to one Web site called Dazibao, run by the Paris-based press-advocacy group Reporters Sans Frontières, and to another site dedicated to dissidents and run by the Digital Freedom Network.

The brutality in Algeria has made worldwide headlines, grabbing the spotlight partly because Algeria is located so close to modern, industrialized Europe; but elsewhere in the world other civil wars rage, often in obscurity—even though their own brutality descends to some of the most horrific depths imaginable. And here, too, journalists caught up in civil war pay a terrible price.

Mohyedin Alempour was one of them.

On Tuesday, December 12, 1995, shortly before his fiftieth birthday, the artist and BBC journalist left his small apartment in an ugly high-rise in the center of Dushanbe, the capital of Tajikistan in Central Asia. He was never seen alive again by family and friends.

Alempour was a well-known figure in that former Soviet republic, a multitalented Renaissance man in a long winter coat, with a thick gray beard. He was famous in this country of 5 million people for his books, films, TV programs, photography, reports for the national news agency, and a popular BBC radio program in Persian. His most recent book was about an Iranian pop star from the 1970s named Gougoush. During a visit to the United States, he did a BBC radio series in the Tajik language, called *From Dushanbe to Los Angeles*, in which he interviewed people he met, including the Iranian shah's family.

With his wife, Osak, and two sons and a daughter, Alempour had remained in his country after most other journalists fled the civil war. He stayed on despite a threat to his life from one of the warring regional clans. In the early 1990s an explosive mixture of clan rivalries, Islamic militancy, and political feuding left over from Soviet days erupted in civil war in Tajikistan, which is squeezed between China, Afghanistan, and two other former Soviet republics. After the collapse of the Soviet Union, Communists in Tajikistan were ousted but seized power again, then squabbled over whether to make concessions to the opposition, which included Islamists. Militias that opposed any concessions overthrew the government after warfare that took the lives of tens of thousands.

Alempour didn't share the government's view that resurgent Islam was a threat. That kind of dissent was dangerous in a country where the government was run by gunmen who had climbed to power over the bodies of their victims. The president, Emomali Rakhmonov, was the former field commander of paramilitaries known for their brutality.

Alempour's body was found near the campus of Tajikistan University in Dushanbe early on the morning of Wednesday, December 13, 1995. He had a bullet wound to the head. His death provoked an outcry. As British journalist Jonathan Rugman put it, Alempour "was so loved and respected a figure . . . that the Tajik media reported his death as a national disaster."

No culprit was found. The government blamed the opposition but offered no proof. The opposition blamed bandits but offered no explanation for why Alempour's gold ring had not been taken. The Committee to Protect Journalists noted that most of the other journalists killed had died at the hands of paramilitary forces under the command of the man who was now president. It added: "Like those of his colleagues, Alempour's murder had all the hallmarks of a political killing."

Alempour's country was the fourth most dangerous for journalists during the 1990s, after Algeria, Colombia and Russia, with a total of twenty-nine deaths, according to the Committee to Protect Journalists. Other press-advocacy groups put the toll as high as sixty. "In sheer numbers," according to a special CPJ report,

> the killings of journalists in Tajikistan rival the worst levels documented . . . in Central America and Argentina in the late 1970s and early 1980s. As in Latin America, the paramilitary death squads responsible for these killings appear to enjoy immunity from prosecution, and are in some cases direct extensions of state internal security forces.

Noting that twenty-five thousand Russian troops remained in the country and had helped set up the paramilitaries, the report charged: "The deliberate killings of journalists could not have been carried out without Russian complicity."

The press-advocacy group Glasnost Defense Foundation reported that during the civil war, thirty independent publications were shut down and some one hundred journalists fled into exile in neighboring countries such as Afghanistan. Alempour had been one of the few to defy the death squads and stay on. Among the others who stayed—and died:

Daviatali Rakhmonaliev, forty-one, reporter and programming director of the state television network, a man with close ties to the pro-Communist government. He was shot dead in front of his home. A U.S. State Department report said: "Opposition forces were probably responsible for the murder."

Khushvakht Haydarsho, a pro-government editor who was planning to publish a series on the country's "criminal and political Mafia." He was shot dead near his home. A State Department report said a rival faction within pro-government forces was believed responsible.

Viktor Nikulin, a correspondent for Russian state television, who had received threats and installed a heavy lock on his door. He was shot and killed in his office. He was the twenty-ninth journalist killed since the civil war began.

On Thursday, December 14, 1995, one day after his body was found near the university campus, artist and journalist Mohyedin Alempour was buried by his family in the village of Aini in the snowbound Pamir Mountains north of Dushanbe. Later the BBC helped set up a foundation in his memory to conserve his photographs and writings. The foundation had one other goal, according to BBC executive David Morton: "the training of a new generation of Tajik journalists."

From the frozen mountains of Tajikistan to the blistering heat of Africa, civil wars continued to take their toll. Vincent Rwabukwizi, director of an opposition newspaper, was one of the victims in a civil war that turned into the single most intensive slaughter of human beings of the entire twentieth century.

In early April 1994, Rwabukwizi was caught by soldiers in front of his home in the Nyamirambo district of Kigali, the capital of Rwanda. This was at the height of the genocide in that small, remote country in equatorial Africa—the slaughter of tribe against tribe that took an estimated 800,000 lives in only four months. It began when the president of Rwanda, from the ruling Hutu tribe, died in a plane crash on April 6. That touched off killings of members of the opposition Tutsi tribe by soldiers and death squads, which in turn touched off bloody reprisals. Entire families were hacked to death, shot, burned alive, or had their skulls crushed.

Among the victims in the first few days, the CPJ's William Orme said, were the nation's leading independent journalists, "systematically pursued and murdered by soldiers and militia." Information from press-advocacy and human rights groups indicates that, of the forty-four journalists who were killed during the hundred days of madness, at least fourteen were singled out because of their work for news media. That death toll made Rwanda the eleventh most dangerous country in the world for the press.

Vincent Rwabukwizi had lived with danger for years, long before the massacre. He was targeted for attack by the government of the majority Hutu tribe, always suspicious of anyone deemed sympathetic to their rivals, the aristocratic minority Tutsis who had once ruled the land. Rwabukwizi was the director of the opposition paper *Kanguku*. He was considered close to the rebel forces of the Tutsi-dominated Rwandan Patriotic Front. And he interviewed the last Tutsi king, in exile in Kenya.

For that interview he was sentenced in 1990 to fifteen years in prison, released after ten months, placed under house arrest, then picked up again and held for four months on separate charges of inciting ethnic unrest and calling for the overthrow of the regime. Released again in September 1991, he went into hiding at times because of continuing harassment. The genocide began on Thursday, April 7, 1994, the day after the Hutu president died in the plane crash. Only a few days later, opposition journalist Rwabukwizi was located by soldiers and shot dead in front of his home.

Other leading journalists were either killed or fled for their lives. Among the unlucky were:

Eudès Nshimiryo, a director of state-run TV Rwanda. He was entertaining guests, some of them opposition Tutsis, at his home on the first day of the massacres. Hutu soldiers attacked his guests. Trying to defend them, Nshimiryo showed the soldiers his press card—and was immediately killed.

Emmanuel-Damien Rukondo, president of the Association of Newspaper Owners and a freelance reporter for the newspaper *Rubyiruko-Rubanda*. In his neighborhood in Kigali, the capital, he was paraded naked in the back of a truck and then cut into pieces.

Jeanne d'Arc Mukmusoni, director of an opposition newspaper. She and her husband tried to flee the capital but were stopped at a militia checkpoint and killed.

The horror of Rwanda may be an extreme case, but the deliberate targeting of independent journalists is all too typical of what happens in any civil war. "On any street corner you can be shot down," said Algerian TV producer and reporter Horria Saihi, another courageous woman in the Algerian press corps. She was on a death list drawn up by the Islamic fundamentalists and was also in trouble with the government for challenging its censorship. Refusing to be silent, she kept working, traveling incognito and sleeping in a different place each night. For her defiance of those who would silence her, she received a Courage in Journalism Award from the International Women's Media Foundation in New York in 1995.

Saihi summed up the attitude of many independent journalists when she explained why she kept going despite the danger: "I know [that] what awaits me in the end is a bullet in the head, but what kills me more is censorship."

9

In the Thick of It

Protests and Riots

PHOTOGRAPHER ROBERT CAPA once said: "If your pictures are no good, you aren't close enough." Being close enough to get the picture and the story is essential for anyone covering the news, but with it comes risk. Journalists who cover protests and riots have to plunge into the thick of things to find out what's going on. And that's when it becomes dangerous.

Photographer Lorescu Voirel was nearly strangled with an American flag in Port-au-Prince, Haiti, as he took pictures for the New York daily newspaper *Newsday* during an anti-American demonstration in front of the U.S. embassy in 1994. During the same scuffle, CNN correspondent Peter Arnett was assaulted. Rastko Kostic, a reporter for student media in Yugoslavia, lost two teeth and suffered two broken fingers, a broken nose, and several cuts when police beat him during an opposition demonstration in Belgrade in 1997. Eight other journalists, both local and foreign, were beaten while covering the protest. Mohammad Quamruzzaman, a reporter for the weekly *Neel Sagar*, was shot dead by police in the northern town of Nilphamari, Bangladesh, in 1996. Witnesses said that after shooting him, police beat and kicked him. He had been covering a police crackdown on a violent protest against election results.

Demonstrations often touch on sensitive issues, and that is one reason that the journalists covering them risk retaliation. People showing how they feel about an issue convey a message to the rest of society and exercise one of their most fundamental rights, especially if they are expressing a grievance against the government. In a healthy democracy, it is essential that journalists be able to tell the full story of these demonstrations and be ready to report any effort by police to suppress protests, but all too often journalists are held back by powerful forces who try to block news coverage.

Sometimes the message of the demonstration is unpalatable for these forces, and other times those opposed to the demonstrators attack them—and don't want the press to publicize how brutal the attack was or how violently and defiantly the demonstrators fought back.

Often it is the photographers and television camera operators who are harassed, shoved, or beaten the most during clashes with police. Why are photographers rather than print reporters singled out for attack during demonstrations? Is it because one picture is considered more damaging than a thousand words? Or is it simply because someone carrying a camera is easier to identify as a journalist—and therefore as "the enemy"—than someone not carrying equipment? Both reasons seem to be true. "Savvy censors and thugs the world over have learned," says Professor Susan D. Moeller of Brandeis, "that a picture is more dangerous than the verbal telling of an event—and that when opportunities to take pictures are denied, international news interest wanes."

There is another reason why photographers are more likely than reporters to be attacked in such clashes. Photographers have to be closer to get the best shot. If they stand back where it is safe, their view of the protest demonstration is obscured by people standing in the way. While a print reporter who misses the action can always get a "fill in" later by another reporter, a photographer who misses the action has no way to recoup. "And, of course," Moeller quite rightly points out, "if photographers are close enough to shoot their pictures, they are more than close enough to get shot."

Also, few things provoke more anger from police or belligerent protesters than having a camera lens pointed at them. One of the surest ways for a photographer to be assaulted is to photograph police beating demonstrators. That happened on a chilly November evening in Warsaw.

The year was 1982. Poland was restive. For eleven months the nation had been living under martial law, with the leaders of the popular pro-democracy Solidarity movement kept in internment by a nervous Communist military regime during the final decade of the Soviet empire. A student protest demonstration was getting under way at an intersection in the center of the capital. Mick Deane, a British journalist based in Rome, was the sound technician for a CNN camera crew covering the protest. I was the CNN correspondent with them.

Suddenly low, squat armored personnel carriers, looking like tanks

without gun barrels, appeared on the streets. They fired tear-gas canis-
ters. Soon the dark, eerie streets were fogged with low-lying mist. Out
of the armored cars poured what looked like Martians in a low-budget
sci-fi film: special antiriot ZOMO police in black uniforms with gas
masks, each wielding a truncheon and beating anyone in sight. The
CNN crew videotaped the police beating the student demonstrators. In
the confusion and chaos, the crew and I became separated. By chance, I
avoided what happened next.

"We couldn't see the way we were going," Deane recalled later. "We
got frightened. It was very surreal when the gas was around."

The ZOMO police turned on the TV crews. "One took a flying
kick at me," Deane said. "He kicked quite hard." Then the journalists
were forced into the back of a truck with student protesters where
everyone, protester and journalist alike, was beaten with truncheons:
"We were made to lie flat. . . . I was hit a lot on the back, fifteen to
twenty times." Deane's cameraman Ron Dean was the next victim,
for resisting ZOMO efforts to take away his camera: "[He] got a
cracked rib and broken nose."

Poland was risky during that brief, tense period of 1981–1982, but
there are other parts of the world where the tension has continued for
generations. Protests and other demonstrations are almost daily occur-
rences in Israel and the territories controlled by the Palestinian Authority. It is one of the most dangerous areas for photojournalists.

Abdel Rahman Khabeisa, twenty-seven, a Palestinian cameraman for the London-based WTN news service, shot video footage of
youths throwing rocks at Israeli troops in the occupied West Bank
city of Nablus in early 1995. Israeli authorities claimed he had incited
the incident. They imprisoned him for three days, then released him
without charge.

During clashes between soldiers and Palestinian demonstrators in
occupied Ramallah, twenty-four-year-old photographer Atta Wessat
apparently did not realize that some of the "Arabs" in the background
whom he was photographing were actually Israeli undercover troops in
disguise. Fellow journalists said that after Wessat photographed the undercover troops, a group of uniformed Israeli soldiers, joined by border
guards, beat him with rifle butts, an assault that included a blow to the
head requiring twelve stitches, and threatened to shoot him at point-
blank range.

Wessat, a Palestinian working for the Israeli photo agency Zoom 77, was hospitalized. A senior Israeli official later wrote to the Canadian Center of International PEN, the press-freedom advocacy group, saying one of the guards had asked Wessat to move "so as not to obstruct the view of the soldiers." But fellow journalists dismissed this dubious explanation and said the real reason for the attack was the fear by undercover agents that their identities would be revealed.

AP photographer John Gaps III, from Des Moines, Iowa, was on assignment in occupied Gaza when an Israeli sniper wearing a green beret shot him above the right knee with a plastic bullet. Gaps said the sniper fired an M-16 rifle equipped with a telescopic sight, from a distance of only about one hundred yards—making it virtually certain the sniper deliberately targeted the journalist. "I saw the guy draw down on us. There were no rocks being thrown or anything," Gaps told an interviewer from his hospital bed. "I was taking pictures of him and then I saw him draw down and I knew he was going to shoot."

After receiving protests from press groups, Israeli officials said the sniper had been trying to disperse demonstrators, although witnesses said a demonstration had already ended ninety minutes before the sniper shot. He was later given a warning by his commander after a disciplinary hearing.

There have been persistent reports of Israeli troops deliberately targeting journalists. In July 1997, as Palestinian demonstrators in Hebron burned an Israeli flag, Israeli soldiers fired rubber-coated metal bullets at cameramen for AP Television, Reuters, ABC, and Abu Dhabi Television, lightly wounding them. Witnesses said the cameramen were at a considerable distance from the demonstrators and their camera equipment made it obvious they were journalists. Israeli officials denied that the journalists had been targeted.

In Cairo, an Egyptian police officer became angered when an AP reporter at a student anti-Israeli demonstration pointed out an example of police brutality to an AP photographer. The Egyptian policeman ordered the reporter's arrest and beat him. When the reporter identified himself as a journalist, the cop interrupted his beating only long enough to snarl: "So what?"

Often the demonstrations that provoke the most trouble are the ones that concern fundamental everyday grievances such as food prices. In August 1996 southern Jordanians rioted in protest over a 200 percent increase in the price of bread. Among four hundred people arrested were the publisher, editor-in-chief, and three reporters of the

During violent clashes between Palestinian demonstrators and Israeli troops in Bethlehem on February 28, 2000, an Israeli soldier points his weapon at a Palestinian news photographer while an Israeli radio reporter (on right) restrains the soldier. Journalists covering riots and demonstrations often risk attack to get close to the action. Credit: AP/Wide World Photos

weekly newspaper *Al-Bilad.* Because of their coverage of the riots, they were charged with inciting sedition and publishing false information—charges that carry a sentence of up to three years in prison. They were released after eight days, pending trial. The publisher had to sign a statement promising not to instigate violence or dissent. "They are trying to teach journalists not to touch sensitive issues," one Jordanian editor said.

When journalists themselves demonstrate, that makes it even worse; now the police have even more reason to beat them. Twenty-six Pakistani reporters protesting police attacks on newspaper offices were themselves assaulted by police during a demonstration in 1997. Two years earlier in neighboring Kashmir, India, fifteen journalists were assaulted by police and five were seriously injured as they demonstrated against violations of freedom of the press.

Obviously, governments are sensitive to any news stories about demonstrations, especially in countries without a deeply rooted tradition of democracy. In some cases the protest rallies are shows of force by the political opposition, and no government has an interest in letting the public know how strong the opposition is. If anti-government rallies continue day after day, growing ever larger, they can help bring down a regime, as happened in Indonesia in 1998. News of the size of the protests and the numbers of students killed by police during the demonstrations played a major role in the collapse of a regime already weakened by the troubled economy.

Governments seem sensitive to protests on certain issues that touch a nerve, such as demonstrations involving the environment. In 1996, Nigerian police arrested Paul Adams, a correspondent of the London-based *Financial Times*, as he covered local protests against oil pollution in a region where the leading environmentalist had been hanged the year before. Adams was charged with possessing "seditious literature" from the protesters. He faced up to two years in prison, but after international pressure the charges were dropped.

In another environmentally related incident, police beat eight journalists in Minsk, Belarus, as they were covering a protest march on the tenth anniversary of the Chernobyl nuclear disaster. Radio Liberty correspondent Eduard Terlitsky required several stitches for his head injury. Oleg Trizno, a freelance reporter for underground opposition newspapers, was arrested at the demonstration and jailed for five days for "insulting a policeman." To show how petty and spiteful they could be, before releasing him police forced Trizno's wife to reimburse them the $6 it had cost to jail her husband.

10

Money at Stake
Economic Secrets

XI YANG GOT a scoop—and risked execution.

His report barely raised eyebrows elsewhere. But in his country it meant a trial and a possible firing squad. The charge: stealing state secrets. And what were those secrets? Not nuclear plans. Not missile data. Not the identities of spies, nor secret codes. Instead the secrets were government plans to sell gold and raise interest rates or keep them at current levels. Hardly the stuff of spy novels. The subject might excite economists but not many others. In the United States, the idea that a journalist might face a firing squad for publishing Alan Greenspan's secret thoughts about interest rates would be unthinkable, not to mention absurd. But it wasn't unthinkable in China, as reporter Xi Yang found out.

He grew up as part of the Beijing elite. His father was an editor of the official Chinese Communist Party newspaper *People's Daily*. As a young man Xi served in the army, then covered sports for eight years as a reporter and editor of the state-controlled journal *Xintiyu* (New Sports). In 1992 he moved to Hong Kong, then a British colony, where his grandfather lived. Xi got a job as a reporter for the respected local newspaper *Ming Pao*. He was one of a number of new hires who spoke the northern Mandarin dialect and had good contacts in mainland China.

Fellow reporters described him as a "man of few words" with a "modest, no-nonsense" working style. He traveled for reporting assignments, including a trip to Singapore to cover talks between Chinese and Taiwanese officials and trips to mainland China to interview a Communist official in the city of Dalian and to Beijing to interview the handicapped son of then-leader Deng Xiaoping for a story on the disabled.

Hong Kong reporter Xi Yang (right) with his sister Xi Ying after his release from a Chinese prison where he served nearly three years of a twelve-year sentence for revealing economic secrets. Xi Yang is shown at a news conference at his newswpaper, *Ming Pao*, on January 25, 1997, in Hong Kong after his release. Credit: AP/Wide World Photos.

The real trouble began in the summer of 1993. Xi went to Beijing and received accreditation to cover Sino-British trade talks and, according to Chinese officials, also contacted a source named Tian Ye who was in a good position to slip him banking secrets. Tian was deputy head of the foreign affairs department of the People's Bank of China, the nation's central bank, equivalent to the Federal Reserve in the United States.

Soon Xi's paper *Ming Pao* was revealing scoops about secret Chinese banking plans, stories that were then picked up by other publications. For example, Japan's Kyodo News Service ran this item referring to Xi's story in *Ming Pao*:

CHINA SET TO SELL GOLD RESERVES FOR FOREIGN EXCHANGE
HONG KONG, July 28 (Kyodo)—China's central bank has decided to sell

some of its precious gold reserves on the international market to boost its foreign exchange holdings, a Hong Kong newspaper reported Wednesday.

The People's Bank of China is preparing to unload an unspecified amount of gold on the market, *Ming Pao* said, quoting bank sources.

That item apparently caught the attention of one of the most powerful Chinese leaders, central bank chairman Zhu Rongji, a fast-rising politician who would later become prime minister. He is believed to have pushed behind the scenes to have reporter Xi Yang punished for breaking this story.

On Monday, September 27, 1993, Xi was arrested at his Beijing hotel, the Jianguo, by agents of the State Security Bureau who seized notes and other documents from his hotel room. Xi, thirty-eight years old, was charged with espionage, a crime that carried with it a maximum sentence of execution by firing squad. His source at the bank, Tian Ye, was also arrested. They were held incommunicado.

Xi's arrest set off alarm bells in Hong Kong, where many people were already apprehensive about the planned handover of the British colony to mainland China in four years. Fellow journalists began a vigorous campaign of protests. Not only were many people in Hong Kong worried what this case might mean for freedom of the press after China took over the city in 1997, but there were real fears for Xi's life. As a headline of the United Press International (UPI) news service put it grimly: "Reporter in China May Face Execution." And in fact, on the same day that Xi was arrested, China announced the execution of eight young financial employees convicted of embezzlement.

Xi and Tian were tried secretly, without being allowed to have defense lawyers present. Xi's family, friends, and employer were not even informed of the trial until three days after it was over. When Xi's father, now retired as an editor of *People's Daily*, got the news that his son had been convicted and sentenced to twelve years in prison, he suffered a heart attack and was taken to a hospital. Tian, the bank official who allegedly passed secret information to Xi, received a prison sentence of fifteen years, three years more than Xi.

Angry protests greeted the news of Xi's conviction and sentencing. Martin Lee Chu-ming, a Hong Kong legislator, said: "Twelve years for a scoop is extremely shocking." Xi began serving his sentence at Beijing No. 2 Prison, where he was required to work twelve hours a day and could receive family visits only once a month. He reportedly suffered from kidney and stomach ailments.

As protests continued in Hong Kong and around the world, Chinese officials felt obligated to explain why they were imposing such stiff punishment for a scoop about gold and interest rates. The state security minister told a Chinese reporter that Xi's story "caused economic losses" for the state. Official Chinese media portrayed Xi as a sinister figure who had come to Beijing "under pretext" of covering Sino-British talks and had been "doing his utmost to pry into major state banking and financial secrets." State television belatedly showed footage of Xi and Tian at the municipal Supreme Peoples' Court, heads bowed, as a judge in military uniform rejected an appeal while a TV announcer called the case against them "very grave." Chinese officials passed word that Xi had been lucky not to be executed.

As the deadline drew near for China to take over Hong Kong, leaders in Beijing apparently decided it was time to toss a bone to democrats so the transition would be smooth. Only five months before the handover, and shortly before the big annual holiday of Chinese New Year, Xi was suddenly told at 8 A.M. on Sunday, January 26, 1997, that he was being released on probation that same day. By noon he was having lunch in Beijing with his family, including his father and younger sister, and that evening he flew to Hong Kong and celebrated with chocolate cake at the offices of his paper, *Ming Pao*. His hair had turned gray. He was forty years old.

Money had been at stake when Xi was arrested and again when he was released, three and a half years later. Chinese bank secrets could be worth billions of dollars if their premature release tipped off speculators to attack the currency, the *yuan*, so Beijing had been willing to risk world opprobrium to try to stop leaks. But China also didn't want to scare off investors, traders, and other customers in Hong Kong by cracking down too hard on journalists. So it released Xi Yang just in time to create a warm, cozy atmosphere for Britain's handover. At the same time, China didn't want journalists to get the idea it had suddenly become a bastion of freedom of the press, so the same month that it released Xi Yang, it also denied parole to imprisoned economic journalist Gao Yu.

With so much money at stake, revealing economic secrets can easily land a reporter in trouble—and not just in China. Four days before Xi's prison sentence was announced, a verdict was handed down in another Asian country in a criminal case involving journalists and eco-nomic secrets. The "crime" was even more absurd in this case: publish-ing a government estimate on how much the economy had grown in the second quarter. And yet, as ludicrous as it might seem in the West, to Singapore's authoritarian regime the growth rate was a deadly serious matter, a secret so important that it must be guarded at all costs, even by threats of prison for any journalist who revealed it.

This secret is known in Singapore as the "flash estimate." It is a quarterly report by the Monetary Authority of Singapore (MAS) on how fast or slow the rate is, in a country that has long prided itself on strong growth. In the three months of April, May, and June of 1992, the economy had not expanded quite as fast as some had predicted—and that embarrassing fact had to be kept quiet. Word of it leaked out when Tharman Shanmugaratnam, director of the MAS economics depart-ment, brought a copy of the secret flash estimate to a meeting with an economist from a brokerage house. Either accidentally or intentionally, depending whether you believe the monetary official or the prosecutor, Shanmugaratnam let the economist get a peek at the secret report. The economist later told Kenneth James, a reporter for the local weekly *Busi-ness Times*, who passed on the information in an E-mail to his editor, Patrick Daniel. The editor decided to publish this scoop, and readers of the June 29, 1992, edition of *Business Times* saw this page-one item:

2ND QTR: FLASH ESTIMATES POINT TO BELOW 5PC GROWTH
But Private Sector Analysts Remain Bullish and
See Higher Growth
By Anna Teo
SINGAPORE—Official flash estimates suggest that economic growth in April and May fell below the first quarter rate of 5.1 per cent.

With a none too encouraging April and May trade record, and a vis-itor arrival growth that did not quite translate to strong tourist spend-ing, the early indications point to a second-quarter growth of 4.6–4.8 percent.

It was hardly the crime of the century, revealing a 4.6–4.8 percent growth rate a few days before the figure was officially released. The news had no impact on the stock market. But still government officials were furious. Seven agents of the Internal Security Department raided the offices of the *Business Times*, seized documents, and questioned the staff. Journalists Daniel and James, monetary official Shanmugaratnam, and two economists were all charged with violating the Official Secrets Act, a crime punishable by up to five years in prison.

Editor Daniel's staff joked about it, giving him a copy of the record *Jailhouse Rock*, but Singapore's authorities found it no laughing matter. Prime Minister Goh Chok Tong said he could not run a government that was "leaking all over the place." The country's attorney general personally prosecuted the case, in one of the longest criminal trials in Singaporean history.

The judge found all five guilty and then, before handing down sentences, noted that past cases involving the Official Secrets Act had ended with prison sentences ranging from nine months to five years. Having thoroughly alarmed the defendants by raising the possibility of jail time, he then ruled that they would not have to serve time and instead ordered them to pay fines. Editor Daniel was fined $3,600 and reporter James $3,150.

A much harsher sentence awaited a journalist in a nearby Asian country, again for daring to reveal economic truths. This time there was a connection between those economic facts and politics. At a time when Vietnam's Communist government was claiming things were fine and getting better every day, a dissident journalist named Doan Viet Hoat published a newsletter that said the economy was a mess. His punishment? Fifteen years at hard labor.

A stubborn, square-jawed man with glasses and a gentle smile, he had been in trouble for a long time. Doan was born in 1942 and met his wife when they were Saigon University students during the Vietnam War. He was also writing for a local newspaper at the time. Later he received a doctorate in education at Florida State University and became associate dean of Saigon's Van Hanh Buddhist University. After the fall of Saigon, a former student denounced him as an opponent of the Communist government. That was the beginning of a series of punishments throughout most of the rest of his life.

In a predawn raid on his home in August 1976, troops seized him in his pajamas and handcuffed and blindfolded him. Hue, one of his three sons, was five years old at the time and later recalled what he saw:

> It was 5 a.m. I woke up and came out from the back and saw him handcuffed, sitting on a chair. I didn't know what was going on. Grandma told us to get out of the way. It was in [our] huge library; police were

searching through every book. . . . When I was brushing my teeth, my father wanted to go to the bathroom. A guard went with him.

That was the last time Hue and his two brothers ever saw their father at home again in Vietnam. While Doan was serving twelve years of "reeducation" at Chi Hoa Prison, his wife smuggled their sons out of the country on fishing boats. They eventually made their way to relatives in Minneapolis. She herself stayed but was able to visit her husband only once a year for fifteen minutes. Ousted from her teaching job, she was forced to sell slippers, nuts, and ice cream to make a living. In 1986 she was arrested and imprisoned for twenty months for asking Amnesty International to campaign for his release.

Doan was released in 1988 and taught at the Agriculture and Forestry University in the now-renamed Ho Chi Minh City (formerly Saigon), but his reeducation had obviously not achieved what the government had intended. He continued to advocate democracy and freedom of expression. Doan published four issues of a ten-page typewritten newsletter called *Dien Dan Tu Do* (Freedom Forum). In it he called for a multiparty democracy and economic reforms—and revealed what the Communist regime wanted kept secret: the extent of economic failure.

He was arrested at his home on Saturday, November 17, 1990, and held without trial for two and a half years. At last he was put on trial behind closed doors for "activities aimed at overthrowing the government." As alleged proof of his crime, the prosecutor cited Doan's article about economic problems, published in his typewritten newsletter in July 1990. Here is an excerpt:

> The poor situation of the Vietnamese economy is no longer tolerable. Soviet and East European aid is now negligible. Overseas investment is still low. Meanwhile discontent within the party and opposition outside it are growing every day. The recent hard line adopted by the authorities to stop demonstrations of discontent only puts off the day when a real solution will have to be reached.

For this and other writings, on March 30, 1993, he was convicted and sentenced to twenty years at hard labor, a sentence reduced on appeal to fifteen years of hard labor to be followed by five years of house arrest. He was moved around to six different prisons and at one point was in solitary confinement in a closet-sized cell, with family visits forbidden, at one of the worst prisons, Thanh Cam, in a remote, malaria-ridden area near the Laotian border, surviving on meals of rice alone. For refusing to do hard labor he was reportedly put in shackles, but he remained defiant and went on a hunger strike.

After three years of being denied contact with him, his wife, having moved to Minneapolis, received a letter in July 1997 in which he wrote: "The light in me burns brighter every day, which makes me happy." Just over a year later he was released as part of a general amnesty and deported to the United States. At the age of fifty-four he had spent nineteen of the past twenty-one years in prison. "I regret that they don't let me stay in Vietnam," he told reporters. "I don't want to leave my country. I love my country. I want to contribute to freedom and democracy."

Criticism of economic failures seems to worry some governments more than others, perhaps because some are less confident of public support and fear that the public's knowledge of the truth could weaken their grip on power. In 1995 in the Central Asian country of Tajikistan, the co-editors of the *Evening Courier*, the only independent newspaper, were abducted and threatened with death and the deaths of their children—simply for publishing a story that criticized economic policies.

Even in the relatively more "civilized" country of Singapore, the criminal prosecution of the journalists who revealed the economic growth rate has reminded government officials of the danger of leaking economic secrets. After the trial, distances between the officials and the journalists widened—literally. As one journalist explained: "When Monetary Authority of Singapore officials meet private sector analysts in the authority's conference room . . . , they now place two tables between them to prevent peeks at official papers."

11

The President's Mistress

Exposés

THE EXPOSÉ IS the lifeblood of many journalists. Sensational revelations are among the most coveted stories and are often the most popular kind of reporting, especially stories that point out the foibles of the
high and mighty. To no one's surprise, this type of reporting is more
popular with the general public than with the powerful figures whose
personal shortcomings are exposed, and that makes the exposé one of
the main causes of attacks against journalists.

Anything to do with sex is bound to hit a nerve.

When a born-again Christian named Frederick Chiluba became his
nation's president, he vowed to base government policy on his strict religious beliefs. The last thing he wanted was a pesky newspaper claiming he wasn't all that pious in his personal life. Yet, after his landslide
election in 1991 in the southern African nation of Zambia, the president
came under constant attack by the nation's leading independent paper,
the *Post* (circulation fifteen thousand, mostly in Lusaka, the capital).

At one point President Chiluba tried to block the return to power of
a foreign-born former president by proposing that only native-born citizens could hold high office. But that backfired when the newspaper alleged that Chiluba himself had been born abroad (in Zaire). Not only
that, but the paper also cited evidence that Chiluba was not really the
president's name and that he had changed his name after he was allegedly expelled from school—charges Chiluba denied.

The attacks escalated. The paper quoted a former cabinet minister
at her drug-trafficking trial as calling Chiluba "a twit." For using that
offending word, the paper's editor and reporter were arrested and
charged under an obscure law against "ridicule of the President." Then
the paper quoted another former cabinet minister, one who alleged that
Chiluba had smoked pot and trafficked in drugs. For that and other

stories, the editor and other staffers were arrested and charged with criminal libel.

The exposés kept coming. The paper revealed that a woman who was the president's personal secretary had a suspiciously luxurious lifestyle. In response, heavily armed paramilitary police stormed the newspaper's offices, seized documents, and delayed printing of the next edition. No reason was given, but the paper speculated that the raid was prompted by rumors that it had obtained compromising photographs of the president with his secretary—rumors apparently touched off by the article about her lifestyle.

In 1995 the newspaper's allegations became even more personal. On Tuesday, June 13, *The Post* ran a bombshell exposé on page one; the headline: "Chiluba's Lover Quizzed." It reported that a Zairean-born woman named Clementine Mutshingi Kabondo had arrived in Lusaka, the capital, from the countryside to demand support payments from Chiluba for her eight-year-old daughter. She claimed that Chiluba was the father, that the child was the product of an alleged twelve-year extramarital affair with the president, and that police had tortured her.

President Chiluba strongly denied the allegations. In a letter published in the paper, he said: "It is obvious that your story is part of your persistent campaign of vilification intended to malign and defame me." He gave the *Post* forty-eight hours to produce the woman and her daughter. The paper refused, in effect saying "See you in court." When the forty-eight hours expired, editor-in-chief Fred M'membe arrived for work at his office on the morning of June 19. A few minutes later, at about 8 A.M., three senior police officers placed him under detention and took him to a police station. Special projects editor Masautso Phiri, also wanted by police, voluntarily went to the police station. He and M'membe were held overnight and charged with criminal libel.

The case dragged through the courts for years, delayed by such issues as whether the president should have to submit to a DNA test demanded by the newspaper, a demand the courts rejected. Meanwhile M'membe's paper ran story after story about the case. One said that a woman friend of the alleged mistress had been interrogated by police. Another story disclosed that an unusually high-ranking police officer had been assigned to drive the alleged mistress to and from court, thus giving her preferential treatment, with the implication that someone was trying to influence her testimony.

While this case dragged on, Chiluba's government arrested editor-in-chief M'membe again and again for other stories. It attached so many other charges to those already pending against him that at one point he faced a potential total of one hundred years in prison. One of the most bizarre charges against him was possession of a prohibited publication—his own newspaper. The government had banned one day's edition for revealing a secret plan to change the constitution. Years later, all of these lawsuits were still pending.

Sex reared its head in another country, and once again a journalist paid a price for his exposé. In the small, impoverished African country of Gabon, Omar Bongo became president in 1967 and more than thirty years later was still the president. While many of the people (population just over 1 million) lacked running water or most other bare necessities, Bongo became one of Africa's wealthiest men, thanks to his cut of revenues from oil and other resources.

When not imprisoning opposition leaders, Bongo was reportedly spending $600,000 a year for splendid suits flown in from Paris. Apparently, more than suits were being flown in. In 1995, Gabon's only independent newspapers, La Griffe and Le Bucheron, reprinted articles from French newspapers that revealed embarrassing details of a prostitution trial in Paris implicating President Bongo. Francesco Smalto, an Italian menswear designer based in Paris, was charged with "aggravated pimping." He testified that Bongo had been his best customer for tailored suits, and in order not to lose him to the competition, Smalto in 1992 and 1993 had sent blonde call girls to accompany shipments of suits to his client in Libreville, Gabon. Smalto explained to the court: "We noticed that a female presence facilitated Mr. Bongo's orders."

What made it even more embarrassing was testimony by Monica, one of the prostitutes, read aloud by the judge: "It went very badly that evening. Bongo didn't want to wear a condom, and as he had a friend who had died from AIDS, I refused to make love to him." The court also heard testimony that Bongo was rumored to be HIV-positive. That was too much for the president. He sued the French newspaper Le Monde for "insulting" him during its coverage of the trial and recalled the Gabonese ambassador from Paris, while Bongo supporters demonstrated outside the French embassy in Libreville, his nation's capital.

Because Gabon's two independent papers, La Griffe and Le Bucheron, had reprinted articles about the trial from Le Monde and other French newspapers, Bongo shut them down, at least temporarily. On April 20 his interior minister ordered printers to stop printing the papers, on grounds that they were publishing articles from French newspapers that had been banned in Gabon. Two weeks later, after protests, Gabon's government let the two papers resume printing.

In Paris, Italian designer Smalto was convicted of pimping, given a fifteen-month suspended prison sentence, fined $120,000, and ordered to pay a symbolic twenty cents in damages to an antiprostitution organization. In Libreville, Bongo somehow survived the embarrassing episode. He issued a statement saying that such matters should be kept private, and in any case, "it is public knowledge that many figures outside of Gabon could be involved in comparable paracommercial practices."

Close behind sex as a favorite exposé subject in newspapers is any scandal involving money.

Captain Valentine Strasser, a young army officer who ruled the diamond-rich African nation of Sierra Leone for four years, bristled at suggestions he was motivated by anything other than public service. In October 1993 the independent weekly the *New Breed* ran a story with the headline: "Sierra Leone's Great Redeemer Becomes a Millionaire While the People Continue to Starve." Understandably, Strasser was not pleased by the headline, nor by the story. It was a reprint of an article from the Swedish newspaper *Expressen*, claiming that Strasser had flown to Antwerp, Belgium, and sold 435 carats of diamonds worth $43 million for his personal benefit. For that exposé, the managing editor and three staffers for the *New Breed* were arrested, held for ten days, put on trial in proceedings that lasted almost two years, convicted of seditious libel and other charges, including publishing a false report likely to harm the image of the government, and fined a total of $888.

In another money exposé, TV station news director Juan Bolivar, one of the most respected journalists in the Dominican Republic, claimed in a book that a businessman had diverted company funds to a presidential election campaign. For that, Bolivar was convicted of defamation and sentenced to six months in prison and a staggering fine of more than a quarter of a million dollars, a sentence later suspended. In Uruguay, a money exposé caused brothers Federico and Carlos Fasano to be locked up in Montevideo Central Prison for insulting the honor of a foreign head of state. In their leftist newspaper they had claimed that President Juan Carlos Wasmosy of the nearby country of Paraguay benefited from his company's alleged overbilling for work on a hydroelectric plant. Undaunted, Federico Fasano continued to edit his newspaper from prison. He and his brother were released after two weeks, and later their conviction was overturned on appeal.

After sex and money, high up on the list of exposés that powerful figures dislike is anything suggesting that their health is less than perfect, since obviously their political enemies could be encouraged by news that the Great Leader might not be around in the near future.

In December 1997 an editor was curious about the behavior of President Paul Biya of Cameroon. The president showed up twenty minutes late for a national championship soccer game in the African nation's capital, Yaoundé. Even more mysteriously, he disappeared at halftime, returned only five minutes before the end of the game, quickly awarded a trophy to the winning team, and left. Editor Pius Njawe learned from three sources that the sixty-five-year-old leader had suffered a heart attack while receiving friends in the presidential box at the stadium. Njawe, his country's most respected journalist and winner of an international press freedom award, revealed this news in his thrice-weekly newspaper, *Le Messager*. A few days later, on Christmas Eve, he was arrested in his office. Njawe was convicted of "spreading false information" and undermining national security and was sentenced to two years in prison and a $800 fine, a sentence later reduced to one year and $500.

In Croatia, former Yugoslavia, a weekly tabloid ran into unexpected problems when it tried to print a special edition about the health of seventy-four-year-old President Franjo Tudjman. He was at Walter Reed Military Hospital in Washington in 1996, undergoing treatment for what was officially termed "digestive problems" at a time of speculation that he had cancer. *Nacional*, the tabloid, began its press run, but then the printing house, which is state controlled, said it could not complete the job because, it claimed, it was out of paper. Editor-in-chief Ivo Pukanic said he later learned there was plenty of paper. The special edition was published a day later; the president had made sure the bad news about his health was delayed. Tudjman died at the age of seventy-seven on December 10, 1999, with no official cause of death given other than "abdominal disorders." Western news reports noted that he had been fighting stomach cancer for three years.

Another leader sensitive about stories concerning his health was President Mobutu Sese Seko, the longtime dictator of Zaire and one of the wealthiest men in the world. One year before Mobutu's death of cancer in September 1997, publisher Michel Luya ran an article in his newspaper *Le Palmares* citing a source in the Swiss city of Lausanne who said Mobutu was riddled with cancer, and that he would be "operated on for throat cancer after undergoing a surgery on his prostate." For reporting that, Luya was arrested at his home. His paper was suspended. An official said his story was not only false but also an "affront" to the president.

Although Zairean officials confirmed that Mobutu had undergone prostate surgery in Lausanne, they insisted he was recovering well and "there is no cause for concern about him." Publisher Luya was kept in prison for ten days and released on bail. The following January, he again revealed news of Mobutu's failing health, reprinting articles from Belgian and French media. Luya was again arrested and held ten more days at Kinshasa's Makala Prison, charged with "seriously threatening the security of the state" because of his exposés on Mobutu's medical condition. Mobutu died of cancer eight months later.

Another type of story that provokes attacks on journalists is the exposé of human rights abuses. Leah Makabenta, a Philippine citizen working in Kuala Lumpur as a correspondent for the international news agency Inter Press, exposed what she called the "slave conditions" of migrant workers on plantations in Malaysia. She cited human rights abuses among an estimated 2.5 million foreign workers, including illegal aliens from Bangladesh, Pakistan, Sri Lanka, Indonesia, Thailand, and the Philippines. Malaysia's government called her article "very negative" and expelled her.

In the West African nation of Mauritania, seventy thousand minority blacks allegedly were expelled or forced to flee to neighboring countries by a government dominated by a different ethnic group—Moors of Arab-Berber descent. One official involved in the expulsions of the minority blacks later became interior minister—and suspended the weekly opposition paper *Le Calame* after it published reports implicating him in the alleged human rights violations. The government also harassed two senior editors of *Le Calame*. Like many Mauritanian journalists, they earned their living as teachers in Nouakchott, the capital, because their newspaper jobs didn't pay enough. Officials ordered them transferred to remote schools hundreds of miles away—including one bordering the western Sahara, in a situation tantamount to internal exile—as obvious punishment for their exposés.

Environmental exposés also rankle the powers that be. Sometimes officials take preemptive attacks to prevent reporters from revealing the truth about the ruination of nature by predatory landowners, especially if the landowners happen to have ties to the officials themselves.

In Indonesia in 1997, logging firms owned by cronies of then-dictator Suharto set off fires to clear huge tracts of jungle. Soon the fires raged out of control. Choking smoke covered much of Southeast Asia and became a health and safety hazard. When editors were about to reveal the names of those behind the haze crisis, Suharto officials pressured them to shift the blame to natural causes. As one journalist put it: "Editors were told . . . to say it was El Niño instead."

Even the most trivial of revelations can land journalists in trouble with those they embarrass. For revealing that Sierra Leone's Captain Strasser, of diamond-selling fame, had smoked pot at a Christmas concert, the head of the journalists' association was arrested and held for seven hours. For reporting that Ethiopian president Negasso Gidada was drunk at a public gathering, two senior editors were detained at the Central Criminal Investigation Office Prison and charged with libel. For photographing boys washing a donkey at a beach in Gaza City, AFP photographer Fayez Noureddin was beaten and kicked by security police who complained that the photo made Palestinians look primitive. For reporting that someone had stolen the portable telephone of the Sudanese interior minister, two journalists were seized by police and held incommunicado for two days.

Perhaps the most ludicrous complaint about an exposé came from the interior minister of Pakistan. When freelancer Zafaryab Ahmad revealed abusive labor conditions of carpet workers, he was arrested and charged with sedition. The interior minister claimed Ahmad had worked secretly with Indian intelligence . . . to discredit Pakistan's carpet industry.

12

We Are Not Amused

Satire

BEIJING DIDN'T LAUGH when a Hong Kong newspaper published satirical cartoons about its human rights record.

The cartoons appeared in the comic strip series *The World of Lily Wong*. One of them alluded to allegations by human rights advocates that mainland China was harvesting organs from executed prisoners and selling them for use as transplants. That cartoon appeared in the Hong Kong newspaper *South China Morning Post* in May 1995, two years before Britain handed over the colony to China.

Beijing had already strongly denied the allegations before the cartoon appeared, pressuring two local TV stations not to air a documentary on the subject, but the issue remained a touchy one as Hong Kong prepared for the takeover. Amid this tension, one day after the "body parts" cartoon appeared the *South China Morning Post* fired staff cartoonist Larry Feign, an expatriate American living in Hong Kong, and canceled his *Lily Wong* comic strip. The word came to him in a fax from his editor.

The newspaper said the reason for canceling *Lily Wong* after a nine-year run was purely economic, as part of budget cutbacks, but few journalists or politicians believed it. Staff members of the *South China Morning Post* said the move was self-censorship, clearly designed to appease Beijing before it took over Hong Kong. In a report on Hong Kong human rights practices, the U.S. State Department noted the *Lily Wong* incident and concluded: "There are reliable indications that media self-censorship is a fact of life, particularly on issues considered to be sensitive to the PRC [People's Republic of China]."

About a year later, on June 15, 1996, the London-based human rights organization Amnesty International, in conjunction with the Hong Kong Journalists Association and the Foreign Correspondents

Cartoonist Larry Feign was fired by the *South China Morning Post* in 1995 the day after the Hong Kong newspaper published this comic strip, a satirical attack on China's alleged sales of body parts from executed prisoners. Journalists and Western diplomats suspected Feign was fired under pressure from Beijing. Later Feign won a Human Rights Press Award for the cartoon. Credit: © Larry Feign.

Club of Hong Kong, gave Feign one of its Human Rights Press Awards for outstanding coverage of human rights issues in the news media. The award for best English-language cartoon cited his "body parts" satire. In a sense, Feign had the last laugh.

Satire is intended to reveal the truth in a humorous way, and it can be a powerful way of sending a message to the public about the gap between myth and reality, but obviously not everyone finds it funny. Tyrants are usually not amused, especially if the joke is on them. That happened in the case of an Ivorian soccer game.

On Saturday, December 16, 1995, the stadium at Abidjan was packed. The fans were there to see the most important soccer game of the year in the Ivory Coast. The national team—ASEC—was playing the visiting Orlando Pirates of South Africa for nothing less than the African Champions Cup. The two teams had tied 2-2 in an earlier game in South Africa, and now in the rematch the Ivorians had the home-team advantage. Fans in the Ivory Coast were excited. They felt that their team had a good chance to finally win its first African championship cup. This match was so important that even the president of the Ivory Coast himself, Henri Konan Bédié, attended the game.

Bédié was a controversial figure. As a government minister in 1978, he had been fired amid allegations of corruption. Two years later he returned as a legislator, rose to become head of the parliament, and in that capacity acceded to the presidency of the republic when the old president died. In 1995 he was elected president in his own right, running on a campaign slogan that emphasized the notion that "Bédié brought good luck to his country."

But his attendance at the game did not help the team. ASEC lost to the Orlando Pirates, 0-1. Fans were angry. A journalist for an opposition newspaper caught the mood when he wrote a satirical article under the headline: "He Brought Bad Luck to ASEC." That article in the opposition newspaper *La Voie* (The Voice) was published on December 18. Eleven days later the journalist received a summons to appear at a police station and explain just what he had meant by saying the president had brought bad luck to the soccer team. The journalist, a lively, wisecracking man of thirty-nine whose pen name was Freedom Neruda, said he knew what was in store: "When they tell you to go to the police, you are on your way to MACA Prison."

Neruda's real name was Tieti Roch d'Assomption. He was born in the western town of Duékoué. He studied political science and economics at Ivory Coast University in Abidjan, one of Africa's largest cities. This was in the 1970s, in the early days of the nation's independence from France.

He taught math, then began work as a journalist at a morning newspaper called *Fraternité Matin* and an evening paper called *Ivoire Soir*. He worked his way up from copy editor to investigative reporter, but he was frustrated. All the newspapers at that time were controlled by the government, under a one-party system. Criticizing the government "would have been unimaginable," Neruda told me. Journalists had to write their stories carefully. For example, because the government's policy was to play down the importance of a revolt in Angola, their leader could be referred to in newspapers only as Mr. Jonas Savimbi, with no mention of the fact that he was the rebel leader.

In 1991, when the one-party system gave way to limited multiparty democracy, independent newspapers appeared. "It was the springtime of the press," Neruda said. He tried to go into the publishing business himself and founded an independent newspaper, *La Chronique du Soir*, intending to do investigative stories. But the paper quickly foundered. Meanwhile there was political unrest. Neruda took part in a protest march after the army attacked students. Later, as a freelance reporter, he covered the trial of opposition leaders who were arrested at that protest march. The trial convinced Neruda that fair treatment was impossible under that government, and he offered his services to the newspaper *La Voie*, whose publisher was deputy leader of the main opposition party.

Neruda and others on the newspaper wrote articles attacking President Bédié and reminding readers that the president had once been fired amid corruption charges. In 1994, Neruda was among five journalists sentenced to a year in prison for insulting Bédié because they had written about allegations he overspent on his predecessor's funeral. The journalists were freed pending appeals. In June 1995, Neruda was called in for questioning about another satirical article, and his publisher allegedly was beaten in the security minister's office during questioning about that article. A few days later Neruda was threatened by police, who allegedly said they would give him seventy-five truncheon blows. After this threat they sent him home. Later that year, in October, a fire bomb destroyed the paper's editorial offices.

Then came the soccer game and Neruda's decision to poke fun at the president by saying he had brought bad luck. At that time Neruda's publisher had just served an eight-month prison sentence, and other journalists were in jail. Did Neruda worry that if he wrote this satire it would land him behind bars? "A lot of people said writing something might cause trouble. We said there is nothing else to write. . . . Journalists have the right to write their opinions." He went ahead with the article and was summoned to the police station. His publisher and another reporter were arrested. After stalling for time so he could make arrangements for someone to take care of his ten-year-old son, Neruda finally went to the police station on January 2, 1996.

"I slept on the floor," he said. "At 3 A.M. I was sent to the court [for arraignment]." He was charged with seditious libel and held without bail. With a wry smile befitting a satirist, Neruda told me: "My case was so serious, I am a very dangerous gangster, so I must stay in prison before the trial." Nine days later he was convicted and sentenced to two years in prison for "offenses against the head of state." He was taken to the main prison, MACA (Maison d'Arrêt et de Correction d'Abidjan— the Abidjan House of Arrest and Correction). He shared a cell with his publisher and the other reporter. Conditions were not as bad as they might have been. "We were three in a cell for four with small beds. That is for the most privileged prisoners of MACA prison, built for Europeans and the high officials of the public administration. . . . Later a fourth prisoner joined us, who had been involved in killing somebody."

Food was adequate but sparse. "They gave us a ball of rice in the morning." He made a fist to illustrate the size of it. "You get two small pieces of yam a day. . . . Thanks to funds from the paper, we had food sent in from outside." He was permitted one visit a week, each Saturday, from family or friends, but he discovered that more visits were possible—for the right amount of bribes. Despite these privileges, life was harsh. "There were 5,000 prisoners in a prison for 1,500. . . . You had sickness, hunger." Neruda said he had an attack of appendicitis and was permitted treatment at a clinic outside the prison: "I might have died in the prison."

Meanwhile the newspaper was shut down for three months by the government. "We replaced it immediately with *L'Alternative*. It was the same paper with another name." Articles began appearing in *L'Alternative* by a mysterious new journalist named Bintou Diawara, apparently a woman. One of the stories exposed a financial scandal. Another revealed that powerful émigré Lebanese in the Ivory Coast were consistently being given more lenient sentences than Ivorians for the same crimes. Bintou Diawara was actually Freedom Neruda, smuggling stories out of prison.

In August, on the national independence day, President Bédié went on television to offer a pardon to Neruda and the other two journalists—but only on one condition. They had to give up their appeal of their criminal conviction. They refused. "Since the process was not over," Neruda said, "we continued. It was very important for the mentality of the people in prison. . . . I think it makes people reflect on this and gives them a bit more courage."

They lost their appeals. Then, in January 1997, after serving one year of the two-year sentence, Neruda and the other two were released.

One year in prison for joking about a soccer game was the price Freedom Neruda paid for indulging his passion for satire. Other journalists around the world have paid similar prices, sometimes for similar jokes involving soccer, which seems to be a touchy subject among despots, perhaps because soccer is such a popular game in most of the world's nations and satirists can use it easily to convey an idea to a mass audience. Tesfaye Tegen, editor of Ethiopia's weekly *Beza* newspaper, published a cartoon portraying government officials as members of a soccer team, with the prime minister much larger than the other players. The government cried foul and carted the editor off to prison. And in Iran, Manouchehr Karimzadeh's cartoon of a one-armed soccer player wearing a turban was published in the magazine *Farad*. Authorities thought he was ridiculing the late Ayatollah Khomeini and had him sentenced to ten years in prison.

Satirical cartoons and illustrations often hit a nerve not related to the funny bone. On September 9, 1991, the leftist Chilean weekly *Punto Final* published a front-page photograph of army leader and former dictator General Augusto Pinochet, a photo that had been turned into a montage by adding a drawing of a Chilean flag as if he were wiping his bloody nose with it. The montage was captioned "Cynicism and Sadism" and referred to his comments about a secret grave site where bodies were economically buried two at a time, one above the other. Pinochet had said, "This represents a savings for the state."

Manuel Cabieses, the editor of *Punto Final*, had been arrested years earlier in Pinochet's right-wing coup, imprisoned for two years, sent into exile in Mexico and Cuba, and then permitted to return to Chile when democracy was restored. Now, for publishing the bloody-flag montage, a military court charged Cabieses with "inciting sedition." Police armed with an arrest warrant raided his home and office, driving him into hiding for eighteen days. He later was tried and acquitted.

In Lebanon in 1994, the pro-Syrian newspaper *Al-Sharq* ridiculed the most revered cleric among Maronite Christians. It published a cartoon showing the Maronite patriarch, Cardinal Nasrallah Boutros Sfeir, hanging women's underwear on a laundry line in Paris. The cartoon accused him of airing "dirty linen" by complaining to French officials about curbs on Lebanese freedom. The public prosecutor threatened legal action against the paper.

In Cambodia a cartoon in an opposition newspaper showed one government leader holding a gun to the head of another. That cartoon, in addition to an article accusing the nation's two co–prime ministers of being thieves, caused editor Hen Vipheak to be convicted of "disinformation" and sentenced to one year in prison and a $2,000 fine. Failure to pay the fine would have added a year to his prison sentence. He served one week in a prison for common criminals and then was pardoned by the nation's king, who cited the Buddhist tradition of tolerance.

And in Turkey a leftist paper published a cartoon alluding to an incident in which soldiers allegedly forced prisoners to eat excrement.

Cartoonist Ahmet Erkanli was convicted of defaming the armed forces and imprisoned for five months.

Satire in Colombia may have led to the death of a popular journalist and peace activist. Jaime Garzon, thirty-nine, was renowned for his radio and TV spoofs ridiculing the rich and powerful in a country crippled by guerrilla wars and drug corruption. In one TV sketch during the 1998 election, he posed as a shoeshine boy polishing the shoes of a female presidential candidate and asked her: "Madam, don't you ever get sick of spouting the same nonsense every day?"

On August 13, 1999, as he drove to work at an all-news radio network in Bogotá, Garzon was gunned down by an assassin on a motorcycle. It was not immediately clear whether he was murdered for his satire or his peace efforts. Garzon had been scheduled later that day to meet with a guerrilla group as part of a peace process. Whatever the motive for his death, it sent the nation into mourning. Thousands of Colombians filed past his open casket. One mourner was quoted as saying: "They've just killed the most beautiful thing in the world. This man was a symbol of honesty, of courage, of truth."

Sometimes a single joke is all it takes to land a journalist in trouble. Take the case of Muhammad Jasim al-Saqr, editor-in-chief of a leading newspaper in Kuwait. On January 5, 1998, he published a four-line joke in the humor column of the newspaper *Al-Qabas*. In the joke, a teacher asks a student why Adam and Eve were expelled from the Garden of Eden. The student replies: "Because they didn't pay the rent." A seemingly harmless little commentary on the high cost of living in the Gulf states, but the government didn't see it that way. The Ministry of Information had al-Saqr and another journalist criminally prosecuted for "insulting the essence of the Divine Being." They were convicted of blasphemy and sentenced to six months in prison. The paper was ordered shut down for a week.

When the humor is more pointedly political and directly attacks a national leader by name, the consequences can be even more serious, as Viktor Ivancic found out. He edits a weekly newspaper that mixes satire, news, and serious commentary in the Balkan country of Croatia, across the Adriatic Sea from Italy. One day Ivancic found himself facing the possibility of three years in prison—because of a joke that the nation's president didn't find funny.

Ivancic, a thin, sardonic man with a beard, began his career in 1983 as a journalist on *Slobodna Dalmacij*, a newspaper published in the coastal city of Split under the post-Tito Communist regime in Yugoslavia, when Croatia was part of Yugoslavia. By that time censorship had eased. "During the last years of communism," Ivancic said, "it was much more flexible than in the sixties and seventies, so from the beginning we were in opposition to the regime." But even with the easing of censorship, satirist Ivancic got into trouble with authorities—eight times. In two court cases he faced possible prison sentences for insulting the president of then-Yugoslavia but was able to win the cases. Then the communist system collapsed, along with the collapse of the Soviet empire—but Ivancic's hopes of a free press were frustrated. "We were expecting in 1990 something else to happen, something better," he said. "But the power of communism is simply replaced by the power of nationalism and the same mentality of the leaders. Lots of them are ex-Communists."

In the early 1990s, *Slobodna Dalmacij* and its weekly magazine *Feral Tribune* attacked Croatian president Franjo Tudjman for allegedly trying to rehabilitate the disgraced pro-Nazi Ustashe regime that had ruled during World War II. In 1993 the government of President Tudjman gained control of the newspaper *Slobodna Dalmacij*. Satirist Ivancic and other journalists quit the paper rather than come under the thumb of the authoritarian president, a former general in the Yugoslav army. "They came to us, a few of us, and told us, 'Please stay. We will give you double salary.' They wanted to buy us. But we did not stay. . . .

"With a few of my colleagues I borrowed money and we formed our own paper," he said. That paper was a spinoff from the weekly that had been part of *Slobodna Dalmacij*—the magazine called *Feral Tribune* (a play on words that combines the Croatian word for "lamp" with the name of the Paris-based international newspaper *Herald Tribune*). Ivancic's magazine mixed news, commentary, and satire. It was popular; circulation rose to seventy thousand. But soon it was in trouble with the government.

On December 28, 1993, the magazine published a photomontage showing a naked Tudjman in bed with an equally naked Slobodan Milosevic, the controversial and authoritarian Serbian leader of Yugoslavia. One week later editor Ivancic, thirty-three, was arrested at his home and taken to army barracks. He was told he was being drafted into military service. Ivancic found a way out of that scrape, but more trouble lay ahead. The government slapped an enormous tax on his magazine, the same type of tax normally imposed on pornographic publications; the government backed down after international protests. Then a gang seized copies of the magazine from news vendors and burned them in the streets of Split. Finally came the biggest threat of all. For months tension had been building up between the press and the president. At one point Tudjman claimed that independent journalists had "sold themselves to the enemies." At another point he awarded medals to journalists in the state-controlled media—but no medals to independent journalists—at a ceremony in which he also awarded himself nine decorations. "These are very hard times for satire," Ivancic wisecracked. "Whatever we write, the state comes up with something far funnier."

On March 29, 1996, the president saw to it that parliament amended the criminal code to protect himself and four other top officials from libel and "insults." The new law provided stiff prison sentences for anyone convicted of injuring the honor and personal integrity of these leaders. Critics suspected the new law was aimed at *Feral Tribune*. One month later Ivancic's magazine published an article titled "Bones in the Blender." It ridiculed the president's ghoulish plan to dig up the bones of fascists from a cemetery and rebury them with the bones of their victims: the remains of some of the tens of thousands of Jews, Serbs, and Gypsies the fascists had massacred during World War II. President Tudjman said the idea was to convert the existing Jasenovac memorial to the victims of fascism, at the site of a former concentration camp, into a memorial to all Croatian victims of war, fascist and nonfascist alike, as a way of making peace among all Croats. But Ivancic saw it differently: "He wanted to relativize the crime."

The satire in Ivancic's *Feral Tribune* was barbed indeed. The cover showed a skeleton draped in Tudjman's presidential sash. A headline said: "President Tudjman's Interesting Proposal: Everyone to Jasenovac!" Inside was the article, headlined "Bones in the Blender." A photomontage showed Croatia's wartime fascist dictator handing Tudjman a model of the Jasenovac monument. Another article compared Tudjman to the late Spanish fascist dictator Francisco Franco. Clearly that was too much for Tudjman.

One week later police took Ivancic and another journalist to a police station and told them they had been charged by the federal prosecutor with "libeling and insulting the president of the republic" under the amended criminal law. They faced up to three years in prison. Ivancic's *Feral Tribune* remained defiant. In a press statement it said it was

The satirical Croatian magazine *Feral Tribune* angered the nation's president in 1996 by showing a skeleton in a presidential sash and ridiculing his proposal to combine the remains of the fascists with those of their victims at Jasenovac Cemetery. The headline at the bottom says "President Tudjman's Interesting Proposal: Everyone to Jasenovac!" Editor Viktor Ivancic faced up to three years in prison on charges of libeling and insulting the president but won acquittal.

"merely surprised that the government which introduced thought crime had not considered a much more effective way of stopping people [from] thinking for themselves—lobotomy." "I think," Ivancic said later, "their mission was not to put me in prison but to punish us, to send a message to the other journalists: 'Don't write critical articles because you could go to prison.'"

Tudjman's attempt to silence his critics failed. After international protests and a trial attended by observers from press-freedom advocacy groups, a court in Zagreb, the capital, acquitted Ivancic and the other journalist. Judge Marin Marcela wrote: "Croatia is a free country in which freedom of expression, including the right to criticize President Tudjman, exists."

Ridiculing leaders in other countries can anger the powers that be. On Saturday night, July 8, 1995, Russian president Boris Yeltsin was portrayed on national television as a drunken bum. A life-sized doll in the popular satirical show *Kukly* (Puppets) was designed to look like Yeltsin. In the skit, the leader of the economically troubled nation was a tramp in a flophouse singing, "Why did I ever see the light of day? Why did my mother give birth to me?"

Parodying Gorky's *Lower Depths*, the show on Russia's independent network NTV portrayed Yeltsin's prime minister Viktor Chernomyrdin as another bum in a ragged T-shirt and an old cap with earflaps who scrapes together a living selling parts of a dismantled gas stove. His cabinet members are fellow vagrants on the minimum wage: $10 a month. Two of them fight over a broken umbrella in a garbage can. An economist who was the architect of the nation's market-based economic reforms plays the violin in an underpass and collects handouts from pedestrians, then sleeps on a sidewalk bench, covering himself with the newspaper *Izvestia*. At the end, Yeltsin is panhandling on a suburban train, holding in his arms a baby who is presidential security chief General Alexander Korzhakov. Yeltsin begs for charity in Christ's name, saying: "We missed our train. . . . We've been living in the station for more than a week."

Shortly after the program aired, Prosecutor-General Alexei Ilyushenko opened a criminal investigation into the show, saying that the country's highest public officials had been "portrayed in an insulting manner." He said they had been the victims of "a conscious and public humiliation of their honor and dignity, expressed in an indecent way." The prosecutor began proceedings under Article 131 of the Russian criminal code, which provides a maximum possible sentence of two years' corrective labor. His action provoked outrage. Producers of the *Kukly* show protested at a press conference, complete with four nodding puppets of Yeltsin and the other Russian leaders who agreed with NTV president Igor Malashenko when he said: "This is an attempt to intimidate the Russian mass media."

Some writers for the show expressed hope that Russia was not returning to the days of Soviet censorship. Referring to the location of a Soviet-era prison camp, writer Viktor Shenderovich said: "If this had happened fifteen years ago I would be giving this interview from Mordovia, but now it's just rather funny." Alexander Levin, who directed the July 8 show, said Russian leaders were too sensitive. "You need to have a certain cultural level to realize that it is not always bad if people laugh at you," he said. "We have a saying in Russia, 'Don't blame the mirror if your face is deformed.' Well, our leaders are trying to smash the mirror."

If that was their intention, the leaders never got the chance. Later in the year Yeltsin was forced to fire his controversial prosecutor, who had taken flak for being overly zealous in attacking Yeltsin's critics at NTV. Also, a report in the Russian media linked the prosecutor's wife to underworld business. The criminal investigation into *Kukly* was dropped. The puppets went on their merry way, continuing to spoof the Kremlin.

Most satires of top officials are based on analogies, comparing the leader to something else. In Romania, President Ion Iliescu took offense when journalist Nicolei Andrei compared him to a pig. Andrei was arrested and charged with "insulting the head of state." In Indonesia, President Suharto objected when a popular magazine published a cover photo of him as a king-of-spades playing card. The satirical point the magazine made was that although there were supposed to be elections for the leader, Suharto always won under a rigged system, so he might as well be a king. The editor was interrogated by police; expelled from the government-linked Association of Indonesian Journalists (PWI), making it impossible for him to find work as a journalist; and threatened with six years in prison. But before he could be prosecuted, Suharto was ousted.

Clashes between the powers that be and journalists who ridicule them are just as inevitable as the conflicts we have seen, in the preceding chapters, between entrenched interests and reporters who cover crime and corruption, separatist movements, civil wars, protest demonstrations, economic secrets, and exposés. In all of these cases, journalists have the powerful weapon of the truth, but satirists have one more weapon: laughter. And while all satirists hope to amuse the public, some also hope to disturb complacent leaders, on the theory that humorous criticism isn't worth a damn unless it stirs up trouble. As *Kukly* writer Viktor Shenderovich put it: "Satire should irritate the king."

PART III

SHOOT THE MESSENGER

Types of Attacks on Journalists

13

We Have Ways

Violence and Imprisonment

WHATEVER THE PROVOCATION, whether a story of corruption or a scoop about economic secrets, the journalist who writes it may suffer a wide variety of retaliations. Violence and imprisonment are among the favorite techniques to punish reporters. One of the most bizarre and extreme examples of violence occurred in the Central African Empire.

In the summer of 1977 the eccentric and bloodthirsty dictator Jean-Bedel Bokassa decided to have himself crowned emperor. Preparations for the $20 million ceremony attracted journalists from around the world to the tiny, impoverished country known as the Central African Empire to write stories about this appalling man, a hard-drinking former French army sergeant who had ordered the murder of children and was rumored to be a cannibal who kept the cadavers of his enemies in a walk-in refrigerator.

Among the journalists on hand to cover the coronation of Emperor Bokassa I was Michael Goldsmith, a British citizen who reported from Africa for the American news agency the Associated Press. He arrived in Bangui, the capital of the Central African Empire, and wrote a story about the absurd preparations for the coronation.

Bokassa read the story and found it insulting. To make matters worse, an innocent mistake was misinterpreted by his oafish security officials. When Goldsmith sent a routine telex message to his office in Johannesburg, South Africa, technical transmission problems caused the words to be garbled. The gibberish was taken by Bokassa's incompetent police to be some kind of secret, coded message. The entire affair would have been comical had it not been for the fact that Bokassa believed Goldsmith to be a spy. The punishment for espionage was death.

At 9 P.M. on Thursday, July 14, 1977, Michael Goldsmith stopped by his hotel in Bangui on his way to dinner with an American diplomat.

Four plainclothes police armed with guns arrested him, put him in handcuffs, and tried, unsuccessfully, to dismantle the built-in radio in his hotel room, mistaking it for a transmitter. The police then drove him seventy miles to Berengo, Bokassa's imperial residence.

The hapless journalist and two policemen stood for half an hour in the palace compound, waiting. At last Bokassa appeared. "A small group approached," Goldsmith later recalled. "In the center, I recognized Bokassa, carrying the heavy embossed stick he uses as a symbol of majesty." The journalist became elated, he said. He was sure that, having interviewed Bokassa earlier, he could now clear up this misunderstanding. He was wrong. "The group stopped in front of me," Goldsmith wrote. "Bokassa looked at me wordlessly, an evil glint in his eye. I bowed and said, 'Your Majesty.' Bokassa raised his stick and brought it down with full force on the left side of my forehead, opening a gashing wound and causing me to fall unconscious. Seconds later I came to, lying on the ground and being kicked by Bokassa and members of his group."

Goldsmith saw his glasses lying on the ground, only inches from his face. Before he could retrieve the glasses, a boot came down and crushed them. A policeman later told him the boot was Bokassa's. Goldsmith fell unconscious again and awoke the next afternoon in a small, dark punishment cell in the central prison in Bangui.

He was handcuffed. Blood flowed from a dozen wounds. Guards ignored his pleas for medical attention. Next day the prison commander tightened the handcuff over a wound on his swollen left wrist and ordered his legs chained. One week after his arrest, Goldsmith was taken to a larger cell and given two blankets to ward off the cold air of rainstorms, and a day after that a doctor treated his wounds. Meals improved but still conditions were harsh:

> My sleeping space was a rough wooden plank. The cell was infested with rats, cockroaches, lizards and malaria mosquitoes that attacked me in clouds every night. The cell light remained on from dusk to dawn.

After almost a month, he was suddenly taken back to Berengo, the imperial residence. A group of cabinet ministers told Goldsmith that his wife had pleaded for his release in an exchange of telegrams with Bokassa and that the emperor had been moved by her appeal.

"Bokassa himself then appeared and spoke to me sternly for two hours, accusing me of espionage, of having threatened the security of the state and having insulted him in a dispatch on the forthcoming coronation."

But Bokassa also said that Goldsmith would be released and sent home. The journalist spent two days in a hotel under police protection, shaving and bathing for the first time in a month. Just before leaving the country, he was told that the emperor wanted to see him yet again.

"At 8 p.m. I was taken into the Emperor's presence in his ornate salon, surrounded by some twenty of his children and a dozen or so of his ministers. . . . He spoke to me without interruption for three hours while the children and ministers sat in silence. He said the love of my wife had saved my life. . . . The discourse ranged over his career and was punctuated by assertions of his unlimited power. With the plane already on the ground and waiting for me in Bangui, Bokassa took leave of me by kissing me three times on each cheek." The bizarre incident later became part of a documentary film about Bokassa, *Echoes from a Somber Empire*, by the German-American director Werner Herzog.

At the same time that Goldsmith had been arrested, his traveling companion Jonathan C. Randal, an American correspondent for the *Washington Post*, also ran afoul of Bokassa. Randal later described it:

> Arrested without warning one midnight, I was held incommunicado and never interrogated or formally charged. A week later, I was finally served up as Exhibit A for the diplomatic corps and the empire's two governments (one for normal affairs, the other for court matters).
>
>   I was thrust barefoot, unshaven and handcuffed before the astounded excellencies assembled in an auditorium at the imperial court about 40 miles southwest of Bangui. His imperial majesty, dressed in a dark leisure suit and occasionally ringing a small bell like an acolyte, denounced me as a spy, then exonerated me.

What had begun as a farcical mixup over a garbled telex had ended with two journalists arrested, one of them physically assaulted by the emperor himself. Not every journalistic encounter results in a head of state beating a reporter unconscious. And in fact Bokassa, being apparently insane, was an extreme example of official violence. But violence against journalists is all too common a reaction when they ask the unwelcome question and reveal the embarrassing fact. It's the old story of "shoot the messenger"; if you don't like bad news, attack the person who brings it.

Why does violence seem to be a more prevalent form of attack against journalists in some countries and not others? While it is difficult to generalize, some analysts say part of the explanation may lie with the behavior of the press itself, often more provocative and boisterous in Latin American and African nations, relatively more restrained elsewhere. In Asia, said former CPJ executive director William Orme, "the murders of journalists, in proportion to the size of the working press, are relatively rare. This may be more of an indication of the caution exercised by the Asian press than of the restraint or broad-mindedness of the region's rulers." Other analysts point to the unsettling nature of rapid economic and social development. Professor Anne Nelson of the Columbia Graduate School of Journalism told me, "Violence against journalists often occurs when society is in transition, when the rules are changing."

In Russia, where radical social change is under way, one of the nation's most prominent—and eccentric—political figures turned violent when confronted by a television camera crew and reporter. On the eve of a May 1997 holiday marking Russia's victory in World War II, Vladimir Zhirinovsky, the ultranationalist leader of the nation's third largest party, was late for a wreath-laying ceremony at the Tomb of the Unknown Soldier just outside the Kremlin. Presidential guards barred him from entry. He became enraged.

A reporter and TV crew from "2x2," a local Moscow station, were at the scene and videotaped him swearing at the guards. In scenes that were later shown on Russian television, Zhirinovsky grabbed the microphone from reporter Julia Olshanskaya, twenty-four, then twisted her arms and pushed her into his Mercedes. His bodyguards attacked cameraman Valery Ivanov, who fled into a nearby van. When the cameraman tried to emerge, Zhirinovsky slammed the van's sliding door shut on his head and cut his face. Cameraman Ivanov said: "The whole thing resembled a scene from a gangster film."

Reporter Olshanskaya, who was in tears, managed to break out of the Mercedes and escape. Later she said she had feared that Zhirinovsky would abduct her. For his part, Zhirinovsky, who enjoys immunity from prosecution as a member of parliament, offered this explanation: "She was a hooligan, that girl. . . . How could I know that she was a correspondent?" Presumably the microphone in her hand and the TV crew with her did not provide him with enough clues.

Violence against journalists takes many forms around the world. Rulers in some parts of the Middle East consider lashing to be an appropriate treatment for journalists who step out of line. In Yemen, the daily newspaper *al-Shoura* accused a leading politician of adultery. The politician, Sheikh Abdel Maguid al-Zindani, sued for libel and won. In a decision in May 1997 that provoked protests from other journalists, a judge suspended the newspaper for six months, barred the editor and a reporter from practicing journalism for a year—and then topped it off by sentencing each man to eighty lashes. In Iran, Abbas Maroufi published an article in his monthly magazine *Gardoon* describing the seventeen years of the Islamic Republic as a period of "depression." For failing to take a more positive attitude, he was convicted of "publishing lies" and insulting Ayatollah Ali Khamenei, the country's spiritual leader. Then he was sentenced to six months in prison, a two-year ban on working as a journalist, and thirty-five lashes for good measure. Maroufi managed to flee to Germany before the sentence could be imposed.

Beatings of journalists are a disturbing development in Mexico. In one month alone in 1997, five reporters for Mexico City news media were severely beaten. The five separate incidents had three things in common: the journalists specialized in police reporting; police were suspected in each beating; and each incident was clearly intended to intimidate. In one case, a television reporter who had accused police of failing to help victims of muggings was assaulted by a group of armed men he believed to be current or former police officers. Among other things, he said, they gagged him and locked him in a car trunk and later fired pistol shots close to him, then warned him to "turn down the volume" on his reporting. In another case that same month, a reporter for the leading newspaper *Reforma* was assaulted and questioned at gunpoint in his car by two federal policemen after he began investigating alleged cocaine trafficking by employees of a prosecutor's office; the police stole his briefcase, documents, and notes.

Elsewhere in Latin America, beatings of journalists are all too commonplace. Honduran radio commentator Jorge Luis Monroy was on the air praising a legislator from the ruling party when two men from the opposition party burst into his broadcast booth. While Monroy was still on the air, one man punched the commentator and broke his nose while the other man assaulted him with more than fifteen blows to the head and body.

In Nigeria, some journalists who investigate those in power pay a high price. A publisher named Chief Oni Egbunine ran an article in 1997 in his newspaper, the *Horn*, exposing alleged corruption by state officials. Eight soldiers arrested him at his office, brought him to a government building—and then horsewhipped him into a coma.

That same year the *News* magazine ran a story by reporter Sunday Orinya revealing strange goings-on at government buildings in the state of Benue—including a series of unexplained fires and the presence of prostitutes at official functions. He later said that after the story was published, he was arrested at his hotel and taken to a government building where fifteen soldiers, led by the state's chief of security, stripped him naked, hit him 120 times with a horsewhip, and dumped him in a bathroom for two hours. "They started kicking and dragging me," Orinya said.

> The [chief security officer] tore my T-shirt. Thereafter, he asked his men to work on me. Instantly, all of them, about fifteen, started beating me with [a] horse-whip. They whipped me for about one hour [and] thirty minutes and I fell down unconscious. They poured water on me to revive me and they started kicking me again. They asked me to walk on my knees over granite for over thirty minutes. . . . I collapsed again and I was dragged into the toilet where I was left till I became conscious after over two hours.

In some cases the enemies of independent journalists seek the ultimate form of punishment for those who expose their misdeeds.

Commentator Rey Bancayrin of the Philippines was on the air, hosting a call-in show at station DXLL in the southern region of Mindanao in 1998, when two gunmen broke into the studio and shot him dead. Bancayrin had made a name for himself as an outspoken opponent of corruption, illegal logging, and drug trafficking.

In Haiti in April 2000, two unidentified assailants shot radio broadcaster Jean Dominique seven times in the head, neck, and chest as he arrived for work just after six in the morning. He died a few minutes later, at the age of sixty-nine. Dominique was the nation's most popular newscaster and commentator, well known for his denunciations of any abuse of power. His memorial service filled a soccer stadium.

In the violent nation of Colombia, radio reporter Norvey Diaz revealed alleged police involvement in the murder of street people. He
also exposed apparent investments by drug criminals in property at vacation resorts in the town of Girardot. He received many warnings in
the form of threatening letters and even ominous funeral wreaths but
persisted in his reporting. Finally, on Friday, October 18, 1996, Diaz left
his home to attend a function. He never arrived at the meeting. His
body was found with a bullet wound to the back of his neck. Investigators said his murder was the work of professionals.

The second most drastic form of punishment after violence is imprisonment. Asia and the Middle East are two regions where many of
the eighty-seven journalists behind bars in December 1999 were being
held. Nineteen of them alone were incarcerated in China. The next
largest jailer of reporters was Turkey, with eighteen, followed by Burma
and Ethiopia with eight each. (Details of prison conditions for journalists are covered elsewhere in this book in such case histories as those of
Gao Yu, Christine Anyanwu, and Ocak Isik Yurtçu.)

For many years, the dictatorship of Libyan leader Muammar el-
Qaddafi had the dubious distinction of holding a journalist for the
longest period of time. According to press-freedom advocacy groups,
authorities arrested journalist and writer Abdullah Ali Al-Sanussi Al-
Darrat in 1973. He was described as a native of the city of Benghazi,
married, and the father of several children. Libyan authorities never
said why he was being held, and no charges were ever brought
against him. Twenty-six years after his arrest, the Committee to Protect Journalists removed Al-Darrat from its imprisoned list. He was
presumed dead.

14

We Have Other Ways

Legal and Economic Pressures

IF THEY CAN'T shoot or beat a journalist into silence, repressors have a wide variety of other weapons at their disposal. Among the most effective are legal and economic pressures, especially the application of an unusual form of libel law.

Reporter Yryspek Omurzakov learned just how effective that law can be. In remote, mountainous Kyrgyzstan, a small country on the border with China, he wrote satirical articles lambasting the government. Despite warnings from officials, he persisted. Prosecutors charged him with smearing the "honor and dignity" of the president, and Omurzakov was given a two-year suspended prison sentence. Still he persisted, criticizing authorities in articles for the leading opposition weekly, *Res Publika*. Repeatedly he was warned to stop.

Finally, in January 1997, he wrote a story exposing poor living conditions at a hostel for workers at the state-owned Frunze Machine Factory. The factory manager filed libel charges—but not the usual *civil* libel charges common in the West, which normally carry a penalty of monetary damages and an apology. Instead, the factory manager sued for *criminal* libel—meaning that, if convicted, the journalist faced a prison term.

Omurzakov was arrested on March 24, 1997, and held for two and a half months while a court reviewed the case and sent it back to a prosecutor for further investigation. His pretrial detention provoked a protest by twenty-five human rights activists in Central Asia, who accused authorities of persecution. Undaunted, the authorities brought him to trial.

Meanwhile, 108 workers at the Frunze plant signed a petition complaining about conditions at the hostel—the very living conditions that Omurzakov had exposed in his story. Fellow journalists sent copies of the petition to the prosecutor, saying this proved he had told the truth, but the prosecutor refused to drop the charges. Omurzakov was convicted of criminal libel against the factory manager and sentenced to three years in a minimum-security penal colony.

That same year three editors and another journalist at Omurzakov's paper were also convicted of criminal libel, in this case for articles alleging corruption by the head of the state-owned gold-mining company. All four were barred from practicing journalism for eighteen months; two were fined $115; and two were sentenced to eighteen months of forced labor. As a result of these criminal libel prosecutions, *Res Publika*, the main opposition paper, was forced to suspend publication. Presumably that was the goal of the authorities in this Central Asian nation that was once part of the Soviet Union and now claims to be a free and democratic society.

Not only in Kyrgyzstan but around the world there is an alarming growth in the use of criminal libel laws to try to silence journalists. "With more countries wielding insult laws and criminal libel statutes to muzzle expression," CPJ executive director Ann K. Cooper says, "more journalists than ever face a stark choice: Exercise self-censorship or risk going to jail for hard-hitting reporting." The use of legal pressures, and economic ones as well, may reflect an awareness by powerful figures that subtler forms of coercion can be just as effective as violence or imprisonment in silencing reporters, without provoking the popular indignation and protest sometimes caused by more overt attacks.

A powerful Mexican businessman used criminal libel lawsuits to harass and intimidate journalists into dropping a damaging story about him. Ricardo Salinas Pliego, owner of a television station, was named by the *Miami Herald* as receiving almost $30 million from a former president's brother who was later convicted of murder and was suspected of money laundering. At least twelve Mexican journalists who tried to follow up on that story found themselves the targets of lawsuits. One of the reporters, Luis Linares of *La Jornada*, said: "Even though Salinas Pliego has no chance of winning, his strategy of using lawsuits to suppress the story has functioned perfectly. Today, no one is writing about it."

Two American journalists in Mexico also faced criminal libel suits and the threat of jail time. This was because their *New York Times* story quoted U.S. officials as suspecting two Mexican governors of protecting drug traffickers. Eventually the lawsuits were dropped, but one of the two journalists—*Times* Mexico City bureau chief Sam Dillon—said the long legal battle distracted him from his job of reporting for two months. A 1997 study commissioned by a Mexican citizens' group found that seventy-four journalists had been sued since December 1994. Previously such lawsuits were rare. The explosion of lawsuits resulted largely from the newly aggressive behavior of independent journalists as Mexican society became more open. (See chapter 1, "'They Are the News': Facing Mexican Druglords.")

In the Baltic nation of Latvia, society is also more open after decades of repression during Soviet occupation, but the return to democracy has not shielded all journalists from imprisonment. Editor Tatyana Chaladze's newspaper, *Baltiskoye Vremya*, was sued for criminal libel by a former official after the newspaper revealed the disappearance of money from the Latvian state treasury. Although ordered to remain in the capital, Riga, pending trial, editor Chaladze moved to Russia for family reasons. Years later she returned on a news assignment and was immediately arrested at the border for having failed to appear in court. She was thrown into Ilguciems women's prison. After two weeks of protests by Latvian politicians and local and foreign journalists, prosecutors dropped all charges.

In Taiwan it was not only Chinese American journalist Ying Chan who felt the threat of imprisonment for libel. (See chapter 3, "Opening the Door: Courage in Asia."). Two other journalists—the editor and publisher of the *Independence Morning Post*—also faced prison time. Their article accused a senior intelligence official of tapping the phones of legislators who opposed a move to expand presidential power. The intelligence official denied ordering the phone taps, demanded a retraction, and sued for criminal libel. Eventually both sides backed down: the paper published a retraction and apology; the official dropped the lawsuit. Citing this case, press-freedom advocacy groups said criminal libel laws should never be used against journalists, and some legislators in Taiwan called for reforms that would make only civil libel—not criminal libel—allowable against newspapers.

In Egypt six journalists got into trouble for an exposé alleging corrupt business dealings by President Hosni Mubarak's sons. The journalists were convicted of criminal libel and sentenced to a year in prison. The sons later dropped the lawsuit while it was under appeal. In an absurd case in the Pacific island nation of Samoa, Prime Minister

Tofilau Eti Alesana took offense at a letter to the editor published in the main opposition newspaper. The letter by a Samoan living in New Zealand claimed (1) the premier was a "wicked man"; (2) he was in ill health; (3) "very soon he will die suddenly from being hit by a mosquito or a fly"; and (4) he would then go to hell. Alesana sued the publisher and editor of the *Samoa Observer* under a law that provides up to six months in prison for criminal libel.

Journalists in Panama, nominally a democratic country, face criminal libel and other onerous measures under "gag laws" that date back to a military dictatorship of the 1970s. The journalists can be thrown into prison for stories that criticize officials, show "disrespect" toward the government, or "spread false, exaggerated or misleading news." Columnist Tomás Cabal linked the president's former law-firm partner to drug dealers—and received a fifteen-month jail sentence. Investigative reporter Herasto Reyes quoted a former official implicating the president in a financial scandal and was slapped with a criminal defamation suit—filed by the president himself. (Three policemen with an arrest warrant raided the reporter's office, but his colleagues surrounded him protectively and thwarted the arrest attempt.) In 1999 the Committee to Protect Journalists wrote to Panama's president, Ernesto Pérez Balladares, accusing him of using these gag laws "to stifle public debate" just before a presidential election. The CPJ said that at least eighty-five journalists were then being prosecuted for criminal defamation—many of them because of articles criticizing the president.

Even in the freest parts of the world, libel laws are sometimes used to try to silence journalists who ask too many questions. Ireland's restrictive libel laws may have led indirectly to the assassination of investigative reporter Veronica Guerin. (See chapter 5, "A Precious Pen: Defiance around the World.") Irish mobsters had discovered that they could hide behind those laws and threaten crippling lawsuits against any newspaper that planned to reveal their names and their alleged crimes. Their strategy was successful and most journalists dared not name names. But Guerin thought she had found a loophole. Her technique was to go to the criminals themselves and confront them face to face. The idea was that this might provoke them into making a comment, on the record, about the allegations against them—a way for her to get their names and the allegations into print without exposing her newspaper, the *Sunday Independent*, to lawsuits.

"What seemed like inexplicable risk-taking to the outside world," one Irish journalist said, "was part of a deliberate strategy to circumvent Ireland's Byzantine libel laws. Those laws, so stifling to journalistic freedom in Ireland, led Guerin to put herself in harm's way." Her defiant approach worked for a while, until she was assassinated just before she could reveal the names of the three biggest heroin dealers in Dublin. On December 6, 1995, six months before her death, Guerin received an award for her courage from the Committee to Protect Journalists and used the awards dinner in New York to denounce legal pressures against independent journalists:

> We write under ridiculously restrictive laws in Ireland. It's a wonderful country, great place to visit, but, unfortunately for journalists, the most difficult thing we have to work within are our restrictive libel laws. It's difficult for publishers because they are the people who have to pay massive amounts of money on a daily basis in courts.

In addition to libel, Irish journalists until 1998 faced another legal restriction—the Official Secrets Act, which provided penalties including imprisonment for revealing without official permission any information contained in any government document. Anything printed by the government, no matter how trivial, was presumed secret unless stated otherwise. "Even the menu in the Oireachtas restaurant was officially a secret," one critic complained.

One Irish journalist, Liz Allen, faced the threat of seven years' imprisonment because she defied the Official Secrets Act. She obtained a police memo indicating that shortly before Ireland's biggest-ever bank robbery ($4.5 million), police had been tipped off that a major theft was being planned.

Allen and her publisher were charged with violating the Official Secrets Act—a prosecution that touched off protests. "The publication of the memorandum may have been an embarrassment to some senior gardai [police officers]," the *Irish Times* commented, "but it was unquestionably in the public interest, since it raised very important issues about the ability of the Garda [police] to combat serious crime." Perhaps because of the protests, Allen and her publisher got off with a small fine. In 1998, two and a half years after her trial, Ireland enacted a Freedom of Information Act that removed the presumption of secrecy and has made it easier for journalists and other members of the public to obtain and publish government documents. But as for Ireland's libel law, repeated calls for reform have not led to any easing of the restrictions.

Some countries try to repress criticism of the powers that be by enforcing so-called insult laws. Since 1993, Jordan has had tough laws that forbid publishing anything that "offends" the king or the royal family. In 1997, the editor of a weekly newspaper was sentenced to six months in prison and fines of $700. The reason: his paper published an interview with a spokesman for the outlawed Islamic Liberation Party, who indirectly criticized then king Hussein and his peace agreement with Israel. The court found that the editor had libeled the monarch and his brother, Crown Prince Hassan—the first time in Jordan's history that a published article caused a journalist to be sentenced to prison.

After protests in Jordan and abroad, an appeals court threw out the conviction. But the situation for journalists grew worse when the government amended the law. Among other new provisions, newspapers could not publish "false news or rumors that offend public interests or state departments." The government suspended thirteen newspapers just before parliamentary elections. Critics protested at home and abroad. The Committee to Protect Journalists named Jordan's prime minister one of the world's ten worst enemies of the press, and the New York–based research group Freedom House moved Jordan from the category of "partly free" to "not free." Later the laws were declared unconstitutional, the premier resigned, and officials eased their legal pressures on journalists.

But the use of insult laws continued unabated elsewhere. In Yemen in 1994, an opposition paper was effectively shut down by a government lawsuit that accused it of insulting senior officials because it had described them as "dinosaurs who would not die." In Cuba, independent journalist Lorenzo Paez Nuñez was sentenced to eighteen months in prison in 1997 for "libelling and insulting" the national police. (Apparently the police in Cuba are very sensitive to any insults.) An opposition editor and a reporter in the Ivory Coast were each sentenced to a year in prison for "insulting the head of state" in 1995; this for questioning whether he was a native of that country and for implicating him in a financial scandal.

Closely related to the criminal libel and insult laws that are used against the press are the laws banning sedition, meaning the incitement of rebellion. Opponents of press freedom stretch that definition to suit their purposes. In Kenya, publisher and opposition legislator Njehu Gatabaki was charged with sedition for articles linking a cabinet minister with the assassination of the foreign minister. In the Pacific island nation of Tonga, which is a constitutional monarchy, an editor was arrested and charged with sedition because his paper published a letter to the editor from a reader who disagreed with the government's claim that Tonga had the best political system in the world.

Sometimes articles that merely make people worried, rather than rebellious, are enough to land journalists in jail. Ethiopia imprisoned an editor in 1996 for "inciting the public to anxiety and insecurity" because of his paper's reports of armed clashes in the country.

Governments use other legal pressures. In 1997, when foreign journalist Gustavo Gorriti revealed the existence of drug money in the president's campaign fund, Panama refused to renew the reporter's work visa; after protests, he was allowed to stay. That same year Peru revoked the citizenship of Baruch Ivcher, the owner of a muckraking TV station that had exposed torture and corruption in the military. When he resisted the move, police escorted pro-government investors into the station so they could seize control.

Sometimes judges use the law to punish journalists who simply annoy them. In 1997 a Canadian reporter for the *Far Eastern Economic Review* served a month in prison in Malaysia for "contempt of the judiciary"—the first such punishment of a journalist anywhere in the British Commonwealth in the past fifty years. His article noted that a judge's wife had received favorable treatment in the speedy handling of a lawsuit, whereas usually such cases move slowly. (She had sued a school for dropping her son from its debate team for alleged cheating.) In passing sentence on the reporter, Judge Low Hop Bing said that, for too long, there had been "unabated, contemptuous attacks by and through the media on our judiciary."

It's not only legal pressures that are used against independent journalists. Economic pressures are also powerful weapons.

In Azerbaijan, an oil-rich former Soviet republic in the Caucusus region, the government owns the printing plant that publishes all the nation's daily newspapers. After the paper *Avrasiya* ran articles criticizing the government, the printing plant refused to print any more copies of the newspaper for weeks. And another Azerbaijani newspaper, *Azadliq*, said it lost advertising revenue after the government pressured companies to remove their ads.

In Mexico, many newspapers give the government favorable coverage rather than risk losing a lucrative source of income, the *gacetillas*—government advertising that resembles news stories. In Armenia in 1994, the government showed its irritation at the independent Russian-language *Golos Armenii* (Voice of Armenia) by raising the price for newsprint, but the attempt to drive the opposition newspaper out of business failed. In Nigeria the authoritarian regime of General Abacha tried to cripple independent newspapers and magazines by creating confusion about their authenticity. It flooded the marketplace with counterfeit copies of *Tell*, the *Sunday Magazine*, the *News*, and *Tempo*, which did cause some confusion, but not enough to ruin them economically.

Sometimes a government doesn't have to make an overt economic threat because it's already implied. In the Philippines, the family of John Gokongwei owns companies involved in food manufacturing, real estate, airline operations, banking, and department stores, as well as one of the nation's oldest newspapers, the *Manila Times*. His family reportedly knows without being told that the government could hurt the Gokongwei business empire in any number of ways. It received a reminder of that in 1999.

The *Manila Times* accused Filipino president Joseph Estrada of being the "unwitting godfather" for an allegedly improper government contract. President Estrada sued the newspaper for $2.6 million in libel, then dropped the lawsuit after an abject page-one apology said the story "was never intended to malign or impugn [your] sterling reputation." That groveling caused managing editor Chit Estella and other top editors to quit in protest over what they considered an overreaction on the paper's part. Estella quoted the paper's owners as saying there had been "nothing really wrong with the story" but that they had apologized anyway because they feared pressure from the government on their other businesses.

In Hong Kong, while it was still a British colony, one publisher experienced unexplained business problems after he criticized a leader of mainland China. Jimmy Lai Chee-ying wrote an article in his publication *Next Magazine* insulting then premier Li Peng by calling him "a turtle's egg" (hermaphrodite)—one of the worst insults for a Chinese. The publisher's clothing chain suddenly had financial and regulatory problems in China, and an investment bank dependent on Beijing's goodwill withdrew from backing the publisher's initial public stock offering for his media group. Whether orchestrated by Beijing or not, the business setbacks were a clear reminder for this publisher—and others in Hong Kong—that there may be an economic price to pay for journalistic free speech.

PART IV

THE MESSENGER REACTS

Responding to Attacks

15

Chilled or Defiant

The Painful Choice

NBC PRODUCER MARK Feldstein had faced danger before. He once had been assaulted and suffered a head injury while investigating labor conditions in Florida, and he had refused to back down when confronting other threats in the past. But now he faced a new situation.

In October 1998 he and correspondent Lea Thompson and two camera crews arrived in Port-au-Prince, the capital of the impoverished, violence-plagued Caribbean nation of Haiti, to shoot interviews and gather information for one section of an investigative piece for *Dateline NBC* about alleged misconduct by United Nations peacekeepers. UN officials were angered by the questions the NBC journalists asked them about alleged torture and other mistreatment of local residents by UN forces in countries where the blue-helmeted troops were stationed.

Then something strange happened.

On a hot, sunny day, after interviewing a Haitian who said he had been mistreated by UN troops, Thompson and her crew were leaving the UN compound when a military-style vehicle pulled alongside their van and forced it off the road. Five men with semi-automatic weapons, carried police-style, ordered everyone out of the vehicle and asked for Thompson's notes from her interviews—not money or jewelry. The gunmen then drove off in the van with all of the NBC equipment and videotapes and notes for the story. "Whether it was the police or the U.N., I don't know," Thompson said later, "but I do know it wasn't a bunch of thugs who came up to us and suddenly decided they wanted television equipment."

When the journalists told the American embassy about being carjacked, they realized they could not expect any help from the Haitian police. "Somehow," producer Feldstein said, "the police had got the erroneous idea that we were there to do a story about them, not the UN.

The U.S. Embassy told us the Haitian police had opened a criminal investigation into us. We were about to be arrested."

The NBC journalists debated what to do, then decided to leave, even though it meant not being able to do additional reporting. (They still had tapes and notes that had not been stolen.) The embassy provided an armed escort to the airport and the NBC team was able to return safely to New York, where they completed the story. "We didn't feel good about leaving but you have to choose your battles," Feldstein said. "It's not a question of being gutless. You calculate the cost-benefits. You are talking about being thrown into prison, a brutal prison system, for what are marginal improvements in the story. I'm in my forties. I have two children. In my twenties I probably wouldn't have left."

Feldstein is typical of journalists who must make a painful choice when pressured to stop reporting: either give in or risk serious personal consequences. It's one of the toughest decisions journalists ever have to make. While it may be admirable to say "publish and be damned," there are times when the pressures are simply too great, when the chilling effect of repression overcomes the reporter's natural drive to get the truth out. This chapter focuses on the effects of repression as measured by the reaction of journalists to the threats of assault, imprisonment, and legal or economic pressures, and whether the pressures leave them chilled or defiant.

One example of the chilling effect—when the forces of repression won—occurred in Jordan. A new, independent newspaper called *Al-Arab al-Youm* had come under government pressure to stop running stories the regime wanted kept secret. The stories published in the paper included items about a failed attempt by Israeli intelligence to assassinate a Palestinian leader, the arrests of alleged arms smugglers, election fraud, and corruption in the Ministry of Tourism. In reaction to these stories, the Jordanian government threatened prosecution and temporarily withdrew advertising from the paper. Apparently the pressures had an effect—as columnist Yousef Gheishan found out.

Despite the warnings not to publish any more items critical of the government, Gheishan wrote and submitted for publication two columns defending an opposition candidate whose son had been arrested on charges of selling drugs. Gheishan hinted that the charges against the candidate's son were phony and were designed by government officials to smear the politician. Although Gheishan apparently felt sure of his sources, his editor refused to run the two columns. For the journalists on this paper it was a clear case of self-censorship under government pressure. When the Jordanian government later amended press laws to further restrict freedom, the self-censorship intensified. "We used to publish the press releases of the leftist opposition parties," one publisher said, "but after the amendments we stopped." As a former member of Jordan's parliament put it: "The journalists are terrified."

Self-censorship occurs elsewhere throughout the Middle East. The Saudi-owned, London-based newspaper *Al-Hayat* is distributed widely in the Arab-speaking world. It is an influential daily that claims to be independent but in fact censors itself to avoid sensitive subjects such as criticism of the feudal Saudi regime. One of the paper's editors put it bluntly: "Our main concern is not to be banned in Saudi Arabia because most of the advertising comes from the Saudi market."

In Peru a TV reporter tried to stand up to threats, but her station's owners apparently caved in to them. Cecilia Valenzuela came under pressure for her investigative reporting for Canal 9 in Lima. An anonymous note—alluding to the secret police—threatened the life of her baby boy after Valenzuela broke a story alleging that Peru's president wasn't born in Peru and therefore was not qualified to be president. More threats came after she exposed the diversion of military funds intended for flood victims and investigated claims that the military had overpaid for weapons. Finally she reported on secret peace talks between Peru and Ecuador over a border dispute. Canal 9 canceled her program. It claimed a lack of advertising—but local journalists said the government forced the station to drop her. Ironically, the name of her program was *Without Censorship*.

Another Peruvian TV journalist landed an interview with the head of the country's controversial intelligence service but then was told by the station's owners to ask only scripted questions. He quit in protest. A third Peruvian TV investigative journalist, César Hildebrandt of station Canal 13, came under year-long criminal investigation for espionage and treason after he discussed the Peru-Ecuador peace talks. Later his station canceled his program, under what he called "pressure" from the government. He was told he could return to the air, but only if he hosted a noncontroversial history program. The criminal investigation against him was dropped after the station canceled his show. Hildebrandt said all of Peru's independent stations feared government legal moves to deprive them of ownership, "so they are censoring themselves."

In Mexico, the chilling effect comes mainly from fear of death at the hands of drug traffickers. *Zeta* editor Francisco Ortiz Franco estimated that "probably 80 percent" of Mexican journalists self-censor. Tijuana reporter Miguel Cervantes Sahagún said:

> A number of journalists fear for their lives, and in some cases that is why they do not do so many drug stories. For us it is suicidal, not only because of the drug traffickers but also the corrupt police.

Cervantes Sahagún said he would need the kind of bodyguards publisher J. Jesús Blancornelas had after the attempt on his life, and he would need a large life insurance policy, before he would venture more into the drug story. "I would fear for my sons' lives," he said. "Who is going to protect me?" The chilling effect is felt also when sources of information dry up. Cervantes said a senior federal law enforcement officer in Tijuana was killed in the 1970s for discussing drug cases with reporters, and "after that, prosecutors shut their mouths."

Some Turkish editors whose newspapers were shut down for covering the Kurdish story were not able to resume publication. The television network ATV closed its bureau in the largely Kurdish city of Diyarbakir after police imprisoned a cameraman for three months. This came after the cameraman interviewed former members of a Kurdish pro-independence party who allegedly had worked undercover for the government. Even Ocak Isik Yurtçu, the Turkish journalist who received the press freedom award in prison, seemed to be muzzled shortly after he was released. When a *New York Times* reporter asked why Turkey's government had been so reluctant to allow broader freedom of the press, Yurtçu smiled wanly and replied: "I can't really say. Please understand that I'm on probation." He added: "You know what that means."

In Kashmir, after a reporter for the international news agency Agence France-Presse was beaten by Indian security forces, other reporters staged a protest but were driven back by police tear gas. "These incidents and the history of unchecked official hostility toward journalists have cowed the local press," according to the Committee to Protect Journalists. "Kashmiri journalists report that self-censorship has become routine." In Kazakhstan, the chilling effect was felt by a newspaper with the odd name of *Let's Survive until Monday*. After journalists blamed high officials for agricultural failures, the founder of the paper came under so much pressure that he fled the country. The paper didn't survive until Monday or any other day.

The use of criminal libel laws against reporters is also taking its toll. (See chapter 14, "We Have Other Ways: Legal and Economic Pressures.") Chinese American journalist Ying Chan expressed concern that some officials in China and Taiwan were citing the repressive laws of Singapore as a shining example of how to control newspapers. "Some publishers now apologize for articles," she said. "It has a tremendous chilling effect."

As a result of this chilling of journalistic ardor in some countries, stories that might have been done and should have been done were left unreported. Exactly how widespread is the drug corruption of democratic institutions in Mexico? How far do Jordanian officials go to smear opposition candidates? How much truth is there to allegations of torture and other abuses by Peruvian secret police? How brutally have Turkish and Indian security forces dealt with ethnic minorities? All these questions are left unanswered when journalists are chilled. And when these questions are left unanswered, voters in democratic societies are left in the dark, too poorly informed to make meaningful policy choices.

But there is another side to the equation. To a surprising degree, independent journalists around the globe stand up to the government officials, security forces, corporations, organized crime syndicates, gunmen, and others who attempt to prevent them from reporting the news. One of the most dramatic examples—seen live by millions around the world—was CNN's persistence in covering student pro-democracy demonstrations in Beijing in 1989, despite orders by Chinese officials forbidding such coverage.

CNN correspondent Mike Chinoy tells the story in his book *China Live: People Power and the Television Revolution*, a fascinating account of his years reporting historic changes in China, starting in the mid-1970s. By 1987 this American journalist had opened CNN's first Beijing bureau. In his book he sheds some light on the motivations of independent journalists, which often are a mixture of selfish and altruistic concerns. Not only did he want to advance his personal career and contribute to the rise of CNN, but he also wanted to fully inform the American public: "I felt we were filling a major gap in public understanding of the largest nation in the world." On April 15, 1989, less than two months before the Tiananmen Square massacre of pro-democracy demonstrators, several thousand students marched through Beijing in a protest that turned out to be one of the precursors of the later massive demonstrations that ended in tragedy. Chinoy writes of his "adrenaline pumping" with excitement at covering this unprece-dented challenge to Communist rule, because "we had witnessed something with potentially momentous consequences for China." His wording helps explain the motivation of journalists in persisting with uncensored coverage despite risks to their freedom and safety.

A few weeks later, in the buildup to the massacre, the government imposed martial law and ordered CNN to stop its live coverage of the student protests in Tiananmen Square, live coverage seen around the world—even in Kennebunkport, Maine, by a vacationing President George Bush. "It was just after nine a.m. on Saturday, May 20," Chinoy writes, "when two officials of the Ministry of Posts and Telecommuni-cations walked into the CNN workspace on the ninth floor of the Sher-aton and ordered CNN to cease its live transmissions from Beijing in an hour." CNN tried to resist, but all it could do was stall for time, pre-tending that it could not stop broadcasting without written orders from the Chinese bureaucracy. Chinoy appreciated this ploy by his producer, Alec Miran: "Alec was doing a brilliant job of giving the Chinese bu-reaucrats a taste of their own medicine." Still, Chinoy realized that this was a dangerous game: "I worried that we were pushing too far. . . . Im-ages of bayonet-wielding soldiers marching into our control room flashed through my mind." After two hours of delaying tactics, CNN reluctantly ended its live coverage.

In the days that followed more student protests filled the streets, and CNN videotaped them and smuggled its tapes out to Hong Kong or Tokyo for transmission to the world. "Although the martial law re-strictions barred reporting of the protests," Chinoy says, "we were de-termined to carry on." Those words—*we were determined to carry on*—are typical of journalists who react with defiance against efforts to silence their reporting of important news events.

Even earlier in China, during some of the most repressive periods of Chairman Mao's rule, a few journalists stood up to him. One of them was Liu Binyan. He was the foremost reporter of his time. From the 1950s to the 1980s, he was repeatedly punished or threatened with pun-ishment for his exposés of corruption within the ruling Communist

Party. "But I would not be silenced," he later wrote in his autobiography, *A Higher Kind of Loyalty*. At another point in the book Liu described his motivation:

> I felt a growing force pushing me forward, and that force came from my readers, readers from all levels of Chinese society. I could feel their breath on my back. By then, I could not stop. I was defiant.

The story of that defiance began before the Communist takeover. Liu, the son of a railway worker, was born in 1925 in Changchun, in the northeast of the country, and moved at the age of six to Harbin. Later, in Beijing, he joined the resistance to Japanese occupation, distributed Communist Party leaflets, and reported for *China Youth News* after the 1949 founding of the People's Republic of China. He soon got into trouble.

In one article Liu noted the contrast between the coldness of doctors and the claim by party propaganda that people were close and warm. The article was spiked. Liu was accused of being "anti-party" but refused to heed the warning and continued to take a more independent stance. During a brief liberalization period in the mid-1950s, he was allowed to travel abroad. He accompanied the top editor of *People's Daily* newspaper on a trip to Moscow and was impressed by the courage of a Russian journalist, Valentin Ovechkin, who wrote of corruption. In Warsaw, Liu was amazed to see Western newspapers on sale.

Inspired by these foreign influences, back in China he encouraged young factory workers to talk to him about their problems—but again this angered officials. Meanwhile, party leader Mao Tse-tung was ending a period of relative liberalization and beginning a crackdown—and the timing could not have been worse for young journalist Liu. While in Shanghai to cover a cotton-mill strike, he noticed that some citizens spoke up and criticized the party while others were afraid to say anything. In an article about the party's cultural policies, Liu mentioned the fear that some had about criticizing those in power—and then he added a phrase that enraged Mao himself: "Considering how often the Party has gone back on its word, you cannot blame the masses for having reservations."

The party going back on its word? This was not the type of comment permitted by Mao's regime. Liu was denounced by a local party official as a "rightist." At the age of thirty-three, Liu was taken by truck to the countryside where he spent the next thirteen years doing farm labor as punishment. His duties included dragging a cart full of manure. Later he was allowed to work on a newspaper, but not as a journalist, only as a librarian and later as a janitor. During the disastrous Cultural Revolution against independent-minded intellectuals and Western influences, he was sent again to a farm and spent one year working in a cowshed, then eight years planting rice and raising pigs. He was so poor that his family had to cut up a mattress to make him padded clothing against the cold.

Then, as political winds shifted due to power struggles within the top party leadership, repression eased slightly, and in the 1970s, Liu was again allowed to report. He investigated cases of embezzlement and of people falsely accused of crimes. In one case of embezzlement, Liu dug deeper into a story that had already been reported. "I had always felt that the full story had never been told," he said. "Something was being held back. Having been an outcast for twenty-two years, I also had a great unsatisfied curiosity about our society. What, exactly, had happened during those years? I felt that the damage of the Cultural Revolution had not been adequately exposed, and of what had been exposed, we had no real understanding."

One of his articles, "People or Monsters?" revealing party corruption, was printed in *People's Literature*, with a circulation of 1.4 million, and reprinted in other papers and broadcast by provincial radio stations. Liu became a reporter for *People's Daily*, the main newspaper, and wrote about party bureaucrats who exploited peasants, enriched themselves, obstructed justice, and committed human rights violations. Liu became the most prominent journalist in China.

By 1984 he was again in trouble. A senior party official warned him he should give up reporting. "But I had no intention of backing down," Liu said. In fact, he wrote an article praising a Chinese dissident intellectual who had been jailed for trying to take a letter for Soviet leader Nikita Khrushchev into the Soviet embassy in Beijing. He noted that the prisoner also had complained of a fellow inmate who was killed for overstepping a prison boundary that was not clearly marked. And, Liu said in his article, the dissident in prison had written to Mao saying the cult of Mao made it impossible for the party to admit mistakes.

Liu came under investigation, was denied publication in mainstream newspapers, and lost opportunities to travel abroad or obtain better housing. Despite all these pressures, he remained defiant. As he put it, "I would not be silenced."

Finally, in 1987, he was expelled from the party, accused of libel and slander. His books were banned, although they still sold on the black market or were copied by hand and privately circulated. Liu felt certain that arrest was imminent, but a *New York Times* reporter intervened on his behalf, and Liu was allowed to visit the United States in 1988. One year later came the Tiananmen Square massacre of students demonstrating for democratic reforms, and in the repressive new climate that followed, Liu was unable to return home. He resettled in Princeton, New Jersey, and edited an émigré journal.

The dilemma of whether to self-censor or speak out is especially acute in Mexico. There, despite the very real risk of assassination, some journalists refuse to be silent about drug corruption. Even if, as *Zeta* editor Ortiz Franco estimated, 80 percent of Mexican journalists self-censor, that still leaves 20 percent who defy drug traffickers and corrupt government and security officials to report the full story of what drugs are doing to Mexican society. Take the case of a newspaper called *La Prensa* (The Press). When its courageous young publisher was murdered, the staff of his newspaper could have taken the easy way out and stopped covering the drug story. But it did not.

The publisher was Benjamín Flores González, a gutsy, flamboyant man of twenty-nine. Eight years earlier he had made a name for himself covering politics for a newspaper in the border city of Mexicali. During the 1989 election, a politician named Ernesto Ruffo from the center-right PAN was elected governor of Baja California, the first opposition candidate to win a major state election in more than half a century. After Flores González covered the campaign, Governor-Elect Ruffo hired him as his personal secretary. Three years later, Flores González returned to his hometown of San Luis Río Colorado, a border city of two hundred thousand people in the northwest corner of Sonora state, about twenty miles south of Yuma, Arizona. There he founded the newspaper *La Prensa*. Friends said the money he used to start up the paper came from politicians and backers of the opposition PAN.

Those who knew him well said Flores González decided that the way to become someone was to do what no one else dared to do and crusade against drugs and corruption. In a feisty muckraking column called "No Confirmado" ("Unconfirmed"), Flores González revealed the names of drug traffickers and corrupt officials. Soon he had

Mexican publisher Benjamín Flores González defied druglords and published exposés on drug trafficking and political corruption in the border town of San Luis Río Colorado. Credit: AP/Wide World Photos.

The body of Flores González lies on the driveway outside his office, where he was shot on July 15, 1997, at the age of twenty-nine. His newspaper staff vowed to carry on exposing drug crime. Credit: AP/Wide World Photos.

converted the paper from a sedate weekly into a lively daily newspaper with a growing circulation.

In 1997 two of his stories attracted special attention. He wrote that about a half ton of cocaine had mysteriously disappeared from the local office of the federal attorney general. And he reported the activities of Jaime González, an alleged local drug trafficker. After that, the alleged trafficker was imprisoned. Officials later said two of González's brothers blamed publisher Flores González for his imprisonment. According to the publisher's lawyer, in June 1997 a lawyer for the imprisoned drug suspect offered Flores's attorney a deal: he would pay $100,000 to the publisher if he did not reveal the fact that the drug suspect had made a secret arrangement with a judge to let him out of prison. If publisher Flores González refused the hush money, he would be killed.

Flores's attorney says he did not even tell his client about the approach, for fear that Flores González would publish news about it in his paper and make himself a target for attack. But the young publisher became aware that he was in more danger than usual. He "worried about rumors that had begun to circulate in June," editor-in-chief Jesús Barraza said. "It was around that time that he told us that an attack was being organized against *La Prensa*. 'What are they capable of doing?' we asked ourselves."

They found out on July 15, 1997. It was the newspaper's fifth anniversary, and Flores González and his staff were planning to have a celebration party that evening after putting the paper to bed. At 4:30 P.M. he parked his pickup truck outside the newspaper office and opened the vehicle door. As he stepped out, a battered gray Chevrolet Impala with California license plates pulled alongside, and a young man holding an AK47 assault rifle jumped out. As the newspaper's staff watched in horror, the gunman fired the entire clip at Flores González, then returned to the Impala and was handed a .22 caliber pistol by an accomplice. The gunman used the pistol to shoot Flores González three times in the head as the journalist lay on the ground. In all, the assassin fired thirty-three bullets. Nine entered Flores's body and killed him.

Police arrested four local thugs and said González's brothers had ordered the hit, but according to the *New York Times*, most people in the town suspected that the order came from much higher up, possibly a politician in the pocket of major drug criminals. What is interesting is the newspaper staff's reaction to this murder. Editor-in-chief Barraza appeared that day on television. Speaking calmly, he said the newspaper would continue Flores's crusading style of journalism. The newspaper went ahead and published on schedule that evening. "When Benjamín Flores fell at the door of the newspaper he had founded five years before," editor Barraza said later,

> we felt like orphans, overwhelmed by a rage that is difficult to describe. But July 15 the presses did not stop, and each of us reaffirmed our commitment to Benjamín and his mission. I took immediate control and saw how the reporters wet the keyboards with their tears, and, at times, cried out with impotence, pain, and rage at the image of our editor bleeding to death on the floor.

While defiant, Barraza also proceeded with caution and at times avoided excessive risk. When he reported that a suspected drug trafficker who had disappeared was cooperating with police investigating Flores's murder, brothers of the suspect visited editor Barraza and complained about his story. Barraza agreed to publish the family's denial of any deal with investigators, causing some tension with other staff members of the newspaper opposed to letting the family of a drug suspect influence editorial decisions. But for all his caution, Barraza also made it clear he would not back down on his commitment to keep reporting the drug story. "The north of Mexico is a very dangerous place for journalists," he said. "[But] if we have to talk of [the drug trade], we talk about it. If we have to talk about government corruption, we do."

That willingness to take risks is echoed in Turkey, where journalist and author Aziz Nesin defied militant Islamic fundamentalists and made plans to publish a Turkish-language version of *The Satanic Verses*, the controversial novel by Salman Rushdie (an author who had to remain in hiding in England for years because Iran deemed his work blasphemous and condemned him to death). Turkish journalist Nesin said he was unable to publish the translation of Rushdie's book because "publishers are scared." When excerpts finally were published in a newspaper, the publishing house was attacked by fundamentalists, while prosecutors seized copies of the newspaper. Worst of all, when Nesin and other Turkish intellectuals who were opposed to religious fanaticism attended a conference in Sivas, a city near Ankara, a fundamentalist mob set their hotel on fire. Thirty-seven writers and other intellectuals were burned to death. Nesin escaped alive.

Nesin, who wrote a regular front-page column, continued to denounce religious extremists. Why did he take such chances despite repeated threats to his life? Nesin indicated he felt a social obligation. "One of the foremost conditions for civil society," he said, "is freedom of expression." And he added that "a writer is responsible for what he has not written as well as for what he has written. He is responsible for everything he doesn't write because of fear."

In Nigeria, during the reign of military dictators, the editor of *Tell* magazine was arrested and the office of another publication was torched, but *Tell* issued a defiant statement: "State terrorism and acts of brutal intimidation will not force us to compromise our belief in freedom, justice and the rule of law." In the Middle Eastern nation of Yemen, a provincial newspaper reporter was held for eight days by security police and told to sign an agreement that would have required him to provide copies of his stories to the government before they were published. Despite pressure on him, he refused to sign. In Colombia, even after the assassination of Guillermo Cano Isaza (see chapter 6, "The General's Mercedes: Crime and Corruption"), his sons continued his crusade against drug corruption.

In his autobiography, Chinese journalist Liu Binyan repeatedly refers to his defiance of repression and suggests this as his epitaph: "Here lies a Chinese who . . . said what he should say." That kind of spirit crosses cultural boundaries and helps explain the phenomenon of independent journalists in many countries who stand up to repressors despite enormous risk to themselves. It is a personality trait that combines idealism and stubbornness, a sense of public duty and a maverick streak, altruism and an almost selfish, combative personality that fits neatly into the Western model of a journalist with an adversarial relationship toward anyone in power.

Pakistani journalist Zamir Niazi, a veteran of many clashes with censors and the author of three books—*The Press under Siege, The Press in Chains,* and *The Web of Censorship*—deems independence of the press to be a patriotic duty: "Look, this country does not belong to the ruling junta alone. It belongs to me also." Niazi sees a fundamental human right at stake. "Every citizen must stand up for his/her rights. It is our right to know. You can't take away people's right to know!" Looking back on fifty years of efforts to report the news his way, Niazi says: "I did not give in. And I did not make any compromises, and just fought, and kept the torch burning."

16

Cat and Computer Mouse

Using the Internet

WHETHER IT'S PUTTING banned radio stations back on the air in Yugoslavia, helping a Nigerian reporter on the run from police, smuggling news into China, or keeping a Belorussian newspaper alive after police close its printing plant, the Internet is emerging as a major factor in the battle between censors and independent journalists. In the words of one editor, whose Arabic newspaper is forbidden on Jordanian newsstands but available online: "[The Internet] has penetrated all borders and made press censorship the joke of the century."

That may be an exaggeration. There still are many problems of access. And censors as well as journalists are learning how to use the Internet. Each side is trying to turn this medium to its own advantage. It's a cat-and-(computer)-mouse game, with occasional victories on both sides.

The stakes in this game are high, as the potential audience grows exponentially. In 1987, some ten thousand computers were linked to one another through the Internet. Two years later the number had jumped to one hundred thousand, and a year later that number had tripled. In 1992 at least 1 million computers were linked to the Internet and more were being added, at the phenomenal growth rate of 20 percent a month. By mid-1999, according to one estimate, there were 165 million people in the world with Internet access.

The overwhelming majority of the 165 million Internet users at that time were in the developed world: 90.63 million of them in North America and 40.09 million in Europe. In contrast, for example, only 880,000 were in the Middle East. Some countries, such as Libya and Iraq, had no Internet access at the start of the twenty-first century, while Syria was just taking its first tentative steps. But throughout the world, even in some of the more repressive countries, year by year more and more people were making use of this powerful medium.

The Internet's threat to government control of information is unprecedented in history. According to a report published by Freedom House: "Censors have dogged every new communication technology since the creation of movable type in the sixteenth century, through the innovation of the telephone, radio, and television in the nineteenth and twentieth centuries. The Internet, however, is the most formidable challenge to the censor. Cyberspace is everywhere, but headquartered nowhere. No single government can yet control a message as it originates in another country."

That fact has created an extraordinary opportunity for reporters to outwit censors, as journalists face the question of how to respond to repression. One of the most inventive uses of the Internet by independent journalists has been the creation of Web sites that can generate sound through the computer's loudspeakers. In this way, banned radio stations are able to resume broadcasting. Yugoslavia's authoritarian leader Slobodan Milosevic tried repeatedly to silence independent radio stations. Each time, journalists and their supporters turned to the Internet for help.

Take the case of B92. On November 17, 1996, political parties opposed to Milosevic won local elections in eighteen municipalities in the Serbian part of Yugoslavia. Milosevic quickly annulled the results. That touched off angry protests. Day after day, demonstrators marched through the snowy streets of Belgrade. Government-controlled Serbian television and radio either ignored the demonstrators or dismissed them as "vandals." But B92 (a Belgrade station at 92 on the FM dial), the only independent radio station in Belgrade, reported what was actually happening. From its scruffy fifth-floor offices in an apartment building, Radio B92 put out daily news summaries and live reports on the demonstrations, mixed with pop music and political satire. Its reports reached an audience estimated at some seven hundred thousand, out of the capital's population of 2 million.

Milosevic clearly was not pleased. Since its founding in May 1989 as a youth-oriented station, B92 had annoyed the regime. Two years after its founding, the station had been temporarily closed down during a crackdown on demonstrations. Now, in November 1996, Milosevic was again trying to silence reports of anti-government protests. On November 27, partial jamming began. B92's broadcasts could still be heard clearly as long as it played only music, but four times during the day when the station switched to its regularly scheduled news reports and live reports from the street demonstrations, listeners could hardly make out the words of the reporters because of mysterious loud background noise clearly broadcast by another transmitter on the same frequency. To try to outwit the jammers, whose orders (presumably from the Milosevic regime) seemed to be to drown out only the news reports and not the music, B92 would suddenly cut into its music shows with unscheduled news reports before the jammers could react. The next day the jamming escalated to block all B92 programing from 9 A.M. to 2 A.M. On December 3, as the daily protest demonstrations persisted, Milosevic pulled the plug entirely on B92. His federal Ministry for Transport and Communications shut off B92's transmitter, claiming the station did not have a valid license to operate.

That could have silenced B92 permanently, but it did not, thanks to a forty-year-old mathematics professor on the staff named Drazen Pantic. He had been planning for the day when the government would try to take the station off the air. His plan was based on exploiting the possibilities of the Internet. Pantic made use of a computer program called RealAudio that makes it possible for sound to be carried over the Internet. He used a long-distance phone line to transmit the radio station's signal by RealAudio to an Internet service provider in Amsterdam called XS4ALL, which then made it available on Radio B92's Web site to anyone in the world, including anyone with a computer and a modem in Serbia. The broadcasts were in Serbo-Croatian, the language spoken in that Balkan region.

"At 9 a.m., the regime shut down our transmitter," Pantic said. "By sunset, Radio B92 was back on the air, not just in Yugoslavia but all around the world."

Americans helped B92 stay on the air. Progressive Networks, maker of RealAudio, heard about B92's efforts to stay alive and donated improved software. The U.S. government's Radio Free Europe/Radio Liberty and Voice of America, as well as the German government's Deutsche Welle, taped the B92 news reports from the Internet Web site and transmitted them over the air by shortwave broadcasts in Serbo-Croatian back into Serbia. So, through this roundabout communication linkup, from Belgrade to Amsterdam to cities elsewhere in Europe, B92 broadcasts of anti-Milosevic marches could still be heard over the air in Belgrade even though its local Belgrade transmitter had been shut off by the government.

On December 5, after domestic and international protests over the attempt to silence B92 (including a message of support from U.S. Vice President Al Gore), the Milosevic regime backed down and turned B92's transmitter back on. Asked what had happened, Serbian officials offered a new explanation: instead of a license problem it had been a technical glitch. Officials claimed water had dripped onto the cables at the power station used by all Belgrade radio stations and disrupted transmission. There was no explanation why pro-government stations had not been affected. A week later, state-owned Radio and Television Serbia agreed to let B92 broadcast over its transmitter.

Milosevic eventually reinstated the election results that he had tried to annul. For a time, the staff of B92 exulted in their apparent triumph thanks to new technology. "The social impact [the] Internet could spread came to me as a gift from heaven," Pantic said.

But the drama was not over.

For the next two years, as Milosevic came under increasing world opprobrium for such atrocities as the "ethnic cleansing" of Serbia's Albanian minority, Radio B92 continued to report the news impartially, broadcasting over the air, through the Internet, and also by satellite. As the result of an alliance with other broadcasters, its reports were available to eighteen TV stations and thirty-three radio stations throughout Serbia that had a combined audience of 1.6 million listeners. Radio B92 and other independent outlets survived thanks to subsidies from the Soros Foundation and other Western pro-democracy groups. While the subsidies helped economically, they made B92 vulnerable politically, since Serbian authorities could claim it was in the pocket of hostile foreigners.

During those two years, while state-controlled media reported only Serbia's side in Milosevic's effort to crush Albanian guerrillas, B92 gave both sides. For example, one day when Serbian police allowed journalists to accompany them to villages in Kosovo to see alleged evidence of Albanian "terrorist" attacks on Serbs, Radio B92 reported not only the sight of Albanian guerrilla weapons and dead Serbians but also the sight of Serbian tanks in the streets and burned mosques of the largely Islamic Albanian population. This was not the picture Milosevic wanted portrayed.

The radio station had taunted him for years. One of its longstanding jokes was to broadcast speeches by Milosevic and other politicians interspersed with the sounds of a flushing toilet. Milosevic waited for an opportunity to remove this annoying thorn in his side once and for

Editor-in-chief Veran Matic (center) of Belgrade's independent radio station B92 and his staff found innovative ways to use the Internet against efforts by Serbian leader Slobodan Milosevic to silence the station. Matic is shown at a March 24, 1999, press conference after police raided B92, ordered it shut down, and held Matic for eight hours. Credit: AP/Wide World Photos.

all. At last, in 1999, the opportunity came in the form of threatened NATO bombing of Yugoslavia to force Serbian withdrawal from Kosovo. Playing on patriotism and war jitters, Milosevic was emboldened to take harsher measures against anyone he could accuse of supporting the enemy.

On March 24, 1999, shortly before the NATO bombing began, police seized Radio B92's editor-in-chief Veran Matic and held him for eight hours. Serbian authorities labeled him and his staff as traitors and collaborators, especially since B92 had begun reporting on civil defense preparations. Officials of the Yugoslav Federal Telecommunications Ministry shut down the station, using the pretext that its broadcast exceeded the permitted power level of three hundred watts. B92 could no longer broadcast over the air from Belgrade but once again stayed alive by transmitting its signal by Internet and satellite hookups, at a time when the Yugoslav people needed reliable information on a critical development: the start of NATO air strikes against targets in their country.

In its reports on the NATO bombings, carried on its Internet Web site, Radio B92 again took an evenhanded, objective approach that contrasted to the propagandistic style of official media. For example, on April 2, its written news summary contained these items: air-raid sirens sounded in Belgrade; an explosion was heard in Pristina; three captured U.S. soldiers are to go on trial; President Clinton said he holds Milosevic responsible for the soldiers' safety; a Milosevic meeting with a Kosovar politician was denounced by Kosovo guerrillas but praised by Russia; NATO officials showed photographs of targets hit; and France said Yugoslav security forces in Kosovo must be reduced before a political solution could be achieved. In its tone and in its selection of news reports, B92 carefully avoided taking sides and stuck to what it could independently verify as true. Its report even contained a cautionary note: "Radio B92 advises readers that in these difficult circumstances our correspondents are unable to report directly from Kosovo."

But while the Internet made it easier for B92 to continue its reporting and bring its audio signal back to Belgrade, the wartime mentality in Yugoslavia made it easier for Milosevic to tighten his grip on the media. All he needed was one more pretext to shut down all B92 operations. He found it, one week after the start of the NATO bombing, in the form of British foreign minister Robin Cook, who told a press conference that Britain would provide Radio B92 with satellite facilities and an exclusive interview. Since Britain was a prime mover behind the

NATO bombing of Yugoslavia, Cook's embrace of B92 lent further credence to Milosevic's claim that the station was on the side of the enemy. On April 2, Serbian authorities—escorted by police—sealed up the doors to B92's studio. As the station went off the air, its last words were: "We will never surrender."

The government replaced Matic with a new director loyal to Milosevic. The staff was told they could keep their jobs as long as their editorial policy was "patriotic." Asked what that meant, they were told it meant support for Milosevic. The staff walked out. Other staff were hired and on Tuesday, April 13, a new B92 went on the air, no longer an independent voice but instead yet another pro-Milosevic station.

Meanwhile, the original staff turned yet again to the Internet. In the Netherlands supporters of Matic and his independent broadcasters set up a mirror site (a copy of their original Web site, using a different Internet server) called "Help B92." By using a server in the Netherlands, the broadcasters avoided dependence on a server in Serbia that could be seized by Milosevic. The Web site address was www.helpb92.xs4all.nl. It posted E-mails it received from people in Yugoslavia describing life in the region during the eleven weeks of NATO bombing. One resident of Batajnica, a Belgrade suburb near an airbase, wrote: "The situation has become unbearable and terrifying."

During this crucial period in 1999 when the Serbian government attempted to silence any independent voice, "the existence of the Internet was the single factor that allowed certain oppositional groups in the former Yugoslavia to maintain [contact] with the outside world," according to *The Enabling Environment for a Free and Independent Media*. It was an important test of the power of the Internet in the struggle over information control.

When the war was over, Milosevic was still in power; the new B92 radio station controlled by him was still slanting the news in his favor, while the staff members of the old, independent B92 were still using the Internet to circumvent censorship and provide news reports free of propaganda. Later in the year, the independent broadcasters found a way to get back on the air directly. Giving themselves the new name "B2-92," they made use of borrowed facilities of Belgrade's Studio B radio and television station, controlled by an opposition leader. Starting on August 2, 1999, anyone tuning in to 99.1 on the FM dial in Belgrade heard the trademark gag of the irreverent broadcasters: the sound of Milosevic's voice interspersed with a flushing toilet.

The old B92 was back on the air, while continuing to use the Internet as a safeguard against any new repression. These precautions paid off. In May 2000, when a pro-Milosevic politician was assassinated, Milosevic blamed opposition groups and, on May 17, used this as a pretext for a 2 A.M. raid by masked police officers on Studio B's broadcasting center. Government officials shut down several independent media outlets, including B2-92. The officials then converted the local radio station into a pro-Milosevic station broadcasting censored news. But the cat-and-mouse game was not over.

The real B2-92 once again used the Internet to transmit uncensored radio news reports from a secret location. On the Web sites it used, www.freeb92.net/index.phtml or www.opennet.org/index.phtml, a listener could hear the shouts of protest demonstrators and the wail of police sirens during clashes in the streets of Belgrade, as part of news reports on reactions to the media crackdown. In London, the BBC picked up B2-92's audio signals and rebroadcast them by satellite back to Serbia to thirty local radio stations and seventeen local television stations.

The Internet also helped keep another independent radio station alive in Yugoslavia. This time it was not in Belgrade, the federal capital, but in Pristina, the provincial capital of Kosovo, at a time when conflicting official statements by Serb forces and NATO made it difficult for Serbs and ethnic Albanians in Kosovo to know the truth of what was happening in their province.

In 1989, Aferdita Kelmendi, a journalist who was a member of the ethnic Albanian majority population of Kosovo, lost her job with the state-controlled radio station in Pristina, the capital of the province, during a purge of Albanians by Serb officials as Milosevic began his process of ethnic cleansing. With her husband, who is a journalist, and a group of friends, she created Radio 21, an independent Albanian-language radio station in Pristina. In 1990, Serbian troops raided the station and ejected its Albanian staff, but Kelmendi managed to keep the radio on the air. "I'm not living by Serbian rules or Yugoslavian rules," she said later. "I'm living by my own rules. I am independent."

Over the years, her ability to retain that independence came increasingly under question. In 1998, as Serbian police escalated their murderous attacks on ethnic Albanians in Kosovo, Kelmendi turned to the Internet as a supplement to her radio station and posted Albanian-language audio reports from Radio 21 on the station's Web site. This was a way of making sure that Albanian émigrés and others around the world were kept aware of news events in Kosovo.

On March 24, 1999, shortly before NATO began bombing and on the same day that police in Belgrade seized Radio B92's director, Serb forces in Pristina ransacked the office of Aferdita Kelmendi's Radio 21. Afraid for her life, she watched from a hiding spot, she said, as the Serbs destroyed her studio, including its equipment for sending out its audio signal over the Internet. She later reported that one of her correspondents, as well as his father and brother, were executed by the Serbs. Kelmendi and her family fled for their lives to Skopje in neighboring Macedonia—and once again she went online to report the news.

With financial help from the Soros Foundation and the U.S. and British governments, she used the Internet to create a proxy radio news service (www.radio21.net) that transmitted reports for two hours a day. Radio 21's Albanian-language Internet reports were picked up by the BBC and Radio Netherlands and broadcast by shortwave back into Kosovo. Radio 21's reports were also picked up off the Internet by SBS radio in Melbourne, Australia, and broadcast to local Albanian émigrés. The Web site also provided audio of English-language translations of its news reports.

During the eleven-week NATO bombing campaign, Radio 21's reports provided an alternative to both Serbian propaganda and official NATO versions of what was happening on the ground. For example, on June 8 the radio's Web site reported:

> Serbian forces are still continuing operations in Kosova, despite reports by NATO spokesman Jamie Shea that there are signs Serbs are withdrawing. NATO reported today that a train full of Serb soldiers left Ferizaj area towards north Kosova. But our correspondent in Ferizah Rizah Reshani reports that there are no signs to prove that information.

During the bombing, Western news organizations outside Kosovo cited Radio 21 as one source of information about events inside the province, often using the station's Internet reports. Within Kosovo itself, owners of shortwave radios could tune in to Radio 21 reports carried by the BBC and other foreign broadcasters. But residents of the province had little chance to hear or read Radio 21 reports over the station's Web site. Few Kosovars owned computers, and those who did faced the problem of lack of access to the Internet because phone lines were cut during the fighting. As Kelmendi later told a conference of journalists in Washington, however, the station's Web site received a large amount of E-mail from émigré Albanians and other people around the world, from places as far away as Malaysia. "So people are listening to us," she said, "and that is great."

When the Serbs withdrew and the NATO bombing ended, Kelmendi and her family returned to Pristina. Money and other assistance from the BBC, the U.S. Agency for International Development (USAID), the United Nations, NATO, the press-freedom advocacy group Reporters Sans Frontières, and other private associations helped her build a new radio station. A U.S. Army truck brought a transmitter in from Macedonia. On the eleventh floor of a largely abandoned office building in central Pristina, a building commandeered by the United Nations, Radio 21 found a new home and on July 15, 1999, began broadcasting a daily news program from 8 to 9:30 A.M. over the air. Foreign shortwave broadcasters continued to carry its reports. Radio Netherlands had a daily Radio 21 segment for two hours each evening. When U.S. Secretary of State Madeleine Albright visited Pristina on July 29 and addressed the Kosovar people, Radio 21 carried her speech live. One report said it reached nearly half the population of the province.

These two instances, involving Radio B92 and Radio 21, both in Yugoslavia, constituted an important initial test of strength between a dictator and independent journalists using the Internet. Who won? In truth, each side could claim a partial victory. Two independent radio stations stayed alive even with transmitters shut down because they had the Internet to carry their signal. But Milosevic, until his ouster in 2000, maintained his tight grip on most Yugoslav media and public opinion, severely hampered the ability of B92 and Radio 21 to reach their audiences inside Yugoslavia, and began taking steps to try to stop them from using the Internet. Still, on balance the emergence of the Internet changed the equation and helped independent journalists stand up to censors. During the NATO bombing campaign, Yugoslavs who had access to computers or shortwave radios could hear reports by fellow citizens that offered an alternative to the official version of what was happening to their country during a crucial period. The Internet made it easier to ensure that an alternative voice was heard.

More and more, that is the case in other countries around the world.

In Nigeria, Managing Editor Babafemi Ojudu of the *News* credited the Internet with enabling him to survive during the Abacha dictatorship. When police seized his weekly paper's phone lines in 1997, he said, "I hooked my laptop to the phones of friends and got in touch with our reporters online." A friend in Washington E-mailed him tips and contributed reporting to such Ojudu stories as an exposé of alleged illicit Nigerian campaign donations to the Clinton reelection campaign. Nigerian reporters also used the World Wide Web to alert public opinion abroad to arrests of fellow journalists.

In the former Soviet republic of Belarus, which became an independent country, President Aleksander Lukashenko imposed severe press restrictions. His Soviet-style regime repeatedly sought to silence the leading opposition newspaper, *Svaboda* (Freedom), for such stories as a 1995 report that President Lukashenko had praised Hitler for "introducing order" to Germany and another report that revealed alleged corruption in Lukashenko's cabinet. In almost eight years of existence, *Svaboda* achieved a circulation of fifty thousand copies, but after $50,000 in fines, lawsuits, and harassment, including having its bank account frozen, the thrice-weekly eight-page paper was finally ordered shut down on November 24, 1997. Editor Ihar Hermianchuk told a Minsk press conference he would find a way to keep the paper alive. The Internet provided the way.

First the editor tried to use the newspaper's existing Web site, but their provider "got scared and took away their Web site," the *Washington Post* reported. Then, on December 1, 1997, the U.S. government's Radio Free Europe/Radio Liberty Web site came to the rescue. It reprinted *Svaboda* articles in text form and also included them in its daily 8 to 9 P.M. GMT live audio feed on its Web site (www.rferl.org/bd/RAschedules/be-realaudio.html). For the next fifty-two days, until editor Hermianchuk could find a way to resume publication, *Svaboda* online reported food shortages, strikes, opposition meetings, health problems from the Chernobyl nuclear disaster, and an opinion poll showing that only 12 percent of citizens felt that life would improve anytime soon. None of these reports appeared in Lukashenko's state-controlled press. How many Belarussians accessed these online reports? No one knew, and editor Hermianchuk was not sanguine: "Very few people in Belarus have access to the Internet."

In the Middle East, one of the most repressive regions of the world for journalists, Daoud Kuttab found a way to outwit censors. After

years of frustration at being arrested by both Israeli and Palestinian police, having his stories spiked, being fired by a newspaper under pressure from Palestinian leader Yassir Arafat, and suffering other repression, in 1996, Kuttab turned to the Internet for help. From his office in
Jerusalem, the Palestinian American journalist and broadcaster created
a censorship-free Web site for fellow journalists. He called it the Arabic
Media Internet Network, giving it the acronym AMIN. (The Web site is
www.amin.org.)

Soon it was carrying stories of alleged torture by both Israelis and
Palestinians, demands that Arafat be ousted, and reports of Jordanian
editors being arrested—items that most mainstream newspapers in that
region dared not print. (As of March 1999, two of the three private
Palestinian dailies had financial or political ties to Arafat's regime, and
the third avoided strong criticism of Arafat for fear of reprisals.) Shortly
before the start of the year 2000, the AMIN Web site was recording an
average of 55,363 visits a day—a small number compared to that of the
Web site of the *New York Times*, for example, but still large enough to
represent an important potential reach into the audience of opinion
molders in the Arab world. As Kuttab put it, the Internet had created "a
bypass that governments are unable to control," and he added: "All the
barriers that governments had created to stop the spread of news [are]
no longer viable."

He soon had a chance to test that idea. In 1997, Kuttab's educational television production company was providing live coverage of
sessions of the Palestinian Legislative Council, the legislative body of
the Palestinian Authority. When the debate shifted to allegations of
corruption in Arafat's administration, transmissions were disrupted
by static apparently caused by jamming from Arafat's Palestinian
Broadcast Authority. To try to get around the apparent jamming, Kuttab distributed a tape of that day's session to other local Palestinian
TV stations—and was arrested.

Taken to a Palestinian police office at 11 P.M. that evening, he was
held without charge in a prison in Ramallah, north of Jerusalem, for one
week, during which he went on hunger strike. News of his imprisonment spread quickly, helped by stories his associates posted on the
AMIN Web site. Soon human rights organizations were demanding his
release. U.S. government officials followed suit. Arafat's police bowed
to international pressure and released him.

Since that incident Daoud Kuttab has continued to use the Internet

Palestinian American journalist Daoud Kuttab spoke to reporters in the West Bank town of Ramallah in 1997 after one of his many clashes with authorities. Kuttab had just been released after being held a week for producing live broadcasts of a Palestinian legislative debate about corruption. To get around print censorship, Kuttab created the Web site AMIN to provide an outlet for Arab journalists unable to get their stories published in Middle Eastern newspapers. Credit: AP/Wide World Photos.

to get word out quickly—and unhindered—whenever there is a story to tell about alleged official misconduct. In October 1999, in an article on his Web site titled "Torture and Democracy," Kuttab asked: "Does the security apparatus of the Palestinian Authority carry out torture?" and answered his own question by citing the case of a consumer activist who was arrested on charges of incitement and held for nineteen days after criticizing terms of a prisoner release agreement with Israel. "He was deprived of sleep for three days, and made to stand almost the entire time," Kuttab wrote. "His eyes were blindfolded with a dirty rag," causing him eye inflammation. (The activist also told TV viewers about his torture when interviewed by Kuttab, so the Web site was not the only way for getting the truth out.)

Being evenhanded, Kuttab also ran an item on his Web site that month about alleged torture in an Israeli prison in occupied South Lebanon. Other items on the AMIN Web site, written by himself and other journalists, revealed Arafat's appointment of an alleged convicted criminal as district attorney for the West Bank, evidence of a massive trade in illegal arms protected by Palestinian Authority security forces, and indications that Arafat was suffering from senility (the article was titled "Arafat Should Resign Now").

Reports such as those were not likely to appear in any Palestinian newspapers. As one newspaper columnist put it: "[The editors] censor about 40 per cent of my articles concerning Palestinian policies, corruption, and mismanagement." That kind of self-censorship had been practiced for decades in conventional Palestinian news media, but now, with the AMIN Web site, there was an uncensored outlet for those sensitive stories. Daoud Kuttab's use of the Internet showed the potential power of this emerging medium in the Middle East.

In Chile, newspaper editors were frustrated in June 1997 when a judge imposed a gag order barring them from covering one of the country's most sensational trials. It involved a businessman who was the alleged leader of a drug-trafficking and money-laundering ring. He was charged with bribing police and court officials. The Santiago daily paper *La Tercera* got around the injunction by using the Internet. Through an intermediary in New York, the newspaper posted exclusive trial reports online (at www.copesa.cl/Casos/Lavado/Carrera8.html). "The information we are including [on the Web site] is a journalistic coup," national editor Luis Alvarez said. After ten days, an appeals court ordered the judge to rescind the gag order.

That use of the Internet in Chile is typical of journalists in relatively democratic countries, going online as a way of getting around a temporary ban on reporting. But in closed societies that lack democratic institutions or easy access to the Internet, it is far more difficult to use this medium. Yet even here some independent journalists make the effort. Take the case of Cuba.

In January 1998, Mario Viera Gonzalez, a Havana journalist, founded the small, unauthorized press agency Cuba Verdad (Cuban Truth). Viera wrote an article accusing Fidel Castro's government of hypocrisy because a Cuban foreign ministry official had advocated an impartial world criminal court—yet Cuba itself had no such independent judiciary. Viera called his article "Morality in Undershorts." He dictated his story over the telephone from Havana to a contact in Miami, who then posted it on the Cuban emigré-run anti-Castro Web site CubaNet (www.cubanet.org). Castro's government quickly reacted. Viera, fifty-nine, was arrested by Cuban police and charged with slandering the foreign ministry official. On Friday, November 27, 1998, about a dozen supporters of Viera staged a rare protest demonstration in the heart of Havana. Gathering in front of the Capitolio, Cuba's former capital building, they denounced Viera's arrest and traded blows and insults with government supporters. Police detained at least five people.

Cuba's action against Viera showed how seriously it viewed unauthorized use of the Internet. Since his arrest it has punished other independent journalists for trying to use this medium to circumvent official controls on the press. Twenty-five-year-old Jesús Joel Díaz Hernández was seized by police on January 18, 1999, and sentenced to four years in prison for "dangerousness" after his reports were posted on the CubaNet Web site. In New York later that year, while he was still in prison, the Committee to Protect Journalists gave him an International Press Freedom Award, noting:

> Díaz Hernández is one of a number of independent journalists in Cuba who show great courage, tenacity and cunning in the inventive use of the Internet to circumvent censorship and confront President Fidel Castro's systematic campaign to suppress free expression.

Not only Cuban émigré organizations but politically independent groups, such as the Digital Freedom Network (www.dfn.org) and

Florida International University (www.fiu.edu), have also posted articles by independent Cuban journalists. But how many Cubans actually have been able to read these online news reports? Most analysts agree the number is small. According to a 1997 report, less than 2 percent of the nation's 11 million people had computers. Many of those devices lacked proper phone-line connections.

Even if they had adequate computer equipment and software, said Professor Nelson Valdes of the University of New Mexico, who studied Internet use in Cuba, "the phone lines are terrible, so there is no rapid connectivity." In addition, costs are prohibitive for most Cubans. Internet connection services cost $340 a month, in a country where the average monthly wage has been between $14 and $27. "Those who have access feel it is so precious that they don't waste it on news but spend time on scientific information they need," Valdes told me. "They don't look at CubaNet because there's nothing new on it; they've already heard the rumors. The Internet is not the solution to Cuban censorship."

Still, the Castro regime saw the Internet as enough of a threat to take steps to control it. Leaders of the armed forces, interior ministry, and other officials met regularly to discuss what to do about it. They restricted access to the Internet to academics, government officials, diplomats, and some business executives and foreign journalists. Anyone else using a private telephone line to go online faced government monitoring and possible arrest, while restrictions on long-distance calls and their high cost made it difficult for Cubans to connect via foreign servers. Most Cubans were forced to use the only permitted Internet provider, the government-controlled Center for Interchange of Automated Information. "We cannot forget," the center's director, Jesus Martinez, said, "that the Internet can be aggressive. It can hurt you."

That threat was clear to other countries as they mounted similar efforts to hold back the tide of uncensored news. In the landlocked southern African nation of Zambia, President Frederick Chiluba personally ordered the removal of an entire issue of the independent daily *The Post* from the archives of the newspaper's Web site (www.zamnet.zm/zamnet/post/post.html). (In addition, President Chiluba banned the print edition and warned that any citizen possessing it could face imprisonment.) The issue in question was dated February 5, 1996. It had revealed a secret government plan to hold a surprise referendum on a controversial draft constitution. To limit debate, the government had planned not to disclose the impending referendum until the last moment, but the *Post* spoiled the little surprise.

Managing Editor Bright Mwape and another top editor were charged with publishing state secrets online. Why did the government take this use of the Internet so seriously? According to an article in the *Columbia Journalism Review*, Zambia feared cuts in foreign aid if it received unfavorable publicity worldwide, and the newspaper had been giving the regime bad PR by aggressively exposing corruption and repression and posting these reports on a Web site that the government later conceded was widely read. As Managing Editor Mwape put it: "The government has been in a literal state of panic ever since the *Post* went on the Net."

India also apparently worried about news from cyberspace. In the summer of 1999 the Indian government claimed its troops had recaptured the strategic area of Tiger Hills in the disputed border region of Kashmir, but the Web site of the respected Pakistani newspaper *Dawn* (www.dawn.com) quoted Kashmiri guerrillas as disputing that claim. India tried to prevent its people from reading such reports, so Internet users in India were denied access to the Pakistani newspaper's Web site. VSNL, India's government-owned international long-distance telecommunications monopoly, said it blocked the site "under instruction from higher authorities."

Some governments have gone to even greater lengths to counter free speech on the Internet. Singapore not only controlled all three servers in that city-state but also, in 1995, began flooding the Internet with massive mailings of pro-government material to try to drown out criticisms of the regime in Singaporean newsgroups. Tunisia's government set up a bogus Web site designed to appear to be that of Amnesty International, the international organization that has denounced alleged violations of human rights by that North African regime. Tunisia arranged things so that Internet users in Tunisia who tried to access www.amnesty.org were shunted to the bogus site, which praised the regime's allegedly sterling record in human rights.

Some analysts have doubted that governments can hold out for very long in their efforts to censor cyberspace, any more than Canute the Great, the eleventh-century king of England, Denmark, and Norway, was able to still the ocean tide by holding up his hand and ordering it to stop. "There has never been a successful attempt to censor the Net," Adam Powell, a vice president of the Freedom Forum, the

U.S.-based press-freedom advocacy group, told a 1999 conference in London. "It is very difficult to remove something once it is online." Powell said authoritarian regimes must choose between censorship and development, and he added:

> More and more, it is development that is winning. They want to restrict information but they have to give access to data for business development—which makes censorship much more difficult.

The Internet not only helps journalists outwit censors but also provides a defensive tool when reporters come under attack.

As we have seen in chapter 3, Chinese American correspondent Ying Chan, another journalist, and their Hong Kong–based magazine *Yazhou Zhoukan* were sued by a Taiwanese politician for criminal libel because of their story about an allegedly illegal offer to make a donation to the Clinton reelection campaign. Ying Chan used the Internet to rally public opinion to her side. Helped by her sixteen-year-old son, Frederick, in New York, Chan spent four days in November 1996 creating a Web site about the lawsuit. Her brother Nicky had registered a domain name for her (www.yingchan.com). "And," the wisecracking journalist said, "when the New York company that rented me server space asked for a $500 fee for hosting the interactive pages, I told the owner to get lost and uploaded the files to the server at Nicky's computer company in Hong Kong."

On her Web site she posted the text of her *Yazhou Zhoukan* article about the alleged $15 million illegal campaign contribution offer, as well as legal briefs in the case, news stories about it, protest letters by press and legal organizations, links to Web sites of free-speech groups, background on campaign finance issues, and an online open letter to the Taiwanese president that anyone could sign. In the course of a year, she said, her Web site received 8,873 "hits" from readers spread as far as Argentina and Finland.

"The Web gave me unlimited space, an unlimited news hole," Chan told me. "I was absolutely fascinated by the liberating power. It's tremendous. Information is power. I have nothing. I'm by myself. I have no clerical support. I have a full-time job, family, groceries. But I have information. I have the means of putting it out quickly. It's empowering."

Chan was able to react more quickly than the Taiwanese government to each new development in the case, and to put her spin on it, thanks to the Internet. "It's a matter of speed, when timing is essential," she said. "I can get information to people quickly. No FedEx, no Xerox. It's economical. Through the Web I can quickly mobilize the international journalistic community to help us. In fifteen minutes I put it on the Web for all the world to see. That creates pressure on the KMT [the then-ruling party in Taiwan]. I put everything there. They attacked me for interfering with the judicial process by putting things on the Web— so I put *that* statement on the Web too. I'm framing the debate. This [form of] democracy is liberating. It is the antithesis of what politicians want. They want to shut down information. But this information is available to everybody."

The ability of reporters to use the Internet to outwit censors and defend themselves against attack has not escaped the notice of their enemies in a number of countries, including China. As we will see in the next chapter, it is in that country that the biggest single battle is taking place between these antagonists over the future role of the Internet.

17

The Great Firewall

China and the Internet

TWENTY-EIGHT CENTURIES AGO, vassal states under the Chou dynasty began building sections of the engineering triumph known today as the Great Wall of China. As completed later by emperors of the Qin and Ming dynasties, it became a defensive shield of stone and brick snaking forty-five hundred miles across the tops of mountains along the northern border. Today it stands twenty to fifty feet high and fifteen to twenty-six feet thick, with watchtowers and a serrated upper level, a structure so large that it is visible from space. The Great Wall of China was designed to help keep out Mongol and other invaders, and it succeeded for many years until barbarian hordes exploited internal weaknesses of later dynasties and invaded China.

By the start of the twenty-first century, China had a new wall—an electronic one, designed to keep out a new kind of barbarian invader: what the Communist government called "spiritual pollution" in the form of harmful influences purveyed over the Internet, ranging from pornography and separatist movements in Tibet and Taiwan to democracy and the Falun Gong exercise-and-meditation cult. Through a complex system of controls, filters, and threats, Beijing erected what some in the cyberspace community called the Great Firewall of China. China's creation of this firewall posed a question for news dissemination: Could citizens of the world's most populous nation be walled off from electronic sources of information about what was happening in their own country and elsewhere?

Chinese censors were forced to take the Internet seriously when they saw the rapid growth in its use in their own country. In 1996, one year after the Internet became publicly available in China, there were only 81,000 users in that country, but a year later the number had jumped to 670,000, and by late 1999 it had shot up to 7 million. Some analysts projected that during the year 2000 there would be 10 million Chinese online.

To be sure, that figure of 10 million would be less than 1 percent of China's total population of some 1.2 billion. But it's still large enough to have some impact. A closer look at who was using the World Wide Web in China in 1999 indicated its potential for influencing public policy. According to a survey of twenty-two thousand Internet users in China, most had academic or technical backgrounds and a working command of English. One-third worked in computer-related fields or were students. As sinologist Greg May put it, "Internet users represent a relatively young, wealthy and highly educated cohort. In short, they are the people most likely to run China in the future."

Faced with that prospect, the existing rulers in Beijing took extraordinary measures to try to shield China's future leaders against alleged harm from the Internet. Under regulations promulgated in February 1996, all private subscribers to Chinanet, the main Internet service provider, run by the state telecommunications monopoly, were required to register with the Public Security Bureau, provide the government with detailed personal information about themselves, and sign a pledge not to "read, copy or disseminate information that threatens state security." All international telephone connections were routed through gateways controlled by the Ministry of Posts and Telecommunications. In addition to the state-run Chinanet, all Internet service providers were required to take steps to filter out anything deemed harmful, primarily pornography and pro-democracy material.

The government took other steps. It blocked access to Web sites of most Western news services, such as Reuters and CNN. The government's New China News Agency also formed a joint venture with Hong Kong business interests to try to create an alternative to the free-wheeling World Wide Web. The alternative was called China Wide Web and was carefully edited to exclude pornography and the politically incorrect while including business-oriented sites in the Chinese language. The effort flopped. Business executives weren't interested in an incomplete, censored web. As a Hong Kong newspaper pointed out: "Trials among 3,000 state-owned, private and foreign-invested enterprises showed they wanted it all."

While that attempt failed, Beijing pursued other efforts to censor the Internet. All servers installed technology to monitor Internet traffic and look for keywords such as "democracy." To intensify the scrutiny, in May 1999 agents of the Ministry of State Security reportedly visited offices of servers in Beijing and connected two monitoring devices to their computers to try to track individual E-mail accounts of their customers. Announcing plans later that year to monitor Internet sites, Information Minister Wu Jichuan said: "We will not allow the introduction of trash that is harmful to the people."

To make sure that everyone knew how seriously the government viewed the threat of free speech on the Internet, in December 1998, President Jiang Zemin warned that computer programmers faced prison sentences if they "endanger state security." One month later the regime made good on its threat. It passed sentence on a Shanghai software entrepreneur who became the first person in China ever to be charged and convicted of using the Internet to try to overthrow the state. His story sheds light on the rise of a new phenomenon: free-speech activists who chip away at the Great Firewall to disseminate uncensored news online. "In China," said one activist, "it's as close as you can get to real journalism."

Lin Hai was an obscure Shanghai businessman, little known to the outside world until his arrest at the age of thirty on March 25, 1998. He was charged with "inciting the overthrow of state power" through the Internet. Lin, who had a wife and a year-old son, denied being a political activist and said he was, instead, a software engineer who had begun to build up a business using his two desktop computers and one laptop to provide job search and marketing information to clients. In hopes of expanding his business, he said, he sought ways to reach more customers and built up a list of Chinese E-mail users for marketing purposes. He agreed to give thirty thousand E-mail addresses to *VIP Reference*, an underground electronic newsletter compiled in Washington by émigré Chinese advocates of democracy and free speech and sent out by E-mail to hundreds of thousands of mainland Chinese. Prosecutors said that from September 1997 until his arrest, Lin passed on these E-mail addresses to what prosecutors called "hostile foreign publications." By doing so, they said, he helped *VIP Reference* "carry out propaganda and incitement by distributing essays inciting subversion of state power and overthrow of the socialist system."

At his closed four-hour trial on December 4, 1998, according to dissident sources, Lin told the Shanghai Number One Intermediate People's Court that he was innocent of any political subversion and that he

had passed on the E-mail addresses in the hope that he could eventually exchange them for other E-mail addresses with *VIP Reference* and in
that way build up his business. But the court did not buy his argument
and found him guilty.

Lin faced a possible maximum term of life in prison. In the months
before his sentencing in January 1999, human rights advocates anx-
iously awaited the outcome of the trial. During that wait, many Western and dissident Chinese publications ran stories about *VIP Reference*,
the newsletter whose use of Lin's E-mail list had landed him in trouble.
The picture that emerged from these articles, and from my own interview with Li Hongkuan, the editor of *VIP Reference*, was that of a wily,
audacious challenge to Chinese censorship. Editor Li saw the Great
Firewall as no great impediment: "I just go over it."

How did he manage to outwit Beijing's massive effort at censorship in cyberspace? Since the government focused heavily on Web
sites, editor Li decided to concentrate instead on a part of the Internet
that was harder to police: E-mail. His strategy was to send massive
amounts of unsolicited E-mail (known as "spamming"), so massive
that it would be almost impossible for authorities to block. In addition, he sent his E-mails at random times of the day so that there was
no predictable pattern.

By the end of 1999 he was claiming to send "close to 1 million"
E-mails of his *VIP Reference* newsletter each day from his computers in
Washington, D.C., to recipients in China. There was no way independently to confirm his circulation claim, but there was some anecdotal evidence that his missives were getting through without being blocked. "I
receive all my e-mail," one dissident in Beijing said. "It includes Da-
cankao [*VIP Reference*]." In terms of feedback, Li said he got two hundred to five hundred E-mail comments daily from readers. And even a
Communist Party official complained that he was being bombarded
with *VIP Reference* mailings. "It takes me ten minutes to open my e-mail
and 30 minutes to clean it every day," he said, adding that he had been
forced to change his E-mail address "as there was no other way to stop
the flood of anti-Chinese information."

By doing massive unsolicited mailings, editor Li made it possible
for recipients plausibly to tell any government investigators that they
had not requested this material and so should not be punished for receiving it. In addition to mass mailings, as a further ploy against the

censors Li said he changed his originating E-mail address every day so that it could not be traced and blocked by Chinese authorities. ("It's a moving target," one dissident Chinese émigré said.)

Each day, using a new address, Li's two computers in an office near Dupont Circle in the heart of Washington sent out a twenty- to thirty-page issue of *VIP Reference*. "It's small enough so that you can download it in a minute, then get offline and read it on your computer," he said. About one-third to two-thirds of the content was news and the rest commentary. Some of it was written by émigré Chinese and some by Chinese living inside the country. Li said that some of those contributors in China were professional journalists writing under pseudonyms. In addition to E-mail, *VIP Reference* articles were made freely available on its Web site (www.ifcss.org/ftp-pub/org/dck) to all Chinese in Hong Kong or to mainland Chinese who knew how to use a proxy server (an Internet service provider that hides the true identity of Web sites) or who could afford to connect to the Internet via long distance to avoid censored local Chinese servers.

Since the newsletter's beginning in 1997, its issues have included reports on arrests of dissidents, allegations of official corruption, attacks on party leaders, exposés of economic problems, essays on democracy, and other items the regime obviously would have liked to suppress—items such as the series of reports *VIP Reference* did on the Falun Gong. In April 1999, an estimated ten thousand members of the exercise-and-meditation cult silently gathered outside the homes of party leaders in Beijing to protest the regime's efforts to suppress the cult. Official Chinese media avoided any mention of the protest for days, but *VIP Reference* said it E-mailed items such as this one to hundreds of thousands of mainland Chinese:

RED SUN RISES IN THE EAST, FALUN GONG EMERGES IN CHINA
Believers of Falun Gong Protesting around
Zhongnanhai Compound
(Beijing April 25) Ten years after the crackdown on the Tiananmin student movement, more than 10,000 believers of Falun Gong are protesting again.

Complaining about being treated unfairly by the state media, the protestors are demanding that Premier Zhu Rongji hear their side of the story.

(The headline was a play on words, based on a famous Communist Chinese slogan, "Red Sun rises in the east, Mao Tse-tung emerges in China.")

Editor Li, who said he had taken part in the Tiananmen Square pro-democracy demonstrations in 1989 and later left China after being relegated to lesser teaching jobs because of his dissident views, was proud that he was able to get items such as that past the censors. He called himself "a pioneer of virtual press freedom."

Another uncensored newsletter, called *Tunnel*, began on June 4, 1997, the eighth anniversary of the Tiananmen Square massacre, and used a similar technique of massive, unsolicited E-mailings. In its inaugural issue *Tunnel* made a bold claim:

> The autocracy in the past was able to block what we see and what we hear and rectify our thoughts because they monopolized the technology for dissemination of information. The computer network has changed this. It disseminates technology onto the desks of each and everyone of us . . . hence it can undermine the two pillars of an autocratic society—monopoly and suppression.

Tunnel's articles were also available on its Web site (www.geocities.com/SiliconValley/Bay/5598).

The Chinese government, faced with these challenges from *Tunnel* and *VIP Reference*, fought back by putting Shanghai software entrepreneur Lin Hai on trial and convicting him of "inciting the overthrow of state power" for supplying the E-mail list to *VIP Reference*. On January 20, 1999, he was sentenced to two years in prison. The court said that because of his crime he deserved to be "punished harshly." It also fined him $1,200 and ordered the confiscation of "the tools of his crime": his two desktop computers, one laptop, a modem, and a telephone.

But if Lin Hai's two-year sentence was intended to intimidate any other would-be collaborators of *VIP Reference*, it apparently failed. A little over seven months later a second Internet user was arrested and charged with subversion. Chinese dissident Qi Yanchen, thirty-five, an official of an agricultural development bank, was detained by police on September 2, 1999, at his office in Botou, 125 miles south of Beijing, dissident sources reported. He was accused of making copies of *VIP Reference*.

Although the case of Qi Yanchen suggested that a number of dissident intellectuals were ignoring official efforts to stop the spread of uncensored news and comment on the Internet, analysts said other intellectuals kowtowed to the government and, for them, the intimidation campaign was working. Self-censorship was evident, even in Hong Kong, the part of China that enjoyed the greatest degree of press freedom. Officially tolerated Web sites admitted that they avoided sensitive subjects. As Alan Knight of Hong Kong University and Queensland University put it: "Creating fear of prosecution and thereby encouraging self-censorship may prove to be the most effective way that Asian governments can master the Internet."

Even without censorship or self-censorship, there were other factors in China militating against early use of the Internet as a mass medium for independent journalists. One of them was cost. The average computer in China cost $1,000 to $1,200, but the yearly per capita disposable income in urban households was only about $600 (according to 1996 government figures). "A computer is so expensive for most Chinese that families save for computers the way American families save for cars," one analyst said.

Even if they could afford a computer, purchasers then had to pay high access fees for Internet service providers such as Chinanet. In 1999 the rate was 240 *yuan* (about $29) for sixty hours a month, plus local phone charges that ran about fifty cents an hour. According to one survey, Chinese users of the Internet cited high prices as one of the most frustrating features of cyberspace. Those high prices applied to the few Chinese who had the telephone lines necessary for Internet connections. By the start of the twenty-first century, less than 10 percent of the nation's overwhelmingly rural population even had telephones.

Still, for those who wanted to know what was going on in their country and the outside world, there were ways to find out. If a curious person in China did not own a computer or work in an office that had one, there was always the *wangba*, or Internet café, that allowed customers to use computers online. By early 2000 there were an estimated one thousand such coffee shops and snack bars in China, many of them in big cities such as Shanghai. At establishments such as the Internet Café on Shan Xi Road South in the center of Shanghai, users were not policed as strictly as those in offices. They did not have to register with the government and usually did not even have to give their name.

"From my café," said Edward Zeng, head of Unicom Sparkice, a chain of cybercafés in China, "you can read anything you want."

In addition to permitting that degree of freedom, the government also relaxed its earlier controls on Web sites, apparently because it saw a need for its citizens to get complete, up-to-date business information. After previously blocking all access to Web sites of Western news outlets such as CNN and the British news service Reuters, in late 1997 Beijing permitted some of them back online, especially if they carried business news, although by the start of the twenty-first century the government still restricted access to the *New York Times*.

Why did China relax some of its controls over Internet access? For one thing, total censorship proved too difficult to enforce. It required more manpower than the government had expected. ("It is going to mean a lot of manual labor," a Hong Kong scholar said after studying the needs.) In addition, authorities learned that their vaunted computer filters were not foolproof. Clever Internet users found ways around them, for example, by sending coded E-mails that avoided suspicious keywords such as *democracy*. "Anyone who has some knowledge of the Internet can find a way to access what they want," a Chinese journalist commented.

But even if China could have overcome the practical obstacles to censoring the Internet, there were important economic and political reasons for relaxing its grip. Having all but abandoned Communist ideology and turned instead to staking its credibility on its ability to deliver higher living standards, the government needed economic growth. That growth needed to be based partly on international trade—which, in turn, required quick, accurate, and complete business-related information, best available on uncensored Web sites. "The new, relaxed attitude," Helen Johnstone wrote in the *South China Morning Post*, "appears to be a recognition that China will not feel the economic benefits of the system if it seeks to restrict it."

"As economic incentives motivate Chinese authorities to get their population onto the information superhighway as quickly as possible, the amount of open, uncensored online debate will inevitably increase," commented Joshua Gordon, a scholar of Internet issues at the East-West Center in Honolulu. "In the interest of the bottom line, the government knows that it must eventually give up its stranglehold on the free flow of information."

Some analysts believed that the government had suffered a major setback in its effort to ward off what it saw as a threat from the prospect of uncensored information in cyberspace. "They can't stop it," one foreign business executive concluded while attending a computer show in Beijing. Media scholar Webster Nolan wrote in *Nieman Reports* that China was experiencing the rise of market-driven news media and an increase in news from the outside world, and "these two powerful forces . . . may falter at times, but in the end they seem unstoppable."

Buoyed by such optimism, dissident journalists who chipped away at the Great Firewall made sweeping claims. Li Hongkuan, editor of *VIP Reference*, said: "We are destined to destroy the Chinese system of censorship over the Internet." And editors of *Tunnel*, the other main E-mail newsletter, predicted: "When we bore through the barrier so that it is ridden with gaping holes, then the collapse is not far away." An executive of the Freedom Forum, a U.S.-based press-freedom advocacy group, went even further. Summarizing news reports from Hong Kong, he concluded: "China has lost its battle to control Internet content."

But whether China indeed has lost remains to be seen. More skirmishes lie ahead in this battle over information control in cyberspace, and the stakes are high. The question is whether a government that rules the most populous nation on earth can prevent all, or a significant number, of its citizens from knowing what is going on in their country and in the world. Because the Internet has gained such importance as a news medium, and because China's population of 1.2 billion represents such a large percentage of the world total (6 billion), the outcome of this battle could well determine which side—independent journalists or censors—prevails in the global battle over press freedom.

18

Send in Uncle Walter

Advocacy Groups

ALIZA MARCUS RECEIVED the ominous notice in September 1995. The American journalist, based in Istanbul, faced the prospect of being locked up in a Turkish prison.

A prosecutor had charged the Reuters correspondent with inciting racial hatred because of her report about the Turkish army's evictions of Kurdish villagers and the torching of their homes. (See chapter 7, "A Veiled Woman: The Separatists.") Her Reuters news agency report had been published by a pro-Kurdish newspaper the previous year. Marcus was charged under Article 312 of the Turkish Penal Code. If convicted, the thirty-three-year-old native of Westfield, New Jersey, faced up to three years behind bars. More than 170 Turkish writers and intellectuals already had been imprisoned for writing that type of story. Now, for the first time, a foreign correspondent faced prosecution under the same law that had put them behind bars.

In New York, the Committee to Protect Journalists swung into action. CPJ, an influential international group that campaigns for press freedom, sought maximum public pressure on Turkey to try to help Marcus. Not only did the CPJ issue a statement ("Criminal prosecution of Marcus would be highly injurious to Turkey's image as a democratic nation and responsible member of the world community"), but it also urged the U.S. government to act. The CPJ helped mobilize prominent U.S. figures, including then senator Bill Bradley, to sign a letter of protest. And it asked the most respected journalist in the United States to lend his prestige to the effort to keep Marcus out of prison.

It sent in Uncle Walter—Walter Cronkite, former anchor of CBS News and honorary chairman of the CPJ.

Cronkite happened to be in nearby Greece working on plans for a televised documentary series about economic development in a high-tech world. When CPJ asked him to help, Cronkite readily agreed. "It was such a flagrant case of political censorship," he told me later. "There was no justification for it."

Cronkite flew from Greece to Ankara, Turkey, and met with Turkish prime minister Tansu Çiller in late September 1995. He told her: "Turkey's international image as a democratic nation will be badly battered if the prosecution of Ms. Marcus moves forward." Cronkite asked to have the charges against Marcus dropped. "She was quite hospitable and understanding," Cronkite recalled later. "She said there were official channels she couldn't interfere with, but she would use her influence."

Apparently she did. After Cronkite's intervention, prosecutors said they had insufficient evidence against Marcus, and on November 9, 1995, a state security court in Istanbul unanimously acquitted her. Did Cronkite's meeting with the prime minister have anything to do with the acquittal? "Absolutely," said former CPJ executive director Bill Orme. "We know from later discussions that his intervention helped convince high officials there that the prosecution of an American foreign correspondent would damage Turkey's image in the United States." And Cronkite himself said: "Possibly I played a role in the sense that it indicated the concern, the fact that I would make this special effort."

Why did CPJ turn to Cronkite? "We asked Walter," said Orme, "because a) he is who he is, . . . and he can get an audience with almost anyone; b) he happened to be nearby (in Greece) and willing and able to go to Ankara; c) and—very important—he was and is seen by Turks as a friend of the country, as he has often visited, and had narrated travel/archeological documentaries focusing on Turkish sites."

Sending in Uncle Walter was a typical move by the Committee to Protect Journalists, which is one of a number of press-freedom advocacy groups around the world that play an important role in the battle over censorship. Like the Internet, these advocacy groups provide a powerful weapon for journalists against those who seek to silence them. The existence of these groups helps explain the phenomenon of independent journalists who survive despite formidable intimidation and repression, but this resource is not always effective.

The Committee to Protect Journalists was founded in 1981 by a group of U.S. foreign correspondents who had seen the brutal treatment of their foreign colleagues by authoritarian governments and other forces opposed to a free press. "The issue of the day was the mass killing of journalists in Latin America," recalled Anne Nelson, a professor at the Columbia Graduate School of Journalism who was one of the first executive directors of CPJ. Cronkite, who gave his support during the creation of CPJ, said: "It was something we felt was needed."

The Committee to Protect Journalists was such a small organization at first that it consisted of little more than a part-time staffer working behind a small desk in a corner of another humanitarian international organization based in New York, a group called Human Rights Watch. But it had the backing of some media stars. "So it was an organization with a very impressive masthead, leading with Walter Cronkite, and a minimal staff," Nelson said.

It used that impressive masthead to let foreign governments think it was bigger and more important than it really was, Nelson added. In addition, CPJ was quick to take advantage of new technology to extend its influence. It was, Nelson said, "one of the early organizations to use e-mail for the urgent action network for journalists in peril."

Twenty years later, the Committee to Protect Journalists has expanded to a full-time staff of sixteen, as well as five part-time researchers, and a budget of $2.3 million. It holds its annual fund-raising dinners in a ballroom of the Waldorf-Astoria Hotel, where the likes of Disney chairman Michael Eisner and network anchors Dan Rather of CBS, Tom Brokaw of NBC, and Peter Jennings of ABC, and other famous journalists, all splendid in tuxedos and evening gowns, pay $500 or more a plate to honor obscure and embattled colleagues.

To a casual observer it seems an odd juxtaposition: superrich American media stars mingling with impoverished reporters from Sri Lanka or the Ivory Coast, flown in to New York at CPJ's expense to receive their International Press Freedom Awards. For some of the prominent guests there was a sense of shame, a sense that American media executives grew rich and played it safe in their own editorial decisions while these foreign journalists working for low pay risked their lives to report the truth. As Ted Koppel of ABC's *Nightline* said, in one speech that silenced the glittering crowd: "We celebrate their courage even as we exhibit increasingly little of our own."

While the annual dinner might present a study in contrasts of rich and poor, courage and caution, it also serves a vital function: raising almost half of the money CPJ needs to do its work. (The dinner in 1999 brought in $1 million, the CPJ said.) Other funds come from charities. In

1999, CPJ listed donations of $100,000 or more from the Ford Foundation; from American news media–related institutes, including the Freedom Forum, the Knight Foundation, and the McCormick Tribune Foundation; and from the Open Society Institute of billionaire financier George Soros. Prominent individuals from the press world, including Katharine Graham of the *Washington Post* and CBS anchor Rather, each gave in the range of $25,000 to $49,999.

From its drab, cramped twelfth-floor offices at 330 Seventh Avenue in New York City, the Committee to Protect Journalists provides one of the strongest international supports available for journalists in trouble. One main focus is a massive lobbying and publicity effort to win the release of imprisoned reporters, editors, publishers, and photojournalists—one of its most difficult and frustrating tasks. CPJ urgently E-mails other press-freedom advocacy groups, human rights groups, foreign governments, U.S. officials, and international bodies. Sometimes CPJ succeeds, but often it fails. Each time that it appeals on behalf of a journalist behind bars, it knows that the chance of success is slim.

Reporter David Rohde, twenty-eight, of the *Christian Science Monitor* revealed a massacre of thousands of Muslims by Bosnian Serb forces after they captured the city of Srebrenica in July 1995. In retaliation, on October 29 the Serb forces arrested and jailed Rohde on charges of espionage. Some in the CPJ feared he might be executed. CPJ chair Kati Marton rushed to Dayton, Ohio, where Bosnian peace talks were under way, and asked to meet with Serbian leader Slobodan Milosevic to urge Rohde's release. Marton was able to meet with Milosevic—perhaps because she happened to be married to the chief U.S. peace negotiator, Richard C. Holbrooke. Whatever the reason, Milosevic discussed the Rohde case with her four times. As *Washington Post* reporter Michael Dobbs put it, "because Marton chairs the Committee to Protect Journalists, whenever the Serbian strongman found himself with a spare moment, he would get an earful from her about the imprisonment of journalist David Rohde."

On November 8, Serb forces released Rohde, who later won a Pulitzer Prize for his stories of the mass graves at Srebrenica. His editor credited the CPJ as well as the U.S. State Department and the United Nations with winning Rohde's release.

The CPJ tries to come to the rescue of not just American journalists but those of any nationality facing imprisonment. Because Turkey for years has jailed more reporters and editors than any other country, the

Committee to Protect Journalists has devoted much of its efforts in that country. Results have been mixed. "Arguing [against] the reasons for censorship is pretty hopeless," Cronkite conceded, "because the whole political culture is different. They don't have the tradition of free speech and free press we have."

Ocak Isik Yurtçu and five other Turkish editors were indeed freed from prison after a high-powered CPJ delegation went to Turkey, lobbied for their release, and drummed up publicity by giving Yurtçu an award in prison. (See the introduction and chapter 7, "A Veiled Woman: The Separatists.") But the Turkish government reneged on its promise of legal reform and proceeded to throw other journalists in jail. By the end of 1999 there were still eighteen behind bars.

In Nigeria during the dictatorship of General Abacha, the CPJ and many other international groups tried without success to win the release of publisher Christine Anyanwu. (See chapter 4, "Guerrilla Journalists: Underground in Nigeria.") "We felt we were beating our heads against the wall," CPJ executive director Cooper said. "It was a horrible situation. The journalists were held in abysmal conditions. Our letters were having a minimal impact." It was only after the death of Abacha that Anyanwu won freedom after three years in prison. But there was a silver lining, CPJ claimed. The order in which the new Nigerian leader released the imprisoned journalists closely paralleled the order of importance that the CPJ had given to the various cases. Anyanwu was released first, and she had been the CPJ's top priority. As Cooper put it: "If you look at the list of journalists and the order of release and how much noise we made, you can see the pattern: the more noise, the more effect."

Because political tides are constantly shifting, it is difficult to predict how governments will react to pressure, but the advocacy group has found that keeping up the pressure increases the chances that when political change does take place, it will include more favorable treatment of journalists. In the mid- and late 1990s, analysts said, many Turkish politicians were under public opinion pressure at home to increase trade with Europe. To do so, they needed better relations with Europe, which in turn meant they needed to reassure Europeans who were concerned about allegations of human rights violations. This provided the CPJ with an opportunity for leverage. "All we can do," former CPJ executive director Orme said, "is ride the political currents, like surfing. What you have to look at is what are the forces in play and how you can exploit them." One force that CPJ has been able to exploit is political change, whether in Nigeria or the former Soviet Union. "Often when there is a change of power," current CPJ leader Cooper said, "the new leader wants to send a message to the international community that things are different. So the thing for him to do is let go political prisoners."

One way the Committee to Protect Journalists puts pressure on governments to release those it has imprisoned is to give the journalists awards for courage and trumpet the news loudly. Each year since 1991, the CPJ has selected four to seven reporters, editors, publishers, photojournalists, or television journalists from widely differing parts of the world and awarded them its International Press Freedom Award. In 1991 the winners were from Cameroon, China, the United States, Russia, and Guatemala, whereas eight years later the winners were from Cuba, Kosovo, Pakistan, and Colombia. Not only does CPJ issue press releases announcing who has been selected, but it hands out the awards at its annual dinner—an event that usually generates publicity because of the American media stars in attendance. Many newspapers around the world publish stories about the plights of the awardees. Newspaper editors are sympathetic to stories about colleagues in distress. All of this helps keep news of these journalists alive instead of subsiding after only a few headlines at the time of their arrests.

If CPJ can't win their release, the next best thing is to buck up their spirits while they remain incarcerated. "We give them the courage to go on," Cooper said. Turkish editor Yurtçu wrote to the CPJ from his cell: "What a pleasure to see a light of hope despite the surrounding prison walls and the deep darkness here."

Sometimes journalists who have been targeted for arrest or other attack turn to the CPJ to help them escape to safety. Nigerian editor Dapo Olorunyomi said that in June 1995, during the Abacha dictatorship, the military issued a "shoot on sight" order against him. He went into hiding. When news of his plight reached CPJ in New York, it secured legal documents for him and obtained funds from the human rights group Amnesty International to pay for his travel. In early 1996 he slipped across the Nigerian border disguised as a trader, having learned that no questions were asked of black marketeers who bribed guards with money and rum. The risky gamble paid off, and Olorunyomi flew to safety in the United States with the help of the Committee to Protect

Journalists. "Without them," he said, "I believe I would be dead or in prison."

The advocacy group also has helped save the lives of TV journalists, including two dramatic rescues in 1999. It arranged to airlift wounded Chilean cameraman Abner Machuca out of Macedonia and provide life-saving surgery after he suffered a sniper's bullet wound to the head; and it helped evacuate Sierra Leonean producer Aroun Rashid Deen out of his African country after his footage of rebel atrocities put him on a death list.

CPJ lawyers come to the rescue of journalists threatened with civil and criminal prosecutions intended to silence them. In June 1996, New York attorney James Goodale, a CPJ board member, flew to Zagreb, Croatia, to present a CPJ legal brief on the opening day of the criminal libel trial of editor Viktor Ivancic and reporter Marinko Culic of the satirical weekly *Feral Tribune*. They faced up to three years in prison for insulting the nation's president. (See chapter 12, "We Are Not Amused: Satire.") Defending the two journalists for their satirical attack on Franjo Tudjman's plan to mix the remains of dead fascists and their victims, Goodale's brief argued: "Croatia's attempts to impose criminal penalties directed against journalists who criticize political leaders is completely at odds with norms of democracy and Western practice." The CPJ brief also denounced all use of criminal libel laws: "Seditious libel statutes are especially pernicious, because they are used exclusively to silence dissent against the governing regime." Three months later the two journalists were acquitted.

One of CPJ's most important functions is a careful accounting of the number of journalists killed, imprisoned, or otherwise attacked. Because CPJ conducts its own painstaking investigations of each reported case of attack and eliminates any statistics that do not involve actual practicing journalists attacked for doing their job, its statistics differ from the tallies of other advocacy groups. For example, CPJ reported that thirty-four journalists were killed for their professional work in 1999, but the World Association of Newspapers (WAN) reported almost twice that number: seventy killed. A closer look at the WAN report shows that it includes *former* journalists, journalists who died while in prison, and others who died from unknown causes. The CPJ figure is a more reliable indicator of the extent of killings directly attributable to the journalists' professional activities.

CPJ publishes an annual book that details, country by country, the various forms of attack on journalists. The annual report also includes a list of the ten worst violators of press freedom. For the year 1999, the enemies list consisted of leaders of Yugoslavia, China, Cuba, Democratic Republic of Congo, Ethiopia, Ukraine, Tunisia, Malaysia, Peru, and Egypt. CPJ's website, www.cpj.org, contains the same information as the annual printed book as well as a quarterly journal called *Dangerous Assignments*, alerts about developments in individual cases of journalists in trouble, and a database with archived reports, although this information retrieval system does not always work well.

In recent years the Committee to Protect Journalists has tried, with mixed results, to encourage the creation and strengthening of professional associations of journalists in their own countries. The main reason for encouraging homegrown associations rather than increasing CPJ's own intervention from outside is that pressure from outside groups such as the CPJ is not always as effective as pressure from an interest group within a country. In some countries, such as Mexico, pressure from Americans may be resented. As former CPJ executive director Orme put it:

> We don't want to introduce . . . gringo meddling accusations into the mix. We would be much more effective in Mexico, and Mexican journalists would be much better protected, if the first line of defense were Mexicans themselves.

In November 1997, with the financial and organizational help of CPJ and other international press advocacy groups, thirty prominent Mexican journalists, including editor and publisher Jesús Blancornelas of Tijuana's *Zeta*, gathered in Mexico City at a dinner to discuss attacks on journalists. They formed a steering committee to begin planning the creation of the Sociedad de Periodistas—the Society of Journalists—a new professional association designed to protect those in the news business. (In a timely reminder of the threat they all faced, only a few days after this meeting Blancornelas survived the assassination attempt described in chapter 1, "'They Are the News': Facing Mexican Druglords.") The Sociedad was formally incorporated in 1998.

What hopes did the Mexican journalists have for this association? "We want to put up an umbrella to protect honest journalists and journalists that do dangerous work," Blancornelas said. The Sociedad listed its main functions as monitoring and publicizing attacks on journalists and ensuring quick, thorough official investigations and prosecutions of those responsible. "Our work is to convince Mexican society that an attack against a journalist is an attack against the whole society and its right to be well-informed," journalist Jorge Zepada said.

Convincing Mexican society of that proposition proved to be more difficult than expected. Weakened by internal rivalries and insufficient funds, the group has had patchy results. One success came when Jesús Barraza, editor of *La Prensa* in the border city of San Luis Río Colorado, was threatened and harassed by drug traffickers. Since his former boss had been murdered by the drug criminals (see chapter 15, "Chilled or Defiant: The Painful Choice"), Barraza had reason to fear for his own life. The government of the state of Sonora provided him with body-guards, then withdrew his official protection, but the Sociedad de Peri-odistas demanded the state government bring back the bodyguards. "The pressure mounted by the Sociedad and other organizations forced them to reinstate the protection," investigative reporter Pedro Enrique Armendares said. The Sociedad also helped bring about government security protection for another threatened journalist, Homero Aridjis, a poet and columnist in Mexico City who received death threats after he attended the November 1997 dinner and denounced the lack of press freedom.

But the professional association has failed to foster better investiga-tions of crimes against journalists. More than two years after the assas-sination attempt against Blancornelas, prosecutors still had brought no charges. "The government doesn't feel obligated to protect journalists that much," freelance reporter Miguel Cervantes Sahagún said. And Blancornelas, as he recovered from his gunshot wounds, conceded that the professional association was having trouble becoming effective: "It will take a long time."

Journalists' associations in other countries have had varied results. The Hong Kong Journalists Association is an important, influential pressure group that has been quick to highlight threats to press freedom since China resumed control of the former British colony. In Argentina, pressure by a national journalists' association, together with protests by Argentine journalists unions and the CPJ, helped bring about the con-victions and life sentences of eight people, including three former po-lice officers, for the Mafia-style assassination of investigative reporter-photographer José Luis Cabezas. But in many other parts of the world,

journalists lack strength and solidarity as a group, partly because journalists tend to be individualistic and competitive with one another.
When an Algerian radio correspondent was abducted by government
security forces in 1995 and disappeared, "the Algerian Journalists Association did not protest," editor Salima Ghezali complained, noting
that her colleagues were "lacking . . . a sense of professional solidarity."

In addition to encouraging local solidarity by journalists, the CPJ
also tries to exert economic and diplomatic pressure on repressive
regimes. After documenting at least twenty-seven murders of journalists in a civil war in the former Soviet republic of Tajikistan in the
early 1990s, the CPJ issued a report that helped lead to diplomatic action. The Organization for Security and Cooperation in Europe referred to the CPJ report when it cited human rights violations as a
reason for withholding further economic aid to the Tajik regime. In
October 1997 in Buenos Aires, President Clinton complained to Argentine leaders about violations of press freedom in that country after
the Committee to Protect Journalists had contacted the White House.
Clinton spokesman Mike McCurry noted at a briefing that Clinton
acted after the CPJ had raised "very serious concerns about the degree of harassment and intimidation" of the Argentine news media.
Argentina later joined all other hemispheric countries (except Cuba)
to create the office of press-freedom ombudsman operating from the
Organization of American States.

The second major international organization devoted to protecting journalists is Reporters Sans Frontières (Reporters Without Borders, or RSF), based in Paris. Like CPJ, it campaigns to free imprisoned journalists. Since its founding in 1989, RSF has campaigned on
behalf of some one hundred journalists. Half of them are now free. It
is not clear how many of those victories can be attributed to RSF's
campaigns, but Nigeria's Anyanwu came to Paris and thanked the
group after her own release.

Early in the year 2000 the advocacy group campaigned energeti-
cally for the release of French photographer Brice Fleutiaux, held
hostage in Chechnya apparently by a pro-rebel militia. As part of the
campaign, RSF's French-language Web site included a "pop-up" page
with pictures of the young photographer and a ticking clock showing
how many days, hours, and seconds he had been held. Fleutiaux was
released on June 12 after eight months in captivity. In his case and that
of many other reporters and photographers in peril, RSF made use of its

good contacts with French and other European newspapers and radio and TV stations to gather signatures on petitions and persuade them to do stories about the cases. Among its strongest supporters is the leading French newspaper, *Le Monde*. In October 1999, RSF coordinated an appeal by some eighty of these news outlets in France and five other European countries to demand the release of imprisoned journalists in Burma, China, Cuba, Ethiopia, Democratic Republic of Congo, Rwanda, Syria, and Vietnam.

In the year 2000, RSF began tracking efforts by repressive countries to restrict access to the Internet. RSF reported:

> At the end of 1999, 20 countries may be considered as "enemies of the Internet," including Burma, Cuba, Tunisia and Vietnam. Their governments control one or more Internet service providers, install filters blocking access to web sites regarded as unsuitable and severely punish users who try to find ways round these obstacles to the free flow of information.

Among other activities, Reporters Sans Frontières awards courageous journalists (1999 winner: Burmese writer Daw San San Nweh); stages charity events, such as an auction of a World Cup soccer ball to raise money for endangered journalists; issues an annual report similar to CPJ's; and produces a monthly "barometer" of press freedom around the world. In its barometer for February 2000, for example, RSF concluded that ninety-five countries had "correct" conditions for the press, sixty-five had "difficult" conditions, and twenty-eight had "very difficult" conditions. The barometer has been published in some newspapers, such as the *Independent* of London. For a while, RSF's Web site also had a section called Dazibao, which published the reportage of journalists banned in their own countries, including Cuba.

RSF has offices in Washington, London, Istanbul, Bangkok, and Abidjan, and it has affiliate branches in Belgium, Germany, Italy, Spain, Sweden, and Switzerland. With its ties to human rights organizations on the European Continent, it is able to mobilize European public opinion, especially in French-speaking France, Belgium, and parts of Switzerland. But it has some weaknesses. Its Web site is badly organized. Not all the items that are on the French-language part of the Web site are translated into English, and those that are translated are sometimes garbled. Because English has become the international language of the Internet, not having a full English-language service limits RSF's ability to influence world public opinion.

Another press-freedom advocacy group, and one that is able to influence public opinion, is known as IFEX, short for International Freedom of Expression Exchange. Created in 1991 with seed money from the Ford Foundation and UNESCO and based in Toronto under the auspices of the Canadian Committee to Protect Journalists, IFEX gathers reports of urgent cases of attacks on journalists and quickly makes them available worldwide on its Web site (www.ifex.org). The reports come in from its fifty member organizations around the world, groups such as the Alliance of Independent Journalists in Indonesia and the Glasnost Defense Foundation in Russia. Some of the groups keep their identities secret, to avoid recrimination in their own countries. That was true of the group of Nigerian journalists who alerted IFEX to reports of beatings, jailings, and murders of their members during the Abacha terror.

For anyone interested in knowing the latest news about attacks on journalists, there is no better source than IFEX's Web site. For example, on February 17, 2000, its list of alerts, with links to fuller accounts, included these summaries:

2000-02-16 COLOMBIA
Journalist remains in captivity
2000-02-16 EGYPT
Human Rights Watch protests Egyptian rights defender's possible imprisonment
2000-02-16 KENYA
Journalist charged, imprisoned
2000-02-16 CHINA
Poet remains imprisoned
2000-02-16 DEMOCRATIC REPUBLIC OF CONGO
Journalist Freddy Loseke expresses fear for his life from his military base prison cell
2000-02-15 FEDERAL REPUBLIC OF YUGOSLAVIA (SERBIA)
ANEM weekly report on media repression
2000-02-15 FEDERAL REPUBLIC OF YUGOSLAVIA (SERBIA)
State media denounces journalist Aleksandar Tijanic
2000-02-15 PAKISTAN
CPJ special report on challenges faced by the press

2000-02-15 COLOMBIA
Journalist killed
2000-02-15 SOMALIA
Journalist killed

IFEX also maintains an excellent archive service detailing every known attack on journalists going back to 1995. As of February 2000, more than six thousand such alerts had been posted in just over five years. The countries most often cited in the alerts were Peru, Nigeria, Turkey, and Yugoslavia. The most common violations of press freedom specified in the IFEX alerts over that period were detention (739 cases), legal action (699 cases), and harassment (440 cases). The total number of journalists killed over that period was 238.

London is the headquarters of an international press freedom advocacy group called Article 19, which takes its name from one part of the Universal Declaration of Human Rights, signed by most nations including China. Article 19 of the declaration states: *Everyone has the right to freedom of opinion and expression; this right includes freedom to hold opinions without interference and to seek, receive and impart information and ideas through any media and regardless of frontiers.* Holding signatories to those words, the group Article 19 publishes articles on threats to freedom in many countries. It led a sustained ten-year international campaign to oppose the Muslim fundamentalist Iranian government's death threat against novelist Salman Rushdie. Eventually a more moderate Iranian regime lifted that threat. Article 19 contributes to public awareness of censorship issues, but its Web site is badly organized and incomplete.

A better organized group is Digital Freedom Network (DFN). From its headquarters in Newark, New Jersey, it uses the Internet to post information from several human rights organizations, including those that specialize in press freedom issues such as Article 19, China News Digest International, CPJ, CubaNet, Index on Censorship, International PEN, and RSF. It has valuable links to the Web sites of opposition newspapers or independent journalists' associations in such countries as Malaysia.

Freedom Forum, based in Arlington, Virginia, is a press-freedom advocacy group established in 1991. It is the successor to a charitable foundation set up by the former chairman of the Gannett Company, whose publishing empire includes *USA Today.* With a billon-dollar endowment, the Freedom Forum sponsors conferences and publishes studies on a wide range of issues, including attacks on journalists worldwide. It has a useful, well-organized Web site (www.freedomforum.org). In Arlington it operates the Newseum, an interactive museum about the news business. Attached to the Newseum is an outdoor memorial to more than thirteen hundred journalists who have been killed while reporting the news. Their names are read aloud by prominent media figures at a solemn sunrise ceremony each year on World Press Freedom Day, May 3.

The United Nations is another important source of support for embattled reporters. It has stood by them in recent years despite complaints from countries such as China. In 1997, on World Press Freedom Day, the United Nations Educational, Scientific and Cultural Organization (UNESCO) instituted an annual award to honor those "who have dedicated their lives to the free, plural and independent exercise of journalism." The first winner of the $25,000 UNESCO/Guillermo Cano World Press Freedom Prize was Gao Yu, who was in a Chinese prison at the time her selection was announced. UNESCO said: "She has paid, and is still paying, with her own freedom for her commitment to media independence."

Beijing denounced the award as "illegal," demanded it be withdrawn, accused UNESCO of "rudely interfering" in China's internal affairs, and threatened to boycott UNESCO activities. But UNESCO's director general Federico Mayor of Spain rejected the Chinese demands and pointedly went to the award ceremony in Bilbao. When Secretary-General Kofi Annan visited Beijing shortly afterward, he, too, made it clear the United Nations was not backing down. While diplomatically avoiding direct comment on China's protest over the prize, Annan said in a statement that human rights, including free speech, remained "an essential element of the world today," and that there was "an incredible desire for democracy from people everywhere." As it turned out, despite its threats China did not boycott UNESCO. Two years later it released Gao Yu, probably to improve the atmosphere before a visit by the U.S. secretary of state.

The UNESCO prize helped focus world public opinion on Gao Yu's plight and may have increased the pressure on Beijing to release her. Whether such pressure could help bring about more fundamental change in the short run is another question. "It is doubtful," Mickey Spiegel of Human Rights Watch said, "whether these prize presentations will help improve China's human rights situation right now, but in the long run the cumulative effect of exposing abuses is bound to help bring changes."

The United Nations has taken other steps to act as an advocate of press freedom. Its headquarters in New York provides facilities for press conferences by the Committee to Protect Journalists. And it was under the auspices of the United Nations and UNESCO that a conference in 1991 in Windhoek, Namibia, issued a major declaration for an independent and pluralistic African press. Each year on May 3, the anniversary of the Windhoek Declaration, the United Nations and other international organizations and press-freedom advocacy groups celebrate World Press Freedom Day, which provides an opportunity for press conferences, press releases, news features, editorials, and columns on the plight of imperiled journalists—an opportunity for publicity and pressure on governments.

These advocacy groups, with their ability to call international attention to attacks on journalists, provide an important function, especially in the newly opened societies that are in transition toward democracy. A study based on research at Oxford University's Center for Socio-Legal Studies concluded:

> It may never be known what elements exactly contribute most—or even essentially—to the creation of a culture of democratic values. Perhaps it is the existence of a vibrant non-governmental sector that is vital, organizations that are sensitive, at any moment, to infringements of journalistic rights. Institutions like the Glasnost Defence Foundation or the Committee to Protect Journalists and Reporters Sans Frontières were, at critical times in transition societies, hawk-like, to identify possible back-sliding and bring international notice to it.

Putting pressure on governments does not always work, but the advocacy groups say it's worth trying. As the CPJ's Ann Cooper put it: "You need to keep pushing because conditions change: the Soviet Union collapsed, [Nigerian dictator] Abacha died." In addition to being ready to exploit those openings, the press-freedom advocacy groups provide the support and encouragement that help some embattled journalists go on. When Gao Yu received the UNESCO prize while in a Chinese prison, she referred to that international support: "This is the chief source of strength and encouragement that I receive behind bars."

Conclusion

Tomorrow's News: The Outlook

BOLSTERED BY ADVOCACY groups and the empowering medium of the Internet, independent journalists at the beginning of the twenty-first century have many weapons in their arsenal as they confront the dictators, politicians, police, armies, druglords, corporations, and other powerful enemies arrayed against them. But their enemies are also well equipped for the struggle. Which side is winning?

In the closing days of the old century and the opening days of the new one, there were conflicting signals. In Latin America, a Uruguayan radio commentator was shot dead by a politician, but the Mafia-linked killers of an Argentine news photographer were finally brought to justice. In Hong Kong, police raided a newspaper office for the first time in recent memory, but legislators rejected a proposal for a government-linked body to investigate complaints against the press. In Russia, the Kremlin kept most reporters from covering the rebel side in the second Chechen war, but a military court threw out treason charges against a Russian journalist who revealed nuclear waste dumping by the navy.

With such a mixed picture, it would be as false to say that independent journalists are bound to win every battle as it would be to say that censors will always prevail. The only safe prediction is that this conflict will go on, and that each side will enjoy victories from time to time. But what of the larger trend? When adding up the victories for each side, is there any pattern that emerges, any indication that one side or the other is gaining the overall advantage? In my view the overall trend shows that conditions are becoming increasingly favorable for independent journalists. These conditions include political change, the rise of the Internet, expanding trade, Western influence, the bonding effect between journalists and the general public, and the persistence of universal human characteristics, including the hungering for knowledge and truth. This concluding chapter expands on all these themes and ends by focusing on Hong Kong as a test case for the future.

POLITICAL CHANGE

While repression remains the dominant condition in a number of countries—including China, the most populous one of all—there are signs that more and more uncensored news is being distributed to more and more people in the world. According to the authors of *The Enabling Environment for a Free and Independent Media*: "Throughout the world, there is a vast remapping of media laws and policies—a change attributable in part to rapid-fire geopolitical changes including the vast move towards democratization."

During the final decade of the twentieth century, hundreds of millions of people saw political change that resulted in the proliferation of newspapers not subject to substantial government control—people in the countries of the former Soviet Union, its former satellites, and Nigeria and Indonesia. These newly free countries of the former Soviet empire plus Nigeria and Indonesia have a combined total population of more than 600 million. To that number add another 100 million in Mexico, where rapid social and political change is resulting in a more open society.

There are many other countries where conditions are favorable for independent journalists. India, the country expected to overtake China at mid-century as the world's most populous nation, with more than a billion people, is a multiparty democracy with a largely free press. It has been so ever since the independent nation's creation in 1947 as part of the breakup of the British Empire. By the start of the twenty-first century, most countries of Latin America were democracies, at least in theory—a change from the military juntas of the past—and Africa, a continent of violent repression and dictatorships, had undergone change as well, with South Africa freed of apartheid and a few countries holding multiparty elections. For example, in Senegal in March 2000 the opposition won a presidential election for the first time in forty years, thanks partly to exposés of corruption revealed by a more aggressive press corps. As the AP put it, "a new breed of young journalists may have played a key role in ensuring the democratic transfer of power in Senegal." Even Iran, for twenty years a repressive Islamic fundamentalist theocracy, was showing some signs of liberalizing and permitting a limited diversity of views, including opposition newspapers.

THE INTERNET

In addition to the hundreds of millions of people living in countries that now have uncensored newspapers because of political change, tens of millions of others have access to uncensored news because of the Internet. By the end of the year 2000, according to one industry estimate, 320 million people were expected to be online throughout the world, and millions more were likely to join them in subsequent years. While many of these Internet users already live in open societies, such as those of the industrialized world, with a largely free press, a growing number of others live in countries such as Jordan or Belarus, where print and broadcast media are subject to government control. In those authoritarian countries, the rise of the Internet means the creation of a new, online press beyond the reach of government censors. That fact greatly improves the chances for independent journalists to overcome efforts to silence them, and it emboldens them to make optimistic predictions. As the director of the AMIN Web site in Jerusalem told me: "Once we are more popular and more local Palestinians access us, we will definitely break many of the taboos in the local press."

As we saw in chapter 16, "Cat and Computer Mouse: Using the Internet," the Internet is also a powerful defensive tool for journalists under attack. Ying Chan's use of the Internet mobilized international pressure on Taiwanese officials. Support poured in as more and more sympathizers saw her Web site. "As a wired woman," she said, "I never felt alone. . . . A global coalition was taking shape through the Net." In the end, helped by the Internet, she and her co-defendants won their criminal libel lawsuit, perhaps providing an example for other embattled journalists in the future.

WORLD TRADE

In addition to the growing power of the Internet to create more favorable conditions for independent journalists, there is another powerful factor: world trade. The twenty-first century has begun during a period of expanding global commerce. UN figures show that total world trade in 1999 was $10.9 trillion, up from $10.5 trillion in 1996. In China alone, trade with other countries grew by 10.6 percent in the first ten months of 1999, for a total of $286.6 billion. As their economies become more and more dependent on global trade, many countries become more and more dependent on the free and rapid flow of information needed for investment decisions and government policy choices, and this increases the need for an uncensored press.

In addition, for many countries without a tradition of a free press, increased trade with Japan and the West increases contact with countries that do have such a tradition, making it more likely that citizens will learn about the utility and desirability of uncensored news and will want it for their own country. As China increases its trade with the United States and other Western countries, its citizens become more aware of the values of these other countries, admired for their affluence much as ordinary Russians admired America during the Soviet period even while their rulers were denouncing the capitalist system. As trade with China grows, more Western journalists establish bureaus in Beijing and attend press conferences where they ask government officials the kind of freewheeling, adversarial questions that are alien to China's own state-controlled journalists. One of the most dramatic examples of this was the extraordinary press conference by U.S. and Chinese leaders during President Clinton's 1998 visit, televised live and uncensored in China. It is impossible to say how long it takes for such democratic influences to help bring about political change in a country without a democratic tradition, but the Soviet example shows that it does happen.

Of course, some analysts say it's still possible to have a vibrant, successful free-enterprise system without a truly free press, and they cite a number of Asian countries, such as Singapore, as examples. It is true that some so-called tiger economies did do well for a while during the boom years of the 1990s without the benefit of a truly free multiparty political system and without a truly free flow of information. But the sharp reverses of fortunes in once high-flying countries such as Indonesia in late 1997 and early 1998 raised questions as to whether the lack of a free press played a role in their demise, depriving them of the ability to see trouble coming in the form of excessively risky investments.

For example, some commentators say that Indonesia might not have experienced an 85 percent decline in the value of its currency if its press had been freer to expose nepotism and other forms of corruption in the ruling Suharto family, corruption that resulted in ill-advised economic projects. *New York Times* columnist William Safire said after the Asian meltdown that these economies were paying the price of basing themselves on the Singapore model that combined freewheeling capitalism with repression of political freedom. Safire said Western corporate executives mistakenly invested in these countries because "the greasing of government palms—without the scrutiny of a free press or the restraint of independent judiciaries—was advertised as a newly stable form of capitalism."

Democracies have a number of built-in safeguards against instability, including a free press. It could be argued that open societies are healthier than closed ones because they foster an unimpeded flow of information and views. They thus generally have a better chance of making sure that disgruntled elements of society get the opportunity to let off steam, to see that their views are taken into account before discontent erupts into unrest; and they have a better chance of anticipating and solving potentially disastrous economic and social problems before it is too late. (That does not guarantee success, of course. South Korea, one of the countries with severe economic problems in the late 1990s, had been evolving into a more open, democratic society at the time of its economic downturn. But the point remains that a country with a censored press has less chance of correcting ill-advised economic policies and investments before it is too late.)

As more and more countries, including newly emerging democracies, look to economic growth to benefit their societies and legitimize their political systems, their leaders become concerned about anything that could harm trade relations with other countries, especially the industrialized, largely democratic countries of Japan and the West. These trade partners have value systems that include a belief in the need for an uncensored press, and any time public opinion in those countries becomes aware of repression of press freedom in another country, it creates an unfavorable impression of that other country—which could harm trade. China has released imprisoned journalists such as Gao Yu shortly before important trade talks with the West. Turkey's occasional relaxing of press controls has coincided with efforts to gain more favorable trade relations with the European community. As Walter Cronkite put it, "Nearly all the countries are interested in their international public relations, particularly in these days of reaching out for investment. They realize that their image is important for their economy."

WESTERN INFLUENCE

All of these economic factors of global trade work to the advantage of independent journalists. In addition, the influence of the United States, the world's only superpower, cannot be underestimated as yet another positive condition for the existence of uncensored news. The United States has, arguably, the freest press in the world. This provides a powerful influence on other countries. Journalists in a number of newly opening societies, including Mexico, emulate the American model. Publisher J. Jesús Blancornelas told me that he was influenced by the American weekly the *Nation*.

A similar influence on emerging nations comes from Great Britain, whose former empire included Nigeria and Hong Kong, places that now have deeply rooted traditions of unfettered journalism. Such British news organizations as Reuters train journalists from Eastern Europe and other newly opening societies, and that training inculcates the value of independent news gathering and distribution. Britain is influential in other ways as well. When I was a foreign correspondent for the AP, *Newsweek*, and CNN, I noticed that in hot spots such as Beirut, most of the journalists, including local reporters, dutifully tuned in to the BBC World Service on their shortwave radios at the top of each hour. They looked to the BBC as a model of largely uncensored news (except, at times, news from Northern Ireland that did not give the Irish Republican Army side of controversies). Other former imperial powers such as France and the Netherlands have left a similar legacy of press independence.

BONDING EFFECT

The influence of the United States, Britain, and other countries with a free press brings with it such journalistic values as an adversarial attitude toward anyone in power (the watchdog role) and an implied populist bonding with ordinary people who constitute the electorate that is being served by having uncensored news. That bonding effect is another positive condition for the survival of an independent press. It was shown dramatically in Argentina, a nation that has taken important steps toward democracy after being one of the hemisphere's least democratic countries. In an opinion poll, Argentines supported the press more than they supported any other institution, including the Catholic Church and the government. And immediately after Argentine investigative reporter–photographer José Luis Cabezas was burned to death in a car in 1997, his murder was protested throughout the nation. "It wasn't just journalists protesting," former CPJ executive director Bill Orme said. "Firemen held a five-minute work stoppage with sirens going on in the fire stations protesting the lack of progress in the investigation. People see independent journalism as defending them, standing up against the state, [as being] their voice, and it seems to be this profound connection which happens almost by a natural process in some societies when it's allowed to happen."

Nigerian journalist Kunle Ajibade was sentenced to life imprisonment (commuted to fifteen years) by the Abacha dictatorship but freed after Abacha's death in 1998. After his release from prison, Ajibade also spoke of the bonding effect between reporters and the people of their countries. "My message to my colleagues is that truth will always prevail," he said. "Journalists are in constant touch with the aspiration of the people. And the people will always win." That may be an exaggeration, but it shows that the connection between journalists and people, in some countries, is a powerful positive condition favoring uncensored news.

HUMAN NATURE

Closely linked to the bonding effect is another positive condition that prevails in many countries: the fact that certain universal attributes of human nature militate in favor of a free press. One of those universal attributes is an individual's natural curiosity about events, which creates a thirst for news. Since news involves information that is new and interesting, suppressing it goes against human nature. Efforts by dictatorships to prevent the public from hearing something unfavorable about them have had limited success throughout history because of the persistence of rumor, underground uncensored publications such as the *samizdat* (self-publishing) phenomenon in the Soviet Union, and contacts with independent sources of news outside the country, often through travelers and businesspeople.

Another universal attribute is the natural human tendency to despise excessive authority and the abuse of power. History is filled with examples of uprisings against tyranny, as well as examples of individuals who resisted oppression at great personal risk. Among those individuals have been independent journalists. In China, despite a repressive regime that vigorously prosecutes dissidents, there are individuals who refuse to be intimidated and who try to give their fellow citizens uncensored reports on economic and social problems. Some of them are journalists who use the Internet to send news from China to émigré groups in the United States. The émigré groups then relay the news to the U.S. government's Radio Free Asia, which in turn relays the reports back into China. As one Chinese émigré put it: "If you talk of the human spirit existing even under extreme conditions, these people show it."

Perhaps equally important as a human factor is the defiant attitude of independent journalists toward the powerful figures who try to censor them. Their defiance points up a significant correlation between freedom and risk. In Russia's first Chechen war (1994–1997), independent journalists had more freedom than in the second round of fighting, and consequently more were killed (or disappeared, presumed dead). In the second Chechen war, which began in 1999, Russia kept the press on a tighter leash, farther away from the battles, and with less access to the rebel side. While that may have reduced the risk to journalists of death, injury, or abduction, it also reduced the likelihood that the full truth of the civilian casualties would be told to the Russian and world public.

More freedom, more risk: that is the pattern in the battleground countries. The pattern does not necessarily apply elsewhere. For differing reasons, there is little risk at both ends of the freedom spectrum. In the most repressive nations, such as North Korea, few "journalists" (actually government employees putting out propaganda) are ever killed or imprisoned for their work, at least not in peacetime. And at the other end of the spectrum, in the freest nations, such as the United States, once again few journalists are ever killed or imprisoned for their work. The greatest number of attacks is concentrated in the countries in the middle, the battleground countries where there is more freedom than in the repressive nations and more risk than in the freest nations. The reason for this is that the limits of journalistic independence have not yet been settled in these countries. Writing in *Media Studies Journal*, William Orme noted that homicide is the leading cause of job-related deaths for journalists and "such killings take place disproportionately in countries or communities where an independent press is just beginning to take root." In newly opened societies, such as Russia, says the CPJ's Ann Cooper, "it is far more dangerous for journalists today than when the state controlled everything. The control was so great that you didn't take a risk. Now journalists try to sort out the rules and limits."

So the fact that twenty-four journalists were killed in 2000 and eighty-one were in prisons at the end of that year does not necessarily mean that the prospects for press freedom are dim. On the contrary, it means that, in many cases, journalists are continuing to push the envelope of what is permitted. They are refusing to back down under pressure. Their push for greater freedom despite the risks in these battleground countries is an encouragement to those who want to see an expansion of uncensored news coverage around the world.

ON THE OTHER HAND . . .

Weighed against all of these favorable conditions—the Internet, world trade, Western influence, the bonding effect, and human nature—are the conditions that militate *against* the ability of journalists to provide uncensored news. They include the survival of some longtime dictatorships, such as those of Saudi Arabia and North Korea; endless rounds of warfare, such as the fighting in Sierra Leone; ethnic strife; Islamic fundamentalist regimes, such as that of the Taliban in Afghanistan, that crush dissent; criminal organizations that grow stronger with illicit profits and the impunity that this buys; state control of broadcasting in many parts of the world; difficulties in obtaining Internet access in some countries; and, perhaps most pernicious of all, self-censorship by the journalists themselves.

In addition, even in the newly opened societies such as Russia and Mexico, where independent journalists have pushed the envelope of what can be reported, the potential for a free press so far has not been fully realized, partly because of official corruption and the failure to enforce a liberal democratic system of law and order.

In Russia, the second Chechen war compounded the problem as former KGB official Vladimir Putin, the hand-picked successor to Yeltsin, made clear his disdain for independent journalists such as Andrei Babitsky, a Russian national who worked for the U.S. government's Radio Liberty. Babitsky reported news from the Chechen rebel side. Under Putin, rather than working to assure Babitsky's ability to report fairly, Russian military forces held Babitsky captive, allegedly beat him, then turned him over to unidentified Chechens under mysterious circumstances. (Moscow said Babitsky was exchanged for Russian soldiers held by Chechen rebels, but Babitsky said Russian troops handed him over not to rebels but to pro-Russian Chechens.) The Kremlin accused Babitsky of conspiring with enemy "terrorists." As Putin put it, "What Babitsky did is much more dangerous than firing a machine gun." For his part, Babitsky said: "The situation with the press, with free speech, is very bad, and it is growing worse."

There were other ominous signs. Soon after Putin was sworn in as Russia's president, armed federal agents in black masks raided the headquarters of Media-MOST, the country's largest private media company, whose flagship television network was NTV, the network that had angered the Kremlin because it broadcast Yelena Masyuk's coverage of the first Chechen war from the rebel side. The media group had continued to take a critical view of the war in Chechnya and of Putin's policies. Later, police arrested the head of the media company and held him in prison for three nights. Politicians and journalists feared that these actions would presage a crackdown on press freedom, despite Putin's assurances that he would support journalistic independence. Other commentators said that even if Putin did not take further steps against journalists, press freedom was threatened by the concentration of media ownership in the hands of a few powerful plutocrats. Writing in *Foreign Affairs* in the spring of 2000, Lee Wolosky concluded that Russia "lacks a free press—not because of government censorship but because of oligarch control of the most meaningful media outlets."

Still, for all these setbacks and obstacles, independent journalists continue to make important gains.

Facing massive international protests, and under pressure from the West at a time that Moscow continued to need Western aid, Russian authorities finally provided information about Babitsky's whereabouts, and after he was freed, they backed off from threats to prosecute him for treason, although he was still under investigation for lesser charges. In

Peru (population 27 million), still a democracy despite efforts by President Alberto Fujimori to suppress dissent and rig elections, the regime backed away from threats to crack down on an independent daily that revealed campaign-law violations. In Mexico, despite the lack of prosecution of those who tried to assassinate publisher J. Jesús Blancornelas, his breezy tabloid *Zeta* went on defiantly exposing drug corruption. Surrounded by bodyguards, Blancornelas refused to give up the fight, saying: "I thought 'if I retire now, it will be as a coward.' What's more, the mafia will use me as an example for other journalists. They'll say what happened to him can happen to you."

While the statistical evidence of attacks on journalists is only partially reliable, due to incomplete data and differences among monitoring groups as to what constitutes an attack that is provoked solely by journalistic activity, there is no question that the most recent indicators show an improvement in the conditions for journalists. According to the CPJ, back in 1994 a record number of journalists were killed: seventy-two. In following years the death toll steadily declined to a low of twenty-four in 1998, rising the next year to thirty-four but then falling again to twenty-four in 2000. The decline in the number killed is not the only encouraging trend. As the CPJ notes: "By another important measure, the number of journalists in prison, press freedom could be seen as improving." At the end of 1996, the CPJ reported a record number of publishers, editors, reporters, and other journalists behind bars: a total of 185. But by 2000 that number had fallen to less than half: eighty-one. That is the lowest number imprisoned in recent years.

While the attacks are disturbing, the number of them is declining, and when they do occur, they often reflect the fact that more and more journalists in these developing countries are out there doing their jobs. The decline in attacks and the evidence that independent journalists are continuing to test the limits of press freedom are encouraging developments that support the thesis of this book: conditions for journalists in the battleground countries are generally improving, although they still have a long way to go.

HONG KONG

At the start of the twenty-first century, one of the biggest test cases for independent journalism in the future is Hong Kong. Former CPJ executive director Bill Orme told me: "Hong Kong is the most important press freedom story of the next five to ten years in the world because whatever happens there, positive or negative, is going to be determinant for all of China and therefore will have enormous impact on the entire world." Despite many predictions that Beijing would crack down on press freedom in Hong Kong after the handover by Britain in 1997, by the start of the twenty-first century that had not happened. There were many examples of surprisingly uncensored news reports by media in the former British colony.

For example, while official state media in Beijing suppressed most information about the Falun Gong, privately held media in Hong Kong openly and freely reported news about the outlawed exercise-and-meditation cult, including news of a demonstration by nine hundred cult members in December 1999. Also, Hong Kong newspapers regularly printed calls for Beijing to release imprisoned political dissidents and independent journalists. In addition, the city's TV news reports included coverage of rallies calling for the resignations of Chinese leaders.

One of the most dramatic examples of uncensored Hong Kong news coverage concerned the March 18, 2000, presidential elections in Taiwan, where voters ignored Beijing's threats and chose a pro-independence candidate. Chinese government-controlled media on the mainland were slow to give more than cursory coverage, but uncensored TV news reports about the election were available to all viewers in Hong Kong and even many viewers on the mainland. (Chinese in the southern provinces near Hong Kong easily get local Hong Kong television. Senior government and military officials in Beijing and elsewhere have access to satellite TV channels in their offices. And even some urban Chinese in upscale housing complexes can see programming from Hong Kong.) In addition to television news from Hong Kong, there is, of course, the enormous amount of information online from Hong Kong newspapers' Web sites, available to an estimated 10 million Internet users in China. And the city's newspapers continue to be outspoken. Even the satirical comic strip *The World of Lily Wong* made a comeback in Hong Kong, this time in a new tabloid in June 2000.

Why did Beijing tolerate such freedom of the press in Hong Kong while suppressing journalists in the rest of China? The answer, many analysts said, was money. "Hong Kong is a money cow for the Chinese leadership, many of whose children profit from Red chip [Communist enterprise] involvement in Hong Kong free enterprise," Alan Knight of Hong Kong University and Queensland University told me. "The immediate imposition of mainland restrictions on Hong Kong would be unacceptable to the business community."

Did that mean Hong Kong would someday end up being the democratic tail wagging the authoritarian dog, the small bastion of press freedom causing the giant of mainland China to end censorship? Experts were divided. Writing in the CPJ publication *Dangerous Assignments*, A. Lin Neumann predicted in 1997 that if Hong Kong were allowed to continue on its free path, "it may open the way toward greater press freedom for all of China." But Francis Moriarty, a political reporter for Radio Television Hong Kong, disagreed: "Hong Kong's history is too different for China to emulate. . . . HK [Hong Kong] simply doesn't have that kind of mass." Alan Knight was moderately pessimistic:

> Hong Kong has been tolerated but there have been no moves to allow its diversity of views across the border. I think Beijing might prefer a Singapore model where the press is privately owned and free to profit from the growing market system. Singapore meanwhile retains tight control of the press through licensing.

Taking a cautious position in the middle, CNN's Hong Kong bureau chief Mike Chinoy told me he believed that China "will probably stumble towards a somewhat more open and benign form of authoritarianism."

If China did someday take that stumbling step, the impact on journalism worldwide could be dramatic, depending on how much easing of censorship took place. If it were a great deal of easing, that could add more than 1 billion people to the plus column for countries with independent journalists—a plus column that already includes the 1 billion in India and the hundreds of millions of others in the free or partly free countries of the West, Japan, Russia, Mexico, Nigeria, and Indonesia. It would not necessarily mean an end to all attacks and pressures on journalists but could greatly improve their working conditions.

Even if China remained a totalitarian dictatorship with rigid censorship, that fact alone would not be enough to cause any major rollback of the press freedoms that already exist elsewhere. But another factor that could cause such a rollback would be any significant increase in the number of wars in the world, since censorship and other acts of suppression of independent reporting are tolerated more readily in wartime, even by democratic societies. There is no way of knowing whether there will be any major increase in the number of armed clashes in the world, and it would be naive to assume that the world will somehow become a more peaceful place anytime soon, especially with the continued tensions among ethnic groups. But armed conflict aside, the factors favorable for press freedom remain strong at the outset of the twenty-first century, factors that include Western influence, the spread of democracy, the rise of the Internet, and expanding global trade.

While the stories in this book are instructive, it is difficult to project in any great detail from the experiences of independent journalists what will be the future of freedom of the press in the world in the twenty-first century. Still, certain overall impressions provide clues. There is no question that the trend is toward more openness. The cold war is over. Literacy and the Internet are expanding. As the twenty-first century began, brutal dictatorships in Nigeria and Indonesia had given way to more democratic regimes. Despite serious setbacks, Mexico and Russia were holding onto their new status as more open societies. Even the Islamic fundamentalist republic of Iran was moving toward a moderate liberalization. And the final chapter had not yet been written on China.

In all of these countries, the behavior of independent journalists faced with repression tells us a great deal about human character. Their experience shows that freedom of the press is an ideal whose viability is tested every day in the hard reality of economic pressures, legal threats, beatings, arrests, imprisonment, and sometimes even death. While it is always dangerous to make predictions, I see some reasons for hope, based partly on a common thread running through the stories of the independent journalists in this book. Whether it's Gao Yu in China, Ying Chan in Taiwan, Veronica Guerin in Ireland, Jesús Blancornelas in Mexico, Yelena Masyuk in Russia, Daoud Kuttab in Palestine, or Femi Ojudu in Nigeria, they all have one thing in common: their defiance of censorship. That universal human trait of refusing to be beaten down into silence is one of the main reasons for hope that independent journalists with their words of fire may yet prevail.

Notes

The opening quotation is from the personal statement of appeal by Chinese journalist Gao Yu to the Beijing Higher People's Court on December 23, 1994. From *China: "Leaking State Secrets": The Case of Gao Yu* (New York: Human Rights Watch/Asia and Human Rights in China Publications, July 1995), vol. 7, no. 8.

NOTES TO THE INTRODUCTION

The initial references to journalists are from publications of the Committee to Protect Journalists (CPJ); the author's interview with Cable News Network (CNN) correspondent Peter Arnett on October 7, 1997; Jon Lee Anderson, "He Got the Story, Then the Story Got Him," *New York Times Sunday Magazine*, December 21, 1997; *Attacks on the Press in 1997* (New York: Committee to Protect Journalists, March 1998); author's interview with Freedom Neruda in New York on October 24, 1997; author's interviews with Ying Chan in Taipei, Taiwan, on April 12, 1997, and in New York City on October 23–24, 1997.

The statistics and overview are from *Attacks on the Press in 1999* (New York: Committee to Protect Journalists, March 2000); William A. Orme Jr., "When the Shield Fails: Veronica Guerin 1959–1996," *Dangerous Assignments*, no. 51 (New York: Committee to Protect Journalists, Summer 1996); Leonard R. Sussman and Kristen Guida, "Death Toll Down, Press Freedom Up," *Editor and Publisher* (January 24, 1998); "Democracy Momentum Sustained as 'Freedom's Century' Ends" (New York: Freedom House, December 21, 1999), at www.freedomhouse.org/news/pr122199.html; *Press Freedom Survey 2000* (New York: Freedom House, May 2000), at www.freedomhouse.org/pfs2000/; "1999 World Population Data Sheet," on Web site of Population Reference Bureau, www.prb.org; Kavita Menon, "Pakistan: The Press for Change," in *Attacks on the Press in 1999* (New York: Committee to Protect Journalists, March 2000).

The Orme quote about political change is from author's interview with William A. Orme Jr. in New York on October 24, 1997.

The reference to the Clinton-Menem meeting is from John F. Harris, "Argentine Nod toward Pollution Plan Expected," *New York Times*, October 18,

225

1997, and transcript of White House press conference from Federal News Service, October 16, 1997.
The study of press and emerging democracies, based on the Oxford research, is from Monroe E. Price and Peter Krug, *The Enabling Environment for a Free and Independent Media: Report for Center for Democracy and Governance* (Washington, D.C.: USAID, 2000).
The quote at the end is from the preface by Jorge C. Castañeda in *Unpublished Crimes against Journalists* (Miami: Inter American Press Association, 1997).

NOTES TO CHAPTER 1

Details of the attack are from author's interview with J. Jesús Blancornelas at his home in Tijuana, Mexico, March 13, 1998; various news reports, including the November 28, 1997, special edition of his newspaper, *Zeta* (Tijuana, Mexico); John Ross, "Mexico's Deadly News," *Nation*, December 22, 1997; Joel Simon, "Breaking Away: Mexico's Press Challenges the Status Quo," in *Attacks on the Press in 1997* (New York: Comittee to Protect Journalists, March 1998).
Details of the drug traffickers are from Molly Moore, "Mexican Priest Lauds Druglord's Charity," *Washington Post*, September 23, 1997; *Zeta*, October 24, 1997; *Zeta*, November 21, 1997.
The death of Héctor Félix Miranda is from author's interview with Mexican journalist Miguel Cervantes Sahagún, former reporter for ABC and *Zeta*, in Tijuana, March 13, 1998; *Unpunished Crimes against Journalists* (Miami: Inter American Press Association, 1997).
Details on violence in Mexico are from Jon Lee Anderson, "He Got the Story, Then the Story Got Him," *New York Times Sunday Magazine*, December 21, 1997; Sam Dillon, "Gunmen Shoot Tijuana Editor, Bodyguard," *New York Times*, November 28, 1997; *Attacks on the Press in 1997*; William Branigin, "Mexican Writer's Death Laid to Ex-Police Chief; 1984 Killing Underlined Journalists' Plight," *Washington Post*, June 13, 1989; Matthew Rothschild, "Who Killed Manuel Buendía?" *Progressive* 49, April 18, 1985; interview with Miguel Cervantes Sahagún; Julia Preston, "Five Reporters Assaulted in Mexico in Efforts to Intimidate Them," *New York Times*, September 21, 1997; Mary Beth Sheridan, "Mexico Fights Drug War on Its Own Terms, Frustrating US Lawmakers," *Los Angeles Times*, March 26, 1998; author's interview with Francisco Ortiz Franco in Tijuana, March 13, 1998.
The reference to U.S. history is from John Nerone, "Lessons from American History," *Journalists in Peril*, Fall 1996 issue of *Media Studies Journal* 10, 4 (New York: Media Studies Center and The Freedom Forum).
The discussion of weak democratic institutions is by Kavita Menon, "Pakistan: The Press for Change," in *Attacks on the Press in 1999* (New York: Committee to Protect Journalists, March 2000).

The section on social change and journalism in Mexico is from Julia Preston, "Challenger in Mexico Wins; Governing Party Concedes," *New York Times*, July 3, 2000; author's interview with Francisco Ortiz Franco; author's interview with Joel Simon, Latin America program coordinator, Committee to Protect Journalists, September 23, 1997; Jorge Zepada, "Mexico's Journalists Move to Secure Press Freedom," Web site of the CPJ; William A. Orme Jr., "Overview: From Collusion to Confrontation," in *A Culture of Collusion*, ed. William A. Orme Jr. (Miami: North-South Center Press, 1997); Raymundo Riva Palacio, "A Culture of Collusion: The Ties That Bind the Press and the PRI," in *A Culture of Collusion*.

The details about Blancornelas are from interviews with him, Ortiz Franco, Cervantes Sahagún, and former mayor Héctor Osuna Jaime in Tijuana, Mexico, March 13, 1998.

The account of Masyuk's capture is from author's interview with Yelena Masyuk in New York, October 25, 1997; Lee Hockstader, "Journalists Become Chechnya's Latest Victims," *Washington Post*, May 27, 1997; *Attacks on the Press in 1997* (New York: Committee to Protect Journalists, March 1998); speech by journalist Roger Rosenblatt to CPJ awards dinner, New York, October 23, 1997.

Background on Masyuk is from *Attacks on the Press in 1995* (New York: Committee to Protect Journalists, March 1996); Yelena Masyuk testimony to joint U.S. House-Senate Commission on Security and Cooperation in Europe and the International Human Rights Law Group, in transcript of hearing "Russian Media in Light of Upcoming Elections," Washington, D.C., May 14, 1996, at www.house.gov/csce/rusmed.htm; "Statement from the Carter Center on Kidnapping of Russian Journalist," press release, May 14, 1997, Carter Center, Emory University, Atlanta, Ga.

The section on Chechnya is from Ellen Mickiewicz, *Changing Channels: Television and the Struggle for Power in Russia* (New York: Oxford University Press, 1997); *Attacks on the Press in 1999* (New York: Committee to Protect Journalists, March 2000); Lee Hockstader, "Brutal and Futile: This Round of Russia vs. Chechnya Will Be No More Conclusive Than the Last," *Washington Post*, October 3, 1999; *Attacks on the Press in 1996* (New York: Committee to Protect Journalists, March 1997); David W. Chen, "Missing; Last Address: Washington, N.J. Last Seen: Chechnya, July 24," *New York Times*, January 21, 1996.

The discussion of press conditions in Russia is based on David Satter, "Murdering with Impunity in Russia: Authorities Fail to Prosecute the Murders of Seven Journalists," in *Attacks on the Press in 1995*; Neela Banerjee, "Russia: Big Business Takes Over," *Columbia Journalism Review* (November–December 1997);

Catherine A. Fitzpatrick, "Russia's Harsh Press Climate," in *Attacks on the Press in 1996*. (An excerpt of this article appeared in *Moscow Times*, August 12, 1996.)

NOTES TO CHAPTER 3

Information on Ying Chan is based largely on the author's interviews with her in person in Taipei, Taiwan, in April 1997; in New York City in October 1997 with her and her colleague Shieh Chung-liang; and in subsequent interviews by telephone and E-mail. Other background information comes from published accounts, including reports by the Committee to Protect Journalists; Shieh Chung-liang and Ying Chan, "Taiwan Involved in America's Election—A Disputed Case of Political Contribution," *Yazhou Zhoukan*, October 25, 1996; Ying Chan, "Fighting Libel Suit with the Internet," *Nieman Reports* (Fall 1997); Amy Singer, "Close the Door and Beat the Dog," *American Lawyer* (July–August 1997).

The section on Hong Kong is from William A. Orme Jr., "The Tail of the Dragon," CPJ Hong Kong Report, January 1998, on Web site www.cpj.org; Notebook section, *Time International* 148, 1 (July 1, 1996); Joseph Kahn, "A Hong Kong Newspaper Softens Its Voice," *Asian Wall Street Journal*, April 22, 1997; "Freedom of Expression in Hong Kong on the Handover to China," joint report by Hong Kong Journalists Association and Article 19, June 1997; A. Lin Neumann, "Press Freedom under the Dragon: Can Hong Kong's Media Still Breathe Fire?" in *Dangerous Assignments*, no. 55 (New York: Committee to Protect Journalists, Fall 1997); author's E-mail interview of November 22, 1997, with Dr. Alan Knight, honorary research fellow at the Center for Asian Studies at Hong Kong University and chair of Journalism and Media Studies at Central Queensland University, Australia; Knight's Web site Dateline Hong Kong, www.geocities.com/Athens/Forum/2365; Keith B. Richburg, "One Hundred Days of Chinese Rule; Hong Kong's People Seem Content as New Leader Promises Prosperity, Not Democracy," *Washington Post*, October 9, 1997; speech by Ying Chan at CPJ awards dinner, New York City, October 23, 1997.

NOTES TO CHAPTER 4

Details of Christine Anyanwu's life and arrest come from the Web sites of the Committee to Protect Journalists, Reporters Sans Frontières, the German Web site Reporter ohne Grenzen, and various news reports including Nick Thorpe, "Beaten but Not Broken," *The Scotsman*, Nov. 8, 1996, and "Siilent Voices, " *Literary Review Online*, July 1997, on Web site www.users.dircon.co.uk/~litrev/199707/97.html.

Background on the Nigerian military and press is from Dapo Olorunyomi, "Defiant Publishing in Nigeria," in *Journalists in Peril*, Fall 1996 issue of *Media Studies Journal* 10, 4 (New York: Media Studies Center and The Freedom

Forum); *Attacks on the Press in 1997* (New York: Committee to Protect Journalists, March 1998); "CPJ Names Ten Enemies of the Press," Web site of the Committee to Protect Journalists, May 3, 1998; Dapo Olorunyomi, "Famished Road to Freedom," *Guardian* (London), January 22, 1996; Murray Seeger, "Nigeria Descends Deep into Disrepute; Rule by 'Medieval Warlords' Is Holding Back Largest Nation on the African Continent," *Baltimore Sun*, December 21, 1997; author's interview with William A. Orme Jr. in New York, October 24, 1997; Stephen Buckley, "In Sub-Saharan Africa, Crackdowns on the Press Are Becoming Commonplace," *International Herald Tribune*, April 9, 1996; Cindy Shiner, "Nigerian Press Defiant in the Face of Repression," *Guardian* (London), December 20, 1995; Kavita Menon, "Pakistan: The Press for Change," in *Attacks on the Press in 1999* (New York: Committee to Protect Journalists, March 2000).

Information about Babafemi Ojudu comes from his article "A Journalistic Journey towards Freedom," on the Web site of Howard University [no date given but the year is probably 1997], as well as Shiner, "Nigerian Press Defiant"; Buckley, "Crackdowns on the Press"; Vukoni Lupa Lasaga, "Media-Africa: Journalists Use Internet to Elude Dicatators," Inter Press Service, November 18, 1997; and Christina Lamb, "Editors Defy Nigerian Reign of Fear," *Sunday Times* (London), December 24, 1995.

NOTES TO CHAPTER 5

The reference to Bazoft is from John Burns, "Days and Nights in Baghdad," *New York Times*, November 11, 1990.

Information about Gao Yu, including her personal statement to the court, is from *China: "Leaking State Secrets": The Case of Gao Yu* (New York: Human Rights Watch/Asia and Human Rights in China Publications, July 1995, vol. 7, no. 8); *Attacks on the Press in 1997* (New York: Committee to Protect Journalists, March 1998); Mike Chinoy, *China Live: People Power and the Television Revolution*, updated ed. (Lanham, Md.: Rowman and Littlefield, 1999); Daisy Li Yuet-wah, "Endangered Species: Press Freedom in Hong Kong," in *Attacks on the Press in 1994* (New York: Committee to Protect Journalists, March 1995); Barbara Crossette, "Unesco Award to Imprisoned Chinese Journalist Angers Beijing," *New York Times*, May 6, 1997; remarks by Timothy Balding to Bilbao Conference, May 3, 1997, in press release of World Association of Newspapers, issued by headquarters in Paris; letter from Gao Yu to Bilbao Conference, quoted in remarks by Timothy Balding; Eric Eckholm, "China Frees Political Journalist as a Visit by Albright Nears," *New York Times*, February 16, 1999; *Attacks on Journalists in 1999* (New York: Committee to Protect Journalists, March 2000); Charles A. Radin, "International Press Institute Honors Fighters for Free Speech," *Boston Globe*, May 4, 2000.

The section about Veronica Guerin comes from "Veronica Guerin in Life and Death," in *Journalists in Peril*, Fall 1996 issue of *Media Studies Journal* 10, 4 (New York: Media Studies Center and The Freedom Forum); Alan Byrne, "In Death—Brave and Brilliant, with a Sense of Mischief," in *Journalists in Peril*, "Ireland," in 1997 report on Web site of Reporters Sans Frontières, www.rsf.fr; *Attacks on the Press in 1995* (New York: Committee to Protect Journalists, March 1996); Michael Foley, "Gag Reflex: Ireland's Libel Laws Muzzle a Free Press," *Attacks on the Press in 1996* (New York: Committee to Protect Journalists, March 1997); "Ireland's Truth-Teller Silenced," in *Dangerous Assignments*, no. 51 (New York: Committee to Protect Journalists, Summer 1996); "Sentencing in Dublin in Reporter's Killing," *New York Times*, July 30, 1999; and "Gilligan Denies Involvement in Murder of Veronica Guerin," *Irish Times*, April 4, 2000.

The quote by Ana Arana is from an article by her, "In America, Justice for Some," in *Journalists in Peril*. The article is about immigrant journalists in the United States who are not afforded the same protection as journalists who are U.S. citizens.

The final quote is from Gao Yu, "My Personal Statement to the Court," December 23, 1994, in *China: "Leaking State Secrets."*

NOTES TO CHAPTER 6

Information about the murder of Dmitri Kholodov comes from Fred Hiatt, "Bomb in Briefcase Kills Probing Moscow Reporter; Victim Investigated Corruption in Russian Military," *Washington Post*, October 18, 1994; David Satter, "Murdering with Impunity in Russia: Authorities Fail to Prosecute the Murders of Seven Journalists," in *Attacks on the Press in 1995* (New York: Committee to Protect Journalists, March 1996); and various news reports.

The section about Kholodov's reporting is from Dmitri Kholodov, "Our Russian Army Is Sliding Down into a World of Crime," *Moskovsky Komsomolets*, June 1994, translated by Olga Podolskaya and Helen Womack in *Independent* (London), November 3, 1994; James Meek, "Russians Mourn Murdered Anti-Corruption Journalist," *Guardian* (London), October 21, 1994; Peter Ford, "MIGs Race BMWs, Soldiers Starve: Russian Army Crumbles," *Christian Science Monitor*, November 25, 1994.

Details about the extent of Russian crime come from Satter, "Murdering with Impunity"; Steven Erlanger, "Images of Lawlessness Twist Russian Reality," *New York Times*, June 7, 1995; John Lloyd, "Violence Turns Moscow into Gun City: Many Businessmen Hire Bodyguards and Pack a Pistol," *Financial Times* (London), September 2, 1995; Peter Ford, "Hopes for Democracy Flicker in Russia with Assault on Press," *Christian Science Monitor*, March 3, 1995; Nanette van der Laan, "Russian Film Depicts Corruption at Top," *Daily Telegraph* (London), May 23, 1997.

Details about the outcome of the Kholodov investigation are from Michael

Gordon, "Russia Arrests Ex-Colonel in '94 Killing of Journalist," *New York Times*, February 13, 1998; Interfax News Agency, Moscow, February 26, 1998, quoted in BBC Summary of World Broadcasts, February 28, 1998; and Interfax News Agency, Moscow, April 30, 1998, quoted in BBC Summary of World Broadcasts, May 1, 1998; Yekaterina Zapodinskaya, "The Person Who Ordered the Hit Still Remains to Be Found," Moscow, *Kommersant-Daily*, February 14, 1998, quoted by *Current Digest of the Post-Soviet Press*, March 18, 1998.

Details about the murder of Manuel Buendía Tellezgirón are from Matthew Rothschild, "Who Killed Manuel Buendia?" *Progressive* 49 (April 18–23, 1985); William Branigin, "Mexican Writer's Death Laid to Ex-Police Chief; 1984 Killing Underlined Journalists' Plight," *Washington Post*, June 13, 1989; and William A. Orme Jr., ed., *A Culture of Collusion* (Miami: North-South Center Press, 1997).

The quote about impunity is from Jorge C. Castañeda's preface to *Unpublished Crimes against Journalists* (Miami: Inter American Press Association, 1997).

The comment on the danger of reporting crime and corruption is from the author's interview with William A. Orme Jr. in New York, October 24, 1997.

The section about Guillermo Cano Isaza and Colombia is from *Attacks on the Press in 1999* (New York: Committee to Protect Journalists, March 2000); "Personal Profile: Guillermo Cano Isaza," in *Unpunished Crimes against Journalists* (Miami: Inter American Press Association, 1997); and press reports.

The other examples of drug violence are in CPJ annual reports for 1994–1997.

The Ahmad Taufik case and details about Indonesia come from Joe Leahy, "Editor Given Two Years for Suharto Insult," *South China Morning Post*, September 12, 1995; Supara Janchitfah, "Indonesia: Freedom of the Press," *Bangkok Post*, February 12, 1995; CPJ Web site, March 16, 1996; Duncan Graham, "Editor Felled by Indonesia's Risky News Business," *Age* (Melbourne, Australia), July 6, 1994; Vikram A. Parekh, "Indonesia—Cracks in the Wall," in *Journalists in Peril*, Fall 1996 issue of *Media Studies Journal* 10, 4 (New York: Media Studies Center and The Freedom Forum); Rory McCarthy, "Indonesian Press Restrictions Severe, Not Improving: Watchdog," Agence France-Presse (hereafter cited as AFP), November 17, 1997; *Attacks on the Press in 1995*; *Suara Independen* Web site, www.gn.apc.org/independen/english/info.htm, maintained by MIPPA (The Indonesian Society for Alternative Press), Surrey Hills, Victoria, Australia; Linda Yeung, "Indonesia's Tireless Fighter for Freedom of the Press," *South China Morning Post*, November 22, 1997; "TV Reporter Dies from Injuries Sustained in Blast at BBC Office," PTI News Agency, September 7, 1995.

NOTES TO CHAPTER 7

The Mushtaq Ali case and background on Kashmir come from Moses Manoharan, "Journalists Walk Thin Line in Kashmir," Reuters, September 11, 1995; UPI,

September 10, 1995; Vikram Parekh, *On a Razor's Edge: Local Journalists Targeted by Warring Parties in Kashmir* (New York: Committee to Protect Journalists, July 1995); John-Thor Dahlburg, "Waning Rebellion May Forever Stain Disputed Region of Northern India," *Los Angeles Times*, September 25, 1995; Surinder Oberoi, "Kashmir Journalists Report on Thin Ice," AFP, July 10, 1996; CPJ annual reports 1994–1999.

Details of the attacks on journalists in Chechnya come from annual CPJ reports, 1995–1999.

The Basque killing was reported in "Basque Guerrillas Are Blamed as Spanish Journalist Is Killed," Reuters, May 7, 2000; and "Death of a Journalist: Killers Could Not Bear to Hear the Truth," *Guardian* (London), May 9, 2000.

The Ocak Isik Yurtçu case and details about Turkey come from Ahmet Emin [pseudonym], "Turkish Journalists on Trial," in *Journalists in Peril*, Fall 1996 issue of the *Media Studies Journal* 10, 4 (New York: Media Studies Center and The Freedom Forum); Stephen Kinzer, "Turkey Jails a Dissident Who Praised Rebel Kurds," *New York Times*, January 28, 1998; CPJ annual reports 1994–1999; author's interview with William A. Orme Jr., October 24, 1997; "Isik Yurtçu Wins 1996 Reporters Sans Frontières—Fondation de France Prize," press release of Reporters Sans Frontières, on Web site of IFEX (the International Freedom of Expression eXchange Clearing House), Toronto, Canada, www.ifex.org; "Isik Yurtçu," on Web site of Reporters San Frontières [no date given], www.rsf.fr.

No reliable source claims to know the exact number of Kurds in Turkey, but these estimates come from Eric Rouleau, "The Challenges to Turkey," *Foreign Affairs* (November–December 1993); and "The Stateless Nation," *Economist*, June 25, 1994.

The Yurtçu quote about mentioning the word *PKK* is from an interview with the Turkish newspaper *Milliyet*, date not specified, as cited on the Web site of the Committee to Protect Journalists.

The Marcus case comes from Aliza Marcus, "Turkish Army Targets Kurdish Villages," Reuters, November 25, 1994; Jonathan Rugman, "Turkish Court Acquits US Reporter of Racism Charge," *Guardian* (London), November 10, 1995; and *Attacks on the Press in 1995* (New York: Committee to Protect Journalists, March 1996).

The Yasar Kemal excerpts are from author's translation of the Kemal article in *Der Spiegel*, January 9, 1995. Excerpts appeared in various publications, including *Neue Zürcher Zeitung*, January 25, 1995; *Die Tageszeitung*, January 14, 1995; and *Time International Edition*, July 17, 1995.

Additional references to Turkey are from Ertugrul Kurkcu, "Turkey: Award for Jailed Reporter Raises New Hopes for Media Freedom," Istanbul, Inter Press Service, July 16, 1997; Aliza Marcus, "Turkish Writers Languish in Jail despite Changes," Reuters, February 20, 1996; Ertugrul Kurkcu, "Human Rights—

Turkey: Jailed for Professionalism," Istanbul, Inter Press Service, December 13, 1996; William A. Orme Jr., "CPJ's 1997 Turkey Campaign: Background and Chronology," in *Attacks on the Press in 1997* (New York: Committee to Protect Journalists, March 1998); Terry Anderson, "Journalist's Release Is Good News for Turkey," *Buffalo News*, August 22, 1997.

The Mark Tully quote is from "India: Press Has Vital Role to Play in Kashmir: Tully," *Hindu*, September 20, 1997, quoted in FT Asia Intelligence Wire.

NOTES TO CHAPTER 8

The section on Algeria is based on CPJ annual reports, 1994–1999; author's interview with William A. Orme Jr., October 24, 1997; Amnesty International Web site, www.amnesty.org; Celestine Bohlen, "Algerian Rights Advocate Says Military and Rebels Share Blame," *New York Times*, December 19, 1997; Julie Wheelwright, "How Danger Helps Women into Top Posts," London, Gemini News Service, 1996, www.oneworld.org/gemini; Geoff Hartman, "Diminishing Possibilities in Algeria; Interview with Salima Ghezali," Middle East Report, Spring 1997, on Web site of MERIP (Middle East Research and Information Project) at www.merip.org; Toufiq Derradji, "Algerian Journalists—Casualties of a Dirty War," in *Journalists in Peril*, Fall 1996 issue of *Media Studies Journal* 10, 4 (New York: Media Studies Center and The Freedom Forum); Salima Ghezali, "Algerian Journalism's Original Sin," speech at October 1995 meeting sponsored by Human Rights Watch and CPJ, translated from the French by Zohra Kherief and published in *Attacks on the Press in 1995* (New York: Committee to Protect in Journalists, March 1996); Saïd Mekbel, "The Torment of a Targeted Journalist," *Le Matin*, [date not specified] 1994, translated from French by Marlé Hammond and published in *Attacks on the Press in 1994* (New York: Committee to Protect in Journalists, March 1995); Salima Ghezali, "Algeria Burning," excerpts of her speech to the European Parliament, *Nation*, February 16, 1998. *Note:* Her first name is spelled variously as either Sélima or Salima, but I have chosen to use Salima, the spelling used by organizations that have awarded her prizes.

The section on Tajikistan is based on Jonathan Rugman, "Obituary: Mohyedin Alempour: War and Culture in Tajikistan," *Guardian* (London), December 16, 1995; "A Retreat to Tyranny: Tajikistan's Unreported War against Press Freedom," in *Attacks on the Press in 1994*; *Attacks on the Press in 1995*; Glasnost Defense Foundation, quoted on the Web site of International Freedom of Expression Exchange Clearing House, in IFEX Communiqué #7–24, June 30, 1998; Abdusattar Khamidi, "Those Who Knew Too Much Were Silenced," *Golos*, no. 17 (April 26, 1993), translated into English and published by Russian Press Digest, May 3, 1993; and various U.S. State Department Country Reports on Human Rights, Washington, D.C.

The section on Rwanda draws information from Carter Coleman, "Remembering What Others Prefer to Forget" (review of book *Season of Blood: a Rwandan Journey*, by Fergal Keane), *Los Angeles Times*, August 4, 1996; CPJ annual reports, 1994–1997; and the Web site of German press advocacy group Reporter ohne Grenzen.

The quote from Horria Saihi is from Alexandra Marks, "Reporters at Risk," *Christian Science Monitor*, November 10, 1995.

NOTES TO CHAPTER 9

The Robert Capa quote is from Susan D. Moeller, "Dangerous Exposures," in *Journalists in Peril*, Fall 1996 issue of *Media Studies Journal* 10, 4 (New York: Media Studies Center and The Freedom Forum).

The incidents in Haiti and elsewhere are from *Attacks on the Press in 1994* (New York: Committee to Protect Journalists, March 1995); "Serb Students Protest Police Brutality," UPI, February 6, 1997; *Attacks on the Press in 1997* (New York: Committee to Protect Journalists, March 1995); "Govt. Gagging Press to Fulfil Its Designs: Khaleda," *The Independent*, June 3, 1998; *Attacks on the Press in 1996* (New York: Committee to Protect Journalists, March 1995); Moeller, "Dangerous Exposures."

The incident in Warsaw involving Mick Deane is based on the author's interview with him, August 5, 1999, and the author's personal recollection of the incident.

The section on Israel and the Palestinian Authority draws from "Israeli Soldier Injured in Kidnap Attempt," AFP, September 21, 1995; "Israeli Army Arrests Palestinian Cameraman," AFP, February 12, 1995; "Soldiers Beat Up Palestinian Photographer, Journalists Say," AFP, January 28, 1994, *Attacks on the Press in 1994*; "AP Journalists Are Under Fire," *Editor and Publisher*, April 2, 1994; "Army Blames Officer in Shooting of Gaps," *Des Moines Register*, October 1, 1994; Margot Dudkevitch and Arieh O'Sullivan, "Rioting Continues in Hebron; Cameramen Hit by Army Gunfire," *Jerusalem Post*, July 14, 1997; "Palestinians Clash with Israeli Troops; Four Journalists Hurt," AP, July 14, 1997; and *Attacks on the Press in 1997*.

The environmental incidents are in Michael Holman, "Nigeria Frees FT Journalist on Bail," *Financial Times*, January 12, 1996; "Nigeria Drops Sedition Charge against FT Correspondent," AFP, April 19, 1996; *Belarus*, Human Rights Country Reports, 1996 (Washington, D.C.: Department of State, February 1997); *Attacks on the Press in 1996*.

The Jordanian bread riot incident is from Sana Abdallah, "Five Jordanian Journalists Arrested," UPI, August 22, 1996; Joel Campagna, "Jordan Reins in the Press," in *Attacks on the Press in 1997*.

NOTES TO CHAPTER 10

The section on Xi Yang is from "Surprise Release; An Attempt to Calm Some Nerves," *Asiaweek*, Hong Kong, February 7, 1997; "China Set to Sell Gold Reserves for Foreign Exchange," Kyodo News Service, July 28, 1993; "Xinhua Carries Explanation of Xi Yang Case," BBC Summary of World Broadcasts, April 13, 1994, English-language translation from Chinese-language text of report by Xinhua, official New China News Agency, dated April 11, 1994; "China Detains Hong Kong Reporter on Spying Charge," Reuters, September 27, 1993; "A Man of Few Words," *South China Morning Post*, September 29, 1993; "Reporter in China May Face Execution," UPI, December 26, 1993; Jeffrey Parker, "Eight Chinese Executed, Reporter Arrested," Reuters, September 27, 1993; Louis Won, "Father of Jailed Reporter Collapses; Jailed Reporter's Father Suffers Heart Attack," *South China Morning Post*, April 4, 1994; "Memories Dim on Silenced Reporter," *South China Morning Post*, September 24, 1995; Niall Fraser, "Whereabouts of Jailed Source Unknown," *South China Morning Post*, January 26, 1997; "Senior Official Describes Attempts to Resolve 'Ming Pao' Reporter Case," BBC Summary of World Broadcasts, November 30, 1993, translated into English from article in Hong Kong newspaper *Ching Pao*, published November 5, 1993; Jeffrey Parker, "China Reaffirms Hong Kong Journalist's Conviction," Reuters, April 15, 1994; and May Sin-Mi Hon, Linda Choy, and Wendy Lim Wan-Yee, "Xi Yang Freed on Parole; 'I Hope This Auspicious Message Will Become a Source of Strength for Hong Kong in 1997,'" *South China Morning Post*, January 26, 1997.

The Singapore economic secrets case is from Warren Fernandez, "The Osa Case: Who Leaked What, and to Whom?" *Straits Times*, November 20, 1993; Salil Tripathi, "By the Way, Is That an Official Secret?" *Asia, Inc.*, June 1994; Anna Teo, "2nd Qtr: Flash Estimates Point to Below 5pc Growth," *Business Times*, June 29, 1993; Ramesh Divyanathan, "OSA Trial: All Five Accused Found Guilty and Fined," *Business Times*, April 1, 1994; "Singapore; Psst—Wanna See a Statistic?" *Economist*, June 26, 1993.

The Vietnam section draws information from Wayne Washington, "She Waits for Husband, Grieves for Homeland; U.S. Officials Are Normalizing Relations with Vietnam, but the Lives of Tran Thi Thuc and Doan Viet Hoat Are Anything but Normal," *Minneapolis Star Tribune*, January 7, 1996; "Vietnam Human Rights Practices, 1993," 1993 Human Rights Report, U.S. Department of State, January 31, 1994; Wendy S. Tai, "Sons Dream of Freeing Father Long Jailed in Vietnam," *Minneapolis Star Tribune*, March 4, 1993; "Excerpt from *Dien Dan To Do*" [Doan's newsletter], Web site of Digital Freedom Network, www.dfn.org/index-ne.html; "Doan Viet Hoat (Vietnam)," Repression, on Web site of Reporters Sans Frontières: www.calvacom.fr/rsf/RSF_MAJ/RSFKill/prisos_VA/viet_hoat.html; "French Writers Adopt Dissident Vietnamese Academic," AFP, May 21, 1995; "Vietnam Denies Jailed Dissident Is Sick," Reuters, May 26, 1994; Ron Moreau, "The Light in Me Burns Brighter," *Newsweek*, Pacific Edition, January 5, 1998; Trini Tran, "Vietnam Dissident Headed for U.S.," *Los Angeles Times*, September 2, 1998.

Death threats in Tajikistan are from *Attacks on the Press in 1995* (New York: Committee to Protect Journalists, March 1996).

The quote about using two tables in Singapore is from Tripathi, "By the Way."

NOTES TO CHAPTER 11

The section on Zambia draws from "Journalists Detained and Bail Denied; Government to Table Legislation on Regulating Media," Media Institute of Southern Africa (MISA), June 20, 1995, on the Web site of International Freedom of Expression eXchange (IFEX) Clearing House, Toronto, Canada, www.ifex.org; "Zambia: A Hard-Hitting Press Subjected to Harassment," on the Web site of Reporters Sans Frontières, May 1997, www.calvacom.fr/rsf/RSF_MAJ/ RSFComm/Comm_VA.html; David Beresford, "'Scandals' Perk Up Zambia Poll," *Guardian* (London), August 17, 1995; "Court Dismisses 'Post' Editors' Applications; Court Proceedings to Continue," Media Institute of Southern Africa (MISA), March 17, 1997, on the Web site of International Freedom of Expression eXchange; Sam Mujuda, "Cops Hunt for Kafupi," *Post* (Lusaka, Zambia), March 6, 1997; "Kauseni Chauffeuring Clementine Kabondo," *Post* (Lusaka, Zambia), January 16, 1997; *Attacks on the Press in 1997* (New York: Committee to Protect Journalists, March 1998); and Stefaans Brummer, "No Peace for Africa's Press," *Mail and Guardian* (Johannesburg), February 9, 1996.

The story of Gabon's leader Omar Bongo is from Stephane Odzamboga, "Désengagement de la France, réseaux de financement occulte: Le Gabon entre pétrole et démocratie," *Le Monde Diplomatique*, Paris, February 1997; Howard W. French, "Prostitution Trial Upsets France-Gabon Ties," *New York Times*, April 23, 1995; *Attacks on the Press in 1995* (New York: Committee to Protect Journalists, March 1996); Tony Allen-Mills, "Paris Couturier 'Was Pimp' for President Bongo," *Sunday Times* (London), April 16 1995; "Court Fines Designer Who Flew Call Girls to Gabon," Reuters, May 16, 1995; "Gabon President Files Legal Proceedings against Le Monde," Deutsche Presse-Agentur, April 14, 1995.

The Strasser incident is from Rod Mac-Johnson, "Sierra Leone: Corruption Claim Lands Editor in Detention," Inter Press Service, October 14, 1993.

The Dominican defamation case is from *Attacks on the Press in 1996* (New York: Committee to Protect Journalists, March 1997).

The Uruguayan brothers' case is from "Court Rules against Wasmosy," BBC Summary of World Broadcasts, October 16, 1997, quoting from Paraguayan newspaper *ABC Color*, October 14, 1997; "Uruguayan Judge Jails Newspaper Chiefs," UPI, May 24, 1996; *Attacks on the Press in 1996*. The account of Paul Biya of Cameroon is from "Letter from an African Jail," Africa News, February 23, 1998; and "Cameroon Eases Reporter's Jail Term," AP, April 15, 1998.

The story of Croatia's Franjo Tudjman is from "Paper Prevented from Issuing Special Edition on Tudjman," AFP, November 18, 1996; and *Attacks on the Press in 1996*.

The incident involving Zaire's Mobutu Sese Seko is from "Newspaper Banned in Zaire Over Mobutu Report," Reuters, September 18, 1996; *Attacks on the Press in 1996*; "Zaire Publisher Detained Over Mobutu Stories," Reuters, January 17, 1997; and David Pallister, "Mobutu, Former Zaire President, Dies; Ex-Dictator Ousted after Thirty-Year Rule Loses Battle with Cancer," *Guardian* (London), September 8, 1997.

The incident involving alleged slave conditions in Malaysia is from Leah Makabenta, "Asia—Labor: Migrant Workers Confront Unfriendly Hosts," Inter Press Service, December 1, 1993; "Asia—Media: Journalist's Expulsion Still Unexplained," Inter Press Service, April 6, 1994; *Attacks on the Press in 1994* (New York: Committee to Protect Journalists, March 1995).

The Mauritania section derives from *Mauritania Human Rights Practices, 1994*, 1994 Human Rights Report, U.S. Department of State, March 1995; "Mauritania Seizes Paper Over Rights Report," Reuters, May 20, 1994; *Attacks on the Press in 1994*.

The Indonesia incident is from Rory McCarthy, "Indonesian Press Restrictions Severe, Not Improving: Watchdog," AFP, November 17, 1997.

The trivia section is from *Attacks on the Press in 1995*; *Attacks on the Press in 1997*; and "AFP Photographer Says PLO Men Beat Him," Reuters, May 14, 1996.

NOTES TO CHAPTER 12

The story of the *Lily Wong* cartoon is from Alan Knight's Web site, Dateline Hong Kong, www.geocities.com/Athens/Forum/2365; Hong Kong Journalists Association and Article 19, "The Die Is Cast: Freedom of Expression in Hong Kong on the Handover to China," June 1997; www.lilywong.net; and *Hong Kong Human Rights Practices, 1995* (Washington, D.C.: U.S. Department of State, March 1996).

The section giving the background on Freedom Neruda is based largely on the author's interview with him in New York City, October 23, 1997; and on Marc Koffi, "Ivorian Officials Play Down Journalist Beating," Reuters, June 19, 1995; *Attacks on the Press in 1996* (New York: Committee to Protect Journalists, March 1997).

The Ethiopia and Iran incidents are from *Attacks on the Press in 1996*. The Pinochet incident is from Web sites of the Committee to Protect Journalists and Reporters Sans Frontières.

The Lebanese cartoon reference is from "Authorities to Charge Beirut Daily for Cartoon," Reuters, November 3, 1994.

The Cambodian cartoon incident is from AFP, August 30, 1996; "Imprisoned Opposition Journalist Freed by Royal Pardon," BBC Summary of World Broadcasts, September 3, 1996, quoting translation from Cambodian in newspaper *Reaksmei Kampuchea* (Phnom Penh), September 1, 1996; Human Rights Country Reports, 1996, U.S. Department of State, February 1997.

The Turkish cartoon is referred to in *Attacks on the Press in 1997* (New York: Committee to Protect Journalists, March 1998).

The section on the Colombian satirist is based on "Colombia Mourns Satirist, Activist," AP, August 14, 1999; and Martin Hodgson, "Jaime Garzon; Colombian Satirist and Journalist Assassinated on the Way to Work," *Guardian* (London), August 18, 1999.

The Kuwaiti joke is referred to in *Attacks on the Press in 1998* (New York: Committee to Protect Journalists, March 1999).

The section on Croatia's Viktor Ivancic is based on the author's interview with Viktor Ivancic in New York City on October 24, 1997; Michael Foley, "Tudjman Tries to Silence Accusers," *Irish Times*, June 2, 1998; "Executive Editor of Satirical Newspaper Arrested," AFP, January 6, 1994; Tony Barber, "Editor Held as Croatia Cracks Down on Critics; Move to Push Prominent Journalist into Military Service Condemned by Colleagues as Tudjman Government Intimidation," *Independent*, January 7, 1994; Drago Hedl, "Croatia—Media: Press Faces Subtle and Severe State Suppression," Inter Press Service, August 4, 1995; Mark Heinrich, "Journalists Face Trial for 'Slander' of Tudjman," Reuters, May 17, 1996; James Goodale, legal brief of Committee to Protect Journalists in support of Viktor Ivancic and Marinko Culic, June 14, 1996; "Europa and the Former Soviet Union: Croatia," on the Web site of Reporters Sans Frontières.

References to the Russian TV program *Kukly* are from Victoria Clark, "For Russians Life's One Big Joke Again," *Observer* (London), July 23, 1995; Yevgeny Popov, "One-on-One with the Screen: Kremlin Tramps," *Sovietskaya Rossiya*, July 11, 1995, as translated from Russian into English and published in *Current Digest of the Post-Soviet Press* 47, 29 (August 16, 1995): 7; Lee Hockstader, "Satirists Skewer Russian 'Puppet' Government," *Washington Post*, July 19, 1995; Jean MacKenzie, "NTV Slams Government Over 'Kukly' Case," *Moscow Times*, July 18, 1995; and Michael Wines, "TV's Impious Puppets: On Kremlin's Hit List?" *New York Times*, June 18, 2000.

The Romanian incident is from *Attacks on the Press in 1994* (New York: Committee to Protect Journalists, March 1995).

The section on Indonesia is from Cindy Shiner, "Indonesia May Sue Magazine: Editor Questioned after Depicting Suharto as King of Spades," *Washington Post*, March 6, 1998; and *Attacks on the Press in 1998*.

NOTES TO CHAPTER 13

The section on Bokassa is from Kaye Whiteman, "Obituary: Jean-Bedel Bokassa: Brutal Excesses of an Egomaniac," *Guardian* (London), November 5, 1996; Jonathan C. Randal, "Weeds Encroach Where Emperor Held Sway," *Washington Post*, February 4, 1987; Michael Goldsmith, "Reporter Tells of Month's Ordeal in Jail of Central African Empire," *New York Times*, August 18, 1977; David Sterritt, "Film Follows African Tyrant's Reign," *Christian Science Monitor*, August 14, 1992; Jonathan C. Randal, "Bokassa: A Brutal Buffoon Who Saw Himself a Napoleon; Bokassa Crumbled with His Empire," *Washington Post*, September 22, 1979.

The Orme quote is from *Journalists in Peril*, Fall 1996 issue of *Media Studies Journal* 10, 4 (New York: Media Studies Center and The Freedom Forum).

The Anne Nelson quote is from author's interview with her, October 23, 1997.

The Vladimir Zhirinovsky incident is from "Nationalist Leader Bashes Two Journalists," *Chicago Tribune*, May 9, 1997; Nanette van der Laan, "Reporter Seized by Zhirinovsky," *Daily Telegraph* (London), May 9, 1997; and "Zhirinovsky Tangles with TV Reporters," *Seattle Times*, May 8, 1997.

The section on lashing comes from "Two Yemeni Journalists to Be Whipped for Defaming Politician," Deutsche Presse-Agentur, May 31, 1997; and *Attacks on the Press in 1997* (New York: Committee to Protect Journalists, March 1998).

The beatings of Mexican journalists are reported in Julia Preston, "Five Reporters Assaulted in Mexico in Efforts to Intimidate Them," *New York Times*, September 21, 1997; and "Two Journalists Kidnapped and Assaulted," report of Reporters Sans Frontières, September 9, 1997, on IFEX Web site.

The Honduran incident is from "Honduras" section of 1997 annual report by Reporters Sans Frontières; and "Journalist Jorge Luis Monroy Assaulted," Committee to Protect Journalists, October 17, 1996, on IFEX Web site.

The Nigerian horsewhipping incidents are recounted in "Letter from CPJ Executive Director William A. Orme, Jr., to General Sani Abacha, Chairman of the Provisional Ruling Council and Commander-in-Chief of the Armed Forces, Nigeria, July 7, 1997," as reported by Africa News Service, July 8, 1997; and IFEX report "Nigeria: Journalist Severely Beaten; Three Others Arrested," as reported by Africa News Service, December 9, 1997.

The murder in Haiti is reported in Amy Wilentz, "A Brave Haitian Voice," *New Yorker*, April 17, 2000; and "Violence Erupts as Haiti Buries Slain Journalist," AP, April 9, 2000.

The incident in the Philippines is in *Attacks on the Press in 1998* (New York: Committee to Protect Journalists, March 1999).

The murder of the Colombian radio reporter is from *Colombia: Country Report on Human Rights Practices for 1996*, Department of State Human Rights Country Reports, February 1997; and *Attacks on the Press in 1996* (New York: Committee to Protect Journalists, March 1997).

The statistics on imprisoned journalists come from *Attacks on the Press in 1999* (New York: Committee to Protect Journalists, March 2000); and the Web site of Reporters Sans Frontières, March 9, 1999.

The quote on Asian violence is from William A. Orme Jr., "The Meaning of the Murders," in *Journalists in Peril*, Fall 1996 issue of *Media Studies Journal* 10, 4 (New York: Media Studies Center and The Freedom Forum).

NOTES TO CHAPTER 14

The section on libel in Kyrgyzstan is from "Press Conference with Oleg Panfilov, Monitoring Service Head of the Glasnost Defense Foundation," Official Kremlin International News Broadcast, Federal Information Systems Corp., July 22, 1996; *Attacks on the Press in 1997* (New York: Committee to Protect Journalists, March 1998); protest letter to President Askar Ayakyev of Kyrgyzstan from Reporters Sans Frontières, October 1, 1997, on the Web site of Reporters Sans Frontières; "Central Asian Activists Protest against Human Rights Abuses," *Res Publika*, published in Bishkek, Kyrgyzstan, June 10, 1997, as quoted by BBC Summary of World Broadcasts, June 16, 1997.

The Ann Cooper quote is from *Attacks on the Press in 1998* (New York: Committee to Protect Journalists, March 1999).

The Mexican lawsuits are covered in Joel Simon, "When Truth Is No Defense," *Columbia Journalism Review* (September–October 1997).

The Latvia incident is in "Journalist Arrested in Latvia Not to Ask Other Precaution Measure," Baltic News Service, March 25, 1999; "Journalist Arrested and Detained," CPJ news release, March 23, 1999, as reported on the IFEX Web site; "Latvian Prosecutors Drop Defamation Charges against Chaladze," Baltic News Service, March 26, 1999.

The incidents in Taiwan and Egypt are from *Attacks on the Press in 1997* and *Attacks on the Press in 1998*.

The Samoan case is from "Samoa's Main Newspaper Facing Criminal Libel Charge," AFP, March 9, 1998, as reported by an Australian news service based in Sydney, AAP Newsfeed of AAP Information Services, and "'Samoa Observer' Case Goes to Court of Appeal," Pacific Islands News Association, December 24, 1997, carried on the Web site of IFEX.

The references to Panama are from "CPJ Calls for Repeal of Panama's Gag

Laws," March 4, 1999, on the Committee to Protect Journalists' Web site; *Attacks on the Press in 1997*; and *Attacks on the Press in 1998.*

The section on Ireland comes from *Attacks on the Press in 1996* (New York: Committee to Protect Journalists, March 1997); Michael Foley, "A Free Press Will Make Mistakes," *Irish Times*, February 23, 1999; Veronica Guerin, acceptance speech at CPJ International Press Freedom Awards dinner, New York, December 1995; Michael Foley, "Shedding Light on the State [of] Freedom of Information," *Irish Times*, February 17, 1999; "Official Secrecy," *Irish Times*, August 4, 1995; "Women: A Hard Act to Follow," *Guardian* (London), January 27, 1997; "Dail Review Body Likely to Back Repeal of Secrets Act," *Irish Times*, December 16, 1995.

The situation in Jordan is covered in *Attacks on the Press in 1997*; "Restrictions on Press Freedom Are Not Ended with New Law," Arabic Media Internet Network (AMIN), 1997, on their Web site jordan.amin.org; author's interview with Dr. Jabbar A. Allawi Al-Obaidi, visiting research professor, University of Michigan, October 30, 1997; Leonard R. Sussman, "Global Warning: Press Controls Fuel the Asian Debacle," in *Press Freedom 1998* (New York: Freedom House, May 3, 1998).

The Yemeni insult laws are referenced in "Coeducation in South Yemen Abolished; Press Censorship Reportedly Introduced," AFP, October 1, 1994, as reported by the BBC, October 3, 1994; *Attacks on the Press in 1997.*

The Cuban incident is from "Mass Arrest," Reporters Sans Frontières, December 1997 report on their Web site.

The Ivory Coast case is from *Attacks on the Press in 1995* (New York: Committee to Protect Journalists, March 1996).

The Kenyan case comes from "Kenya: Publisher Restrained," IFEX (International Freedom of Expression eXchange) Clearing House, Toronto, Canada, citing Africa News Service, December 29, 1998.

The incidents in Tonga and Ethiopia are from *Attacks on the Press in 1996* and *Attacks on the Press in 1997.*

The story of Gustavo Gorriti in Panama is from *Attacks on the Press in 1997.*

Peru's attack on Baruch Ivcher is covered in Calvin Sims, "Lima TV Station Critical of Fujimori Is Seized," *New York Times*, September 20, 1997.

The Malaysian incident is from Seth Mydans, "Malaysia Court Jails Canadian Reporter Over Magazine Article," *New York Times*, September 5, 1997; and *Attacks on the Press in 1997.*

The two incidents in Azerbaijan are from Nicholas Daniloff, "Mixed Signals: Press Freedom in Armenia and Azerbaijan," in *Attacks on the Press in 1997.*

The Mexican *gacetillas* are referenced in William A. Orme Jr., ed., *A Culture of Collusion* (Miami: North-South Center Press, 1997).

Armenian economic pressures are covered in *Attacks on the Press in 1994* (New York: Committee to Protect Journalists, March 1995).

The counterfeiting of Nigerian publications is from *Attacks on the Press in 1995*.

The Manila Times incident comes from "Manila Times Editors Quit," AP, April 8, 1999.

The Hong Kong incident is in A. Lin Neumann, "Press Freedom under the Dragon: Can Hong Kong's Media Still Breathe Fire?" in *Dangerous Assignments*, no. 55 (New York: Committee to Protect Journalists, Fall 1997).

NOTES TO CHAPTER 15

The Haiti incident is based on the author's interview with *Dateline NBC* producer Mark Feldstein, April 21, 1999; and "NBC Crew Carjacked in Haiti," *News Media and the Law* (Winter 1999).

The story of the Jordanian columnist is from Joel Campagna, "Jordan Reins in the Press," in *Attacks on the Press in 1997* (New York: Committee to Protect Journalists, March 1998).

Saudi newspaper self-censorship is referred to in *Attacks on the Press in 1997*.

The incidents in Peru come from Linda Diebel, "Peruvian Journalist Lives in Fear," *Toronto Star*, November 10, 1997; "Journalist Receives Death Threat," on IFEX Web site, May 29, 1998; *Attacks on the Press in 1998* (New York: Committee to Protect Journalists, March 1999); Anthony Faiola, "Peruvian Government Targets Critical Media," *Washington Post*, July 13, 1999.

The quotes from Mexican journalists Francisco Ortiz Franco and Miguel Cervantes Sahagún are from the author's interviews with them in Tijuana, Mexico, March 13, 1998.

The references to Turkey are from *Attacks on the Press in 1997*; and Stephen Kinzer, "A Terror to Journalists, He Sniffs Out Terrorists," *New York Times*, September 1, 1997.

The references to Kashmir are from *Attacks on the Press in 1997*.

The closing of the Kazakh newspaper is in *Attacks on the Press in 1996* (New York: Committee to Protect Journalists, March 1997).

Ying Chan's comments are from a CPJ press conference at the United Nations, New York, October 23, 1997.

The section on China is from Mike Chinoy, *China Live: People Power and the Television Revolution*, updated ed. (Lanham, Md.: Rowman and Littlefield, 1999); and Liu Binyan, *A Higher Kind of Loyalty: A Memoir by China's Foremost Journalist* (New York: Pantheon Books, 1990).

The section on Mexican publisher Benjamín Flores González is from Jon Lee Anderson, "He Got the Story, Then the Story Got Him," *New York Times Sun-*

day Magazine, December 21, 1997; "Flores Killing Condemned by CPJ," CPJ Web site, July 16, 1997; Joel Simon, "Breaking Away: Mexico's Press Challenges the Status Quo," in *Attacks on the Press in 1997*; Dudley Althaus, "Latin Journalists Find Freedom of Speech a Deadly License; Reporters the Target of Violence as Stories Focus on Drug Traders," *Houston Chronicle*, December 21, 1997.

The quotes from Turkish journalist Nesin are from Aziz Nesin, "Fanaticism's Flames," in *Attacks on the Press in 1994* (New York: Committee to Protect Journalists, March 1995).

The Nigerian newspaper statement is in *Attacks on the Press in 1995* (New York: Committee to Protect Journalists, March 1996).

The reference to Yemen is from *Attacks on the Press in 1997*.

The quotes from Pakistani journalist Zamir Niazi are from the author's E-mail interview with him, June 23, 2000, and an interview with him in *News* (Karachi), March 14, 1999.

NOTES TO CHAPTER 16

The Jordanian editor's quote is from *Attacks on the Press in 1998* (New York: Committee to Protect Journalists, March 1999).

Figures on the growth of the Internet are from "Internet Timeline" on the PBS Web page Life on the Internet, at www.pbs.org/internet/timeline; Bruce Sterling, "Short History of the Internet," on the Web site of the University of Illinois at Urbana-Champaign, w3.aces.uiuc.edu/AIM/scale/nethistory.html; "According to Computer Industry Almanac the U.S. Has More Than Half of Worldwide Internet Users at Year-End 1998," press release of Computer Industry Almanac, July 6, 1999, www.c-i-a.com/199907ciaiu.htm; Graham Lea, "European Internet Users to Pass US by 2003—IDC," on the Web site of *Register*, London, July 13, 1999, at www.theregister.co.uk/990913-000004.html; Sharon Machlis, "U.S. to Have 133m Internet Users Next Year," *Online News*, July 7, 1999, on the Web site www.computerworld.com; Howard Schneider, "In a Spin Over the Web," *Washington Post*, July 26, 1999.

The quote from Freedom House is from *Press Freedom Survey 2000* (New York: Freedom House, May 2000), at www.freedomhouse.org/news/pr122199.html.

The section about the original B92 radio station in 1996–97 is from *Attacks on the Press in 1996* (New York: Committee to Protect Journalists, March 1997); Anthony Loyd, "Belgrade Rebels Tune In to Discontent," *The Times* (London), January 9, 1997; Dejan Kovacevic, "Web, Airwaves, Print Wrestle the Word Out," *Pittsburgh Post-Gazette*, January 14, 1997; Steve Crawshaw, "Protesters Pull the Plug on Milosevic's Cosy Vision of Serbia: Battle of the Airwaves," *Independent* (London), January 24, 1997; Lindsay Nicolle, "Freedom Finds Its Net Voice," *Times* (London), January 29, 1997; Bob Schmitt, "An Internet Answer to

Repression," *Washington Post*, March 31, 1997; Richard Reeves, "Yugoslavian Broadcasts Lessons of Freedom," *Baltimore Sun*, October 14, 1997. The section about B92 during the 1999 NATO bombing is from "War on the Web," PBS Online NewsHour, March 29, 1999, at www.pbs.org/newshour; Cara Cunningham, "Banned Radio B92 from Yugoslavia Still Live on the Web," *InfoWorld Electric*, Infoworld Media Group, April 1, 1999, at Web site archive.inforworld.com; "Radio B92 Open Yugoslavia, News," April 2, 1999, on www.opennnet.org/B92 and www.b92.net/news; "CPJ Update: Radio B92 Shut Down, Foreign Correspondents Detained in Novi Sad," April 2, 1999, on CPJ Web site; Elisabeth Mahoney, "Silence of the Banned Radio Waves," *Scotsman*, April 2, 1999; Veran Matic, "Letter from Belgrade," *Guardian* (London), April 5, 1999; Margie Wylie, "Computers Put Modern War Online," Newhouse News Service in *Times-Picayune* (New Orleans), April 11, 1999; Michael Dobbs, "Yugoslav Media Muzzled, Fearful," *Washington Post*, April 11, 1999; "Radio Closed on Eve of NATO Raids, Back on the Air," AFP, April 14, 1999; Simson Garfinkel, "Banned in Belgrade," *Boston Globe*, April 15, 1999; Frances Katz, "Net a New Dimension in the Coverage of War," Cox News Service, April 19, 1999; Monroe E. Price and Peter Krug, *The Enabling Environment for a Free and Independent Media: Report for Center of Democracy and Governance* (Washington, D.C.: USAID, 2000).

The section on the creation of B2-92 draws from Katarina Subasic, "Serbia's Leading Independent Radio Team Set to Return to the Airwaves," AFP, July 27, 1999; William Branigin, "News to Belgrade: Station to Return," *Washington Post*, July 31, 1999; "Independent Radio Station Is Back on the Air in Serbia," Reuters, in *New York Times*, August 3, 1999; Tim Cuprisin, "Independent Radio Returns to Serbia," *Milwaukee Journal Sentinel*, August 4, 1999; R. Jeffrey Smith, "Belgrade Shuts TV Station and Paper," *Washington Post*, May 18, 2000; Steven Erlanger, "Protests Flare as Belgrade Takes Control of TV Station," *New York Times*, May 19, 2000.

The references to Radio R21 are from Chrystyna Lapychak, "Radio Station Director Vows to Revive Her News Operation," in *Dangerous Assignments*, March 4, 1999, from the Web site of CPJ; "Hillary Meets Kosovo Refugees," UPI, April 13, 1999; "The (New) Media Project—RTV21," no date given but apparently after March 24, 1999, on the Zurich Web site of Medienhilfe Ex-Jugoslawien, www.medienhilfe.ch; "Kosovar Deportee/Refugees to Meet Reporters Friday after Week of Administration, Congressional Meetings," press release on U.S. Newswire, April 15, 1999; Robert Tinsley, "Ethnic Albanian Women Practice Journalism amid the Harsh Reality of Kosovo," no date given but apparently June 1999, on the Web site of International Center for Journalists, www.icfj.org; "Albanian 'Activists' Deny NATO Report on Serb Withdrawal from Kosovo," report by Radio 21 translated by BBC Summary of World Broadcasts, June 8, 1999; Sara Nathan, "Media Matters," *Scotsman*, July 2, 1999;

"Kosovo's Albanians Find Their Voice," *Financial Times*, July 9, 1999; "Pristina Broadcasting Station to Resume with International Head," AFP, July 24, 1999; "Radio 21 Starts on FM in Pristina," from Albanian newspaper *Bota Sot*, translated by BBC Summary of World Broadcasts, July 30, 1999; Jane Perlez, "Albright Tells Kosovars Not to Act Like Their Oppressors," *New York Times*, July 30, 1999.

The Nigerian reference is from Vukoni Lupa-Lasaga, "Media-Africa: Journalists Use Internet to Elude Dictators," Inter Press, November 18, 1997, and author's interview with Dapo Olorunyomi in Washington, D.C., July 16, 1998.

The section on Belarus is from Peter S. Green, "Belarussian Editor Braves Regimes' Tightening Noose," *International Herald Tribune*, December 11, 1997; *Svaboda* online version December 17, 1997, and January 9–21, 1998, on the Web site of Radio Free Europe, www.rferl.org; Fred Hiatt, "On the Front Line of Free Speech," *Washington Post*, December 8, 1997; Howard Jarvis, "From Freedom's Ashes," *Minsk News*, online version December 3, 1999, reprinted from *Transitions*, January 1999, www.ijt.cz/transitions.

Information about Palestinian journalist Daoud Kuttab and his Web site AMIN was gathered from Daoud Kuttab, "Torture and Democracy," AMIN, October 14, 1999, www.amin.org; Brian Whitaker, "Computing and the Net: Holes in the Censors' Net," *Guardian* (London), March 11, 1999; author's interviews by E-mail with Khaled Abu Aker, director of AMIN Web site, January 2000; "Statement of Purpose," AMIN Web site, www.amin.org/En/amin_stat.htm; Virginia N. Sherry, "Torture in Khiam Prison: Responsibility and Accountability," AMIN Web site, October 28, 1999; Daoud Kuttab, "Torture and Democracy," AMIN Web site, October 14, 1999; Edward Said, "Paying the Price for Personal Politics," AMIN Web site, September 30, 1999; "Jordanian Editor Detained for 14 Days," AMIN Web site, August 23, 1999; "Internet Site Created by Kuttab Helps Foster Free Press," *International Press Freedom Awards* on CPJ Web site 1996; "Daoud Kuttab Arrested by PA," letter from Human Rights Watch, on Web site News from Peace Groups, aaa.ariga.com, May 1997; "Turkish, Mexican, Indian Journalists among Press Awardees," Inter Press, November 26, 1996; Stephanie Nolen Ramallah, "Palestinians Find a State in Cyberspace," *Independent* (London), July 21, 1997; Joel Greenberg, "Host of TV Show Says He Was Tortured by Palestinian Jailers," *New York Times*, October 14, 1999; Daoud Kuttab, "Bypassing the Censors," *Jerusalem Post*, February 25, 1999.

The columnist's quote about self-censorship is from *Attacks on the Press in 1998*.

The reference to Chile is from "Chile Paper Skirts Gag Rule on Web," Reuters, June 22, 1997; and "Las Llamadas a la moneda de 'El Cabro Carrera," from *La Tercera* online reports on Web site www.copesa.cl.

The section on Cuba is from "International Press Freedom Awards," Online NewsHour, PBS Web site; Tracey Eaton, "Poor, Poor Cuba Puts the Byte on

Internet Revolution," *Toronto Star*, October 25, 1997; author's interview with Professor Nelson Valdes, University of New Mexico, February 12, 1998; various items from the Web site of Digital Freedom Network, www.dfn.org; "Who's Who in the Cuban Independent Press," Web site of Reporters Sans Frontières, December 4, 1999; "Cuba: Fracas at Journalist's Trial," *New York Times*, November 28, 1998; "Retiran permiso de salida a periodista independiente," October 11, 1999, on the Web site of CubaNet, www.cubanet.org; Mario J. Viera of Cuba Verdad Agency, "By the Path of Our Traditions," May 6, 1999, on the Web site of Florida International University, www.fiu.edu.

The references to Zambia are from the Web site of *Post*, www.zamnet.zm/zamnet/post; *Attacks on the Press in 1996*; Mathew Leone, "Under the Boot, Out on the Net," *Columbia Journalism Review* (November–December 1996).

The India incident is from R. Frank Lebowitz, "India Blocks Pakistani Newspaper's Web Site," July 13, 1999, Digital Freedom Network website, www.dfn.org

Singapore's ploys are mentioned in *Attacks on the Press in 1996*.

Tunisia's ploys are covered in Whitaker, "Computing and the Net."

The quote from Adam Powell is from Whitaker.

The section on Ying Chan is from the author's interviews with her, in person in Taipei in April 1997, and with her and Shieh Chung-liang in New York in October 1997, as well as in subsequent telephone and E-mail interviews; Ying Chan, "Fighting Libel Suit with the Internet," *Nieman Reports* (Fall 1997); and Amy Singer, "Close the Door and Beat the Dog," *American Lawyer* (July–August 1997).

NOTES TO CHAPTER 17

The history of the Great Wall of China is from the *Encyclopaedia Britannica*, at www.britannica.com.

The section on Chinese users of the Internet and government restrictions derives from Bobson Wong, "Improving Internet Access in China," a paper presented at the Computers, Freedom & Privacy 1999 conference in Washington, D.C., April 8, 1999, and posted on the Digital Freedom Network Web site, www.dfn.org.; Adam Clayton Powell II, "China Losing Battle to Control Internet Content," December 11, 1997, on the Web site of Freedom Forum, www.freedomforum.org; Barbara Crossette, "The Internet Changes Dictatorship's Rules," *New York Times*, August 1, 1999; Frank Langfitt, "Taking Dissent Online in China," *Baltimore Sun*, May 11, 1999; Helen Johnstone, "Beijing Opts Out of Plan for Censors on the Net," *South China Morning Post*, December 11, 1997; "Computer Sales Jump in China," AP, February 28, 1999; Murray Fromson, "China and the Internet: People Will Talk," *Online Journalism Review* (August 4, 1998), at ojr.usc.edu; Webster K. Nolan, "In China, a New and Profitable

Journalism Emerges," *Nieman Reports*, Fall 1999; author's E-mail interview with Dr. Alan Knight, November 22, 1997; Michael Laris, "Beijing Turns the Internet on Its Enemies," *Washington Post*, August 4, 1999; Iain S. Bruce, "Enter the Dragon," *Scotsman*, March 23, 1999; "China Clamps New Controls on Internet," Reuters, December 30, 1997.

The references to Lin Hai are from Maggie Farley, "China Sentences Computer Entrepreneur for Subversion," *Los Angeles Times*, January 21, 1999; *Attacks on the Press in 1998* (New York: Committee to Protect Journalists, March 1999); Erik Eckholm, "Trial Will Test China's Grip on the Internet," *New York Times*, November 16, 1998; Elaine Kurtenbach, "China Determined to Tighten Secrecy," AP, November 25, 1998.

The section on *VIP Reference* is from the author's interviews by phone and E-mail with its editor, Li Hongkuan, December 1999 and January 2000; Greg May, "Spamming for Freedom," *Washington Post*, February 19, 1999; inaugural statement of *Tunnel* from its Web site, www.geocities.com/SiliconValley/Bay/5598; author's interview with Shen Tong, head of Democracy for China Fund, May 4, 1998; "Red Sun Rises in the East, Falun Gong Emerges in China: Believers of Falun Gong Protesting around Zhongnanhai Compound," *VIP Reference* Web site, April 25, 1999, at www.ifcss.org/ftp-pub/org/dck/xiaocankao/9904/990425.txt, excerpt translated from the Chinese by Li Hongkuan; "'Internet Guerrilla' Thwarts Beijing's 'Cyberpolice,'" Bernama-Kyodo wire service story carried by *Financial Times Asia Intelligence Wire*, June 2, 1999; Sharon Behn, "US-based Dissidents See Baby Steps toward Democracy in China," AFP, November 21, 1999; Elisabeth Zingg, "China Internet," AFP, January 9, 1999; Mark Landler, "Spiritual Group Meets in Hong Kong," *New York Times*, December 13, 1999.

The reference to Qi Yanchen is from "Chinese Intellectual Detained for Alleged Internet Crimes," AFP, September 3, 1999; and "Chinese Dissident Arrested for Printing Internet Newsletter," *Newsbytes*, Post-Newsweek Business Information, Inc., September 5, 1999.

The reference to self-censorship is from Alan Knight, "Virtual Censorship: Policing the Internet in Asia," report to Freedom Forum conference in Hong Kong, March 18, 1997, reprinted on Web site Dateline Hong Kong, www.geocities.com/Athens/Forum/2365.

The information on costs is from Wong, "Improving Internet Access in China"; "Computer Sales Jump in China"; and Bruce, "Enter the Dragon."

The section on cybercafés and relaxed controls draws from Jennifer Lee, "The Net May Promise Change, but Young Chinese Just Want to Frag Their Friends," *New York Times*, June 29, 2000; Fromson, "China and the Internet"; Bruce, "Enter the Dragon"; Johnstone, "Beijing Opts Out"; Langfitt, "Taking Dissent Online in China"; Sharon Machlis, "U.S. to Have 133m Internet Users Next Year," *Online News*, July 7, 1999, at www.computerworld.com; Nolan, "In

China, a New and Profitable Journalism"; Maggie Farley, "Dissidents Hack Holes in China's New Wall," *Los Angeles Times,* January 4, 1999; inaugural statement of *Tunnel;* Powell, "China Losing Battle to Control Internet Content."

NOTES TO CHAPTER 18

The section on Turkey draws information from "Turkish Court Tries U.S. Journalist," UPI, October 12, 1995; Jonathan Rugman, "Turkish Court Acquits US Reporter of Racism Charge," *Guardian* (London), November 10, 1995; Shawn Olson, "Reuters Correspondent Acquitted; Faced Charges in Turkey Based on Information in Her Stories," *Editor and Publisher,* November 25, 1995; *Attacks on Journalists in 1995* (New York: Committee to Protect Journalists, March 1996); author's interview with Walter Cronkite, February 14, 2000; author's E-mail interview with William A. Orme Jr., January 22, 2000.

The section on the CPJ is from author's interview with executive director Ann Cooper, January 21, 2000; *Attacks on Journalists in 1995;* author's interview with Anne Nelson, October 23, 1997, and E-mail communication, February 3, 2000; author's attendance at CPJ Awards Dinner, October 23, 1997; *Attacks on the Press in 1998* (New York: Committee to Protect Journalists, March 1999); Sherry Ricchiardi, "Journalism's Red Cross," *American Journalism Review* (December 1997); Michael Dobbs, quoted by Christine Spolar in "Bosnian Serbs Free Reporter after Pressure; U.S. Credits Milosevic in American's Release," *Washington Post,* November 9, 1995; author's interview with William A. Orme Jr., October 24, 1997; annual reports of CPJ; author's interviews with Dapo Olorunyomi, Washington, D.C., July 16, 1998; J. Jesús Blancornelas, Tijuana, Mexico, March 13, 1998; Miguel Cervantes Sahagún, Tijuana, Mexico, March 13, 1998; and with various CPJ officials; Web site of World Association of Newspapers (WAN) www.wan-press.org/press_ freeedom/killed.99.html; Jorge Zepada, "Mexico's Journalists Move to Secure Press Freedom," Web site of the CPJ; author's E-mail interview with Mexican journalist Pedro Enrique Armendares, January 31, 2000.

The references to Argentina are from Amelia R. Barili, "Anti-Press Violence in Argentina," *Quill,* December 1997; Laurie Goering, "Photographer Killing Still a Murky Picture," *Chicago Tribune,* December 9, 1997; *Attacks on the Press in 1998;* "Eight Convicted in Argentina Murder," AP, February 3, 2000.

The Ghezali quote is from *Attacks on the Press in 1995* (New York: Committee to Protect Journalists, March 1996).

The reference to Tajikistan is from Ricchiardi, "Journalism's Red Cross."

President Clinton's intervention in Argentina is reported in Ricchiardi, "Journalism's Red Cross"; transcript of White House press conference from Federal News Sevice, October 16, 1997; John F. Harris, "Argentine Nod toward Pollution Plan Expected," *New York Times,* October 18, 1997; John F. Harris and

Anthony Faiola, "Clinton Eases South American Concerns; President Promotes Partnership as Hostility Wanes, Economies Grow," *Washington Post,* October 19, 1997.

The section on RSF is from its Web site, including such features as its press-freedom barometer, its 1999 survey, petitions, newsletters, press releases, and map; reference to Fleutiaux in Chris Stephen, "Chechen Conflict Threatens Georgia Again," *Scotsman,* June 14, 2000.

The references to IFEX are from www.ifex.org/about; www.ifex.org/alerts/browse/statistics.html?what=countries; Anne Nelson, "Monitoring Press Freedoms," *Crosslines Global Report* (May/June 1997).

The discussion of Article 19 draws from its Web site, www.article19.org; Universal Declaration of Human Rights, at www.un.org/Overview/rights.html.

The section on Digital Freedom Network draws from www.dfn.org.

The reference to Freedom Forum is from www.freedomforum.org; and Paul Farhi, "Freedom Forum Dates Back to 1935," *Washington Post,* March 23, 1993.

The UN section is from Timothy Pratt, "Publish and Be Shot," *Times* (London), May 7, 1999; "Press Prize for Jailed Writer," *Independent* (London), March 22, 1997; "Freedom Prize Vow from Jail," *South China Morning Post,* May 4, 1997; Tom Korski, "UN Chief in Prize Row," *South China Morning Post,* May 9, 1997; Barbara Crossette, "Unesco Award to Imprisoned Chinese Journalist Angers Beijing," *New York Times,* May 6, 1997; Oxford-based research in Monroe E. Price and Peter Krug, *The Enabling Environment for a Free and Independent Media: Report for Center of Democracy and Governance* (Washington, D.C.: USAID, 2000); author's interview with Cooper; "Gao Yu Honored," *China Rights Forum* (New York and Hong Kong: Human Rights in China, Summer 1997).

NOTES TO THE CONCLUSION

The summary of conflicting signals comes from "Uruguay: Former Official Kills Journalist, Self," at www.cpj.org/news/2000/Uruguay08march00na.html; "Eight Convicted in Argentina Murder," AP, February 3, 2000; Mark Landler, "Hong Kong Tabloid Is Front-Page News after Its Office Is Searched," *New York Times,* December 6, 1999; "Worry Over Hong Kong Media Move," AP, November 14, 1999; "Russian Journalist Wins Libel Case," AP, February 8, 2000.

The section on political change draws from Monroe E. Price and Peter Krug, *The Enabling Environment for a Free and Independent Media: Report for Center of Democracy and Governance* (Washington, D.C.: USAID, 2000); speech by Vice President Al Gore in "Building a Better Future in Africa," White House conference on Africa, June 26–27, 1994, at www.state.gov/www/regions/africa/presetal.html; "Reporters Play Key Role in Senegal," AP, March 22, 2000.

The references to the Internet are from press release of Computer Industry Almanac, July 6, 1999, at www.c-i-a.com; E-mail from Khaled Abu Aker, director of AMIN Web site, November 24, 1999; Ying Chan, "Fighting Libel Suit with the Internet," *Nieman Reports* (Fall 1997).

The section on world trade is from author's interview with Greta Salsbury, statistician, Department of Economic and Social Affairs, United Nations, June 13, 2000; "China's Exports Up 4.3 Percent in January–October," *People's Daily* Web site, November 15, 1999, at english.peopledaily.com.cn/special/trade/1999111500A101.html; Nicholas D. Kristof, with Sheryl WuDunn, "Of World Markets, None an Island," *New York Times*, February 17, 1999; William Safire, "Gravy Trains Don't Run on Time," *New York Times*, January 19, 1998; author's interview with Walter Cronkite, February 14, 2000.

The information about the bonding effect and human nature is from an Argentine opinion poll reported in *Attacks on the Press in 1997* (New York: Committee to Protect Journalists, March 1998); Kunle Ajibade, "The Pen Is Still Mightier," in *Attacks on the Press in 1998* (New York: Committee to Protect Journalists, March 1999), reprinted from the *News* of Nigeria; author's telephone interview with dissident Chinese émigré who asked that his name and location in the United States not be revealed, May 4, 1998; William A. Orme Jr., "The Meaning of the Murders," in *Journalists in Peril*, Fall 1996 issue of *Media Studies Journal* 10, 4 (New York: Media Studies Center and The Freedom Forum); author's interview with Ann Cooper, January 21, 2000.

The section "On the Other Hand . . ." draws information from Robert Coalson, "Babitsky's 'Crime' and Punishment," in *Dangerous Assignments*, on the CPJ Web site, February 28, 2000, at www.cpj.org/dangerous/2000/Babitsky/Babitsky_frameset.html; Daniel Williams, "Babitsky Reveals Russian Abuses," *Washington Post*, February 29, 2000; Emma Gray, "Putin's Media War," *Briefings: Press Freedom Reports*, March 16, 2000, on the CPJ Web site at www.cpj.org/Briefings/Russia_analysis_March00/Russia_analysis_march00.html; Celestine Bohlen, "Putin Tells Why He Became a Spy," *New York Times*, March 11, 2000; Andrei Babitsky's quote from "For the Record," *Washington Post*, March 8, 2000; Celestine Bohlen, "Russian Security Agencies Raid Media Empire's Offices," *New York Times*, May 12, 2000; David Hoffman, "Russian Media Fight to Live; TV Mogul's Political Battle Also Highlights Financial Woes," *Washington Post*, June 28, 2000; Lee Wolosky, "Putin's Problems," *Foreign Affairs* 79, 2 (March–April 2000); Anthony Faiola, "Power Play in Peru: Rival Candidates Say Fujimori's Quest for Control Threatens Democracy," *Washington Post*, March 22, 2000; Timothy Pratt, "Publish and Be Shot," *Times* (London), May 7, 1999; statistical evidence in various annual reports of CPJ (with some later revisions); Ann K. Cooper, "Introduction," in *Attacks on the Press in 1999* (New York: Committee to Protect Journalists, March 2000).

The section on Hong Kong is from author's interview with William A.

Orme Jr., October 24, 1997; Elisabeth Rosenthal, "Beijing Says It Will Wait to See How Victor Acts," *New York Times*, March 19, 2000; author's E-mail interview with CNN Hong Kong bureau chief Mike Chinoy, March 23, 2000; Damien McElroy, "Hong Kong Lily Back to Bait Beijing Flunkies," *Sunday Telegraph* (London), June 18, 2000; author's E-mail interview with Alan Knight, March 16, 2000; A. Lin Neumann, "Press Freedom under the Dragon: Can Hong Kong's Media Still Breathe Fire?" in *Dangerous Assignments*, no. 55 (New York: Committee to Protect Journalists, Fall 1997); author's E-mail interview with Francis Moriarty, March 26, 2000.

Bibliography

Attacks on the Press in 1999. New York: Committee to Protect Journalists, March 2000. Also see previous issues of this annual report.

Binyan, Liu. *A Higher Kind of Loyalty: A Memoir by China's Foremost Journalist*. New York: Pantheon Books, 1990.

Buckman, Robert. "Specter of Death Haunts Mexican Border Journalists." *Editor and Publisher*, April 4, 1998.

China: "Leaking State Secrets": The Case of Gao Yu. Vol. 7, no. 8. New York: Human Rights Watch/Asia and Human Rights in China Publications, July 1995.

Chinoy, Mike. *China Live: People Power and the Television Revolution*. Updated ed. Lanham, Md.: Rowman and Littlefield, 1999.

Dangerous Assignments. No. 55. New York: Committee to Protect Journalists, Fall 1997.

"From Tempo to Tempo Interaktif: An Indonesian Media Scene Case Study." Paper presented at AusWeb97 Conference, July 5–9, 1997, at Southern Cross University, Lismore, Australia. Saiful B Ridwan, Tempo Interaktif, PDAT, PT Grafiti Pers, Jl. Proklamasi 72, Jakarta 10320, Indonesia.

Hachten, William A. *The World News Prism: Changing Media of International Communication*. 5th ed. Ames, Iowa: Iowa State University Press, 1999.

In the Shadow of Buendía: The Mass Media and Censorship in Mexico. London: Article 19, July 1989.

Jernow, Allison Liu. *"Don't Force Us to Lie": The Struggle of Chinese Journalists in the Reform Era*. New York: Committee to Protect Journalists, 1993.

Journalists in Peril. Fall 1996 issue of *Media Studies Journal* 10, 4. New York: Media Studies Center and The Freedom Forum.

Knightley, Philip. *The First Casualty: From the Crimea to Vietnam: The War Correspondent as Hero, Propagandist, and Myth Maker*. New York: Harcourt Brace, 1976.

Maringues, Michèle. *Nigeria: Guerrilla Journalism*. Paris: Reporters Sans Frontières, 1996.

Mickiewicz, Ellen. *Changing Channels: Television and the Struggle for Power in Russia*. New York and Oxford: Oxford University Press, 1997.

Nelson, Anne. "Monitoring Press Freedoms." *Crosslines Global Report*. Cambridge, Mass. May–June 1997.

Orme, William A. Jr., ed. *A Culture of Collusion: An Inside Look at the Mexican Press*. Miami: North-South Center Press, 1996.

Parekh, Vikram. *On a Razor's Edge: Local Journalists Targeted by Warring Parties in Kashmir*. New York: Committee to Protect Journalists, July 1995.

Rothschild, Matthew. "Who Killed Manuel Buendía?" *Progressive* 49, April 18, 1985.

Seeger, Murray. "Nigeria Descends Deep into Disrepute; Rule by 'Medieval Warlords' Is Holding Back Largest Nation on the African Continent." *Baltimore Sun*, December 21, 1997.

Sheridan, Mary Beth. "Digging Deeper in Mexico." *IPI Report*. Los Angeles: International Press Institute, First Quarter 1998.

Unpunished Crimes against Journalists. Miami: Inter American Press Association, 1997.

U.S. Department of State. Various human rights country reports.

Web sites of various press-freedom and human rights advocacy groups including:
Committee to Protect Journalists—www.cpj.org
Reporters Sans Frontières—www.rsf.fr
International Freedom of Expression Exchange—www.ifex.org
Freedom Forum—www.freedomforum.org
International Press Institute—www.freemedia.at

Index

Abacha, Sani: Ajibade case, 51, 216; Anyanwu case, 44, 45, 47, 199; counterfeit periodicals circulated by, 149; as number-one enemy of press freedom, 47–48; Ojudu and guerrilla journalists challenging, 51, 177; shoot on sight order against Olorunyomi, 200
ABC (Mexican newspaper), 23
Abiola, Kudirat, 48
Abiola, Moshood K. O., 45, 48, 50
Abubakar, Abdulsalam, 45, 47
Adams, Paul, 104
advocacy groups for journalists, 7–8, 195–209; Alliance of Independent Journalists, 74, 75, 206; Article 19, 207; Digital Freedom Network, 94, 181, 207; Freedom Forum, 183–84, 194, 198, 207–8; Freedom House, 2, 3, 4, 5, 147, 168; Glasnost Defense Foundation, 95, 206; Hong Kong Journalists Association, 42, 120, 203; IFEX (International Freedom of Expression Exchange), 206–7; Independent Reporters and Editors, 62; Sociedad de Periodistas, 202–3. *See also* Committee to Protect Journalists (CPJ); Reporters Sans Frontières (Reporters Without Borders; RSF)
Afghanistan, 4, 218
Africa: Cameroon, 117; Central African Empire, 135–37; Democratic Republic of the Congo, 202; druglords attacking journalists in, 73; Gabon, 115–16; Ivory Coast, 121–24; Kenya, 148; Mauritania, 118; political change in, 211; Rwanda, 96–98; Senegal, 211; South Africa, 3, 211; Sudan, 119; violence against journalists in, 138; Windhoek Declaration on press freedom for, 209; Zaire, 117–18. *See also* Ethiopia; Nigeria; North Africa; Sierra Leone; Zambia

African Concord (Nigerian magazine), 50
Agafonov, Sergei, 33
Agence France-Presse, 79, 156
Ahmad, Zafaryab, 119
AJI (Alliance of Independent Journalists) (Indonesia), 74, 75, 206
Ajibade, Kunle, 51, 216
Al-Arab al-Youm (Jordanian newspaper), 154
Albanians, 170, 174–76
Albats, Yevgenia, 32
Al-Bilad (Jordanian newspaper), 103
Albright, Madeleine, 176
Al-Darrat, Abdullah Ali Al-Sanussi, 141
Alempour, Mohyedin, 94–96
Alesana, Tofilau Eti, 145
Alferyev, Vadim, 68
Algeria: Algerian Journalists Association, 204; *Al-Hourria*, 93; Armed Islamic Group, 91, 93; attacks on journalists during civil war in, 89–94, 98; *Horizons*, 92; *La Nation*, 91, 92, 93; *Le Matin*, 92; *Le Soir d'Algérie*, 89; as most dangerous place in the world for reporters, 70, 81
Algerian Journalists Association, 204
Al-Hayat (Saudi newspaper), 155
Al-Hourria (Algerian newspaper), 93
Ali, Mushtaq, 78–79, 88
Allen, Liz, 146
Alliance of Independent Journalists (AJI) (Indonesia), 74, 75, 206
Al-Qabas (Kuwaiti newspaper), 126
al-Saqr, Muhammad Jasim, 126
Al-Sharq (Lebanese newspaper), 125
al-Shoura (Yemeni newspaper), 139
Alvarez, Luis, 180
Alyakina, Natalya, 81
al-Zindani, Abdel Maguid, 139
AMIN (Arabic Media Internet Network) Web site, 178, 180, 212

255

Amnesty International, 120, 183
AM News (Nigerian newspaper), 51
Anderson, Terry, 86, 87
Andrei, Nicolei, 131
Annan, Kofi, 208
Anyanwu, Christine, 44–47, 46, 199, 204
Arabic Media Internet Network (AMIN) Web site, 178, 180, 212
Arafat, Yassir, 178, 180
Arana, Ana, 62
Arellano Félix, Benjamín, 13–14, 15
Arellano Félix, Ramón, 13–14, 15
Argentina: Cabezas case, 203, 210, 216; Committee to Protect Journalists' pressure on, 204; journalists' association in, 203; public opinion on the press in, 216
Aridjis, Homero, 203
Arizona Republic (U.S. newspaper), 62
Armed Islamic Group (Algeria), 91, 93
Armenia, 149
Arnett, Peter, 34, 86, 87, 99
Article 19, 207
Asia: Bangladesh, 5, 99; Cambodia, 125; economic boom with press freedom in, 213; imprisonment of journalists in, 141; murder of journalists as rare in, 138; Myanmar (Burma), 4, 141; press freedom in, 3. See also China; India; Indonesia; Japan; Malaysia; North Korea; Pakistan; Philippines; Singapore; South Korea; Taiwan; Vietnam
Asian News International, 79
attacks on journalists. See violence against journalists
Australia: press freedom in, 3, 58; SBS radio, 175
Avrasiya (Azerbaijani newspaper), 148
Azadliq (Azerbaijani newspaper), 148–49
Azerbaijan, 148–49

Baba, Mukhtar Ahmed, 80
Babangida, Ibrahim, 45, 50, 51
Babitsky, Andrei, 219
Balding, Timothy, 57
Baltic republics: Latvia, 144; press freedom in, 3
Baltiskoye Vremya (Latvian newspaper), 144
Bancayrin, Rey, 140
Banerjee, Neela, 33

Bangladesh, 5, 99
Baron, Marie-Guy, 86
Barraza, Jesús, 164–65, 203
Barrón Corona, David, 14, 17
Basayev, Shamil, 28
Basques, 81
Bazoft, Farzad, 53–54
BBC. See British Broadcasting Corporation
beatings of journalists, 139–40
Bédié, Henri Konan, 121–22, 123, 124
Belarus: banned newspaper posted on Web site, 8; journalists beaten in, 104; journalists using Internet in, 177; press freedom lacking in, 4; Svaboda, 177
Berg, Alan, 62
Beza (Ethiopian newspaper), 124
Biya, Paul, 117
Blancornelas, J. Jesús, 13–25; attack on, 13, 16–20; criticisms of, 24–25; International Press Freedom Award for, 15; journalistic career of, 22–25; the Nation as influence on, 215; paying a price for his journalism, 25; photograph of, 12; refusing to give up, 220; and Sociedad de Periodistas, 202, 203; as typical of new breed of independent journalist, 21
B92 (Yugoslav radio station), 168–74, 176
Bokassa, Jean-Bedel, 135–37
Bolivar, Juan, 116
Bolles, Don, 62
bonding effect, 215–16
Bongo, Omar, 115–16
Brazil, 5
Britain: Financial Times, 104; influence of, 215; Observer, 53; Reuter News Agency, 79, 84, 187, 193, 195, 214; Yugoslav Internet broadcasts aided by, 172–73, 175. See also British Broadcasting Corporation (BBC)
British Broadcasting Corporation (BBC): Alempour as Tajikistan correspondent for, 94, 96; Jameel as Kashmir correspondent of, 78–79; World Service, 215; Yugoslav radio stations aided by, 174, 175, 176
Brokaw, Tom, 197
Bruton, John, 61
Buendía Tellezgirón, Manuel, 15–16, 69–70
Bulgaria, 3

Burma (Myanmar), 4, 141
Business Times (Singapore weekly), 109–10
Byrne, Alan, 58, 60

Cabal, Tomás, 145
Cabezas, José Luis, 203, 216
Cabieses, Manuel, 125
Cahill, Martin, 58
Cambodia, 125
Cameroon, 117
Canada, 3, 58
Canadian Committee to Protect Journalists, 206
Cano Isaza, Guillermo, 70–72, 166
Capa, Robert, 99
Carrillo Fuentes, Amado, 20
Carrington, Walter, 48
Carter, Jimmy, 34
Castañeda, Jorge C., 9, 70
Castro, Fidel, 181, 182
censorship: Chinese attempt to control Internet, 186, 193; in Croatia, 127; Index on Censorship, 207; and the Internet, 167, 168, 183–84; journalists refusing to be censored, 1–2; in Russia, 31–33; self-censorship, 155–57, 161, 192; in Turkey, 87, 88, 199; uncensored news on the Internet, 212; of war coverage, 6, 223
Center for Socio-Legal Studies (Oxford University), 8–9, 209
Central African Empire, 135–37
Cervantes Sahagún, Miguel, 23, 25, 156, 203
Chaikova, Nadezhda, 31
Chaladze, Tatyana, 144
Chan, Ying, 36–43; as American citizen, 36; court finding in favor of, 40; on criminal libel laws' effects, 157; International Press Freedom Award for, *41*; Internet used by, 1, 39, 184–85, 212; on legal terrorism against Asian journalists, 43; out-of-court settlement and apology refused by, 39; smear campaign against, 39; strategy of, 40; worldwide campaign of, 39
Chechnya: Babitsky reporting on war in, 219; Fleutiaux held hostage in, 204; journalists killed in, 81; Masyuk's coverage of war in, 26–35; Russia restricting coverage of war in, 29, 210, 217

Chernomyrdin, Viktor, 32, 130
Chiapas, 77
Chile, 125, 180–81
Chiluba, Frederick, 73, 113–15, 182
Chiluba, Vera, 73
China: CNN coverage of pro-democracy demonstrations, 157–58; computer costs in, 192; on CPJ list of worst violators of press freedom, 202; cybercafés in, 192–93; Falun Gong, 186, 190–91, 221; Feign's satire of, 120–21; Gao Yu case, 54–58, 208, 214; Hong Kong's press freedom tolerated by, 221–22; individuals refusing to be intimidated in, 217; international trade of, 213; and the Internet, 185, 186–94, 217; journalists imprisoned in, 4, 82, 141; Lin Hai case, 188–89, 191; Liu Binyan case, 158–61; press freedom lacking in, 4; releasing journalists before trade talks, 58, 214; repression as still dominant in, 211; Tiananmen Square protests, 42, 55, 158, 161, 191; and Universal Declaration of Human Rights, 207; Xi Yang case, 105–8. *See also* Hong Kong
Chinanet, 187, 192
China News Digest International, 207
China Wide Web, 187
Chinoy, Mike, 157–58, 222
Christian Science Monitor (U.S. newspaper), 198
Çiller, Tansu, 196
civil wars, attacks on journalists during, 89–98
Clinton, Bill, 1, 8, 36–37, 204, 213
CNN: Chinese government blocks Web site of, 187, 193; Chinese pro-democracy demonstration coverage, 157–58; Gulf War coverage, 34; Polish police attack journalists, 100, 101; Russian attack on journalists in Chechnya, 81
Colombia: Cano Isaza killing, 70–72, 166; as deadliest Latin American country for reporters, 15; Diaz killing, 141; *El Espectador*, 70; Garzon killing, 126; as second most dangerous place for journalists, 70, 81
Committee to Protect Journalists (CPJ), 196–204; on Abacha as number-one enemy of press freedom, 47–48; annual

CPJ *(continued)*
dinner of, 197, 200; annual report of,
202; and associations of journalists in
other countries, 202–4; award for Blancornelas, 15; *Dangerous Assignments*
journal of, 202; on decline in attacks on
journalists, 220; Digital Freedom Network posting information from, 207;
economic and diplomatic pressure on
repressive regimes, 204; funding of,
197–98; on Jiang Zemin as enemy of
press freedom, 4; on Jordanian prime
minister as enemy of the press, 147;
journalists protected by, 7–8; on Kashmiri lack of press freedom, 80; on Kashmiri self-censorship, 156; on killing of
journalists in Tajikistan, 95; in Marcus
case, 195–96; on Panamanian criminal
defamation prosecutions, 145; on Russian government threat to NTV, 29; statistics on attacks on journalists, 201;
Web site of, 202; in Yurtçu case, 86, 199,
200; on Zouabri as enemy of the press,
90. *See also* International Press Freedom
Award
computers: cost in China, 192; Nigerian
police destroying journalists', 8. *See also*
Internet
Cook, Robin, 172–73
Cooper, Ann K., 143, 199, 200, 209, 218
corruption: and attacks on journalists, 6,
65–76; in Mexican justice system, 20–21
Courage in Journalism Award, 98
CPJ. *See* Committee to Protect Journalists
Crime News (Zambian periodical), 73
criminal libel, 142–47; Chan case in Taiwan, 36–43; chilling effect of, 157; Committee to Protect Journalists denouncing, 201; M'membe and Phiri case in
Zambia, 114; Singapore using, 39, 157
Croatia: exposé on Tudjman's health, 117;
Feral Tribune, 127, 128, *129*, 201; as
fourth most dangerous place for journalists, 81; Ivancic's satires of Tudjman,
126–30, 201; *Nacional*, 117; *Slobodna Dalmacij*, 126–27
Cronkite, Walter, 195–96, 197, 199, 214–15
Cuba: on CPJ list of worst violators of
press freedom, 202; insult laws in, 147;
journalists using the Internet in, 181–82;

and OAS press-freedom ombudsman,
204; press freedom lacking in, 4
CubaNet (Web site), 181, 182, 207
Cuba Verdad (press agency), 181
Culic, Marinko, 201
cybercafés, 192–93
Czech Republic, 3

D&R (Indonesian newsweekly), 76
Dangerous Assignments (CPJ journal), 202
Daniel, Patrick, 109, 110
Dawn (Pakistani newspaper), 183
Daw San San Nweh, 205
Dazibao (Web site), 94, 205
Dean, Ron, 101
Deane, Mick, 100, 101
Deen, Aroun Rashid, 201
democracy: Chinese monitoring Internet
traffic for references to, 187, 193;
Ghezali awarded Sakharov Prize for, 93;
move to democratization, 211; and
press freedom, 3, 5, 8–9, 21; safeguards
against instability in, 214
Democratic Progressive Party (Taiwan), 38
Democratic Republic of the Congo, 202
demonstrations: by journalists, 103; jour-
nalists attacked during, 99–105
Deng Xiaoping, 56, 105
Deutsche Welle, 169
DFN (Digital Freedom Network), 94, 181,
207
Diawara, Bintou, 124
Diaz, Norvey, 141
Díaz Hernández, Jesús Joel, 181
Dien Dan Tu Do (Vietnamese newsletter),
111
Digital Freedom Network (DFN), 94, 181,
207
Dillon, Sam, 144
Doan Viet Hoat, 110–12
Dobbs, Michael, 198
Dominican Republic, 116
Dominique, Jean, 140
Drici, Yasmina, 89
druglords: Blancornelas challenging,
13–25, 220; Buendía murder by, 16–17,
69; Cano Isaza murder by, 70–72; Diaz
murder by, 141; drug culture eroding
Mexican institutions, 16; Flores
González murder by, 1, 15, 161, 164;

journalists harassed and killed by, 72–73; Mexican government bribed by, 20–21

East Timor, 77
Ecevit, Bulent, 86–87
economic pressures on journalists, 148–50
economic secrets, journalists attacked for revealing, 105–12
Economics Weekly (Chinese periodical), 55, 57
Egbunine, Oni, 140
Egypt: on CPJ list of worst violators of press freedom, 202; criminal libel lawsuits in, 144; journalists attacked during protests in, 102
Eisner, Michael, 35, 197
Elbaum, Cynthia, 31
El Espectador (Colombian newspaper), 70
E-mail: Chan using, 39; Chinese government tracking, 188, 189; Committee to Protect Journalists using, 197
Enabling Environment for a Free and Independent Media, The, 211
environment, the, 104, 118–19
Erkanli, Ahmet, 126
Escobar Gaviria, Pablo, 71–72
Estella, Chit, 149
Estrada, Joseph, 149
ETA (Basque separatist group), 81
Ethiopia: *Beza*, 124; on CPJ list of worst violators of press freedom, 202; editors charged with libel in, 119; journalists imprisoned in, 141, 148; Tegen case, 124
ethnic separatist movements: and attacks on journalists, 6, 77–88; China fearing, 186
Europe: Internet use in, 167; press freedom in, 3. *See also* Western Europe
Evening Courier (Tajik newspaper), 112
Excelsior (Mexican newspaper), 69
exposés, journalists attacked because of, 113–19

Fahassi, Djamel, 91–92
Falun Gong, 186, 190–91, 221
Farad (Iranian magazine), 125
Fasano, Carlos, 116
Fasano, Federico, 116–17
Fawelhinmi, Gani, 52

Feign, Larry, 120, 121, *121*
Feldstein, Mark, 153–54
Félix Miranda, Héctor, 14–15, 23, 24, 25
Feral Tribune (Croatian magazine), 127, 128, *129*, 201
Financial Times (British newspaper), 104
Fitzpatrick, Catherine, 31
Fleutiaux, Brice, 204
Flores González, Benjamín, 161–65; assassination of, 1, 15, *163*, 164; drug traffickers and corruption challenged by, 15, 161; photograph of, *162*
Florida International University, 182
Ford Foundation, 198, 206
Foreign Correspondents Club of Hong Kong, 120–21
former Soviet Union: Armenia, 149; Azerbaijan, 148–49; Kazakhstan, 156–57; Kyrgyzstan, 142–43; Latvia, 144; political change in, 211; press freedom in, 3; threats to press freedom in, 6; Ukraine, 202. *See also* Belarus; Chechnya; Russia; Tajikistan
France: Agence France-Presse, 79, 156; influence of, 215; *Le Monde*, 115, 205
Freedom Forum, 183–84, 194, 198, 207–8
Freedom House, 2, 3, 4, 5, 147, 168
freedom of the press. *See* press freedom
free-market economy, 3, 213, 214
Free Press (Ghanaian periodical), 73
Fujimori, Alberto, 220

Gabon, 115–16
Gannett Company, 207
Gao Yu, 54–58; arrests of, 55, 56; imprisonment of, 56; as independent journalist, 4; international support for, 57; photograph of, *54*; release from prison, 58, 214; on sacrificing herself, vii, 62; *Spring*, screenplay of, 54; UNESCO press freedom award for, 57, 72, 208, 209
Gaps, John, III, 102
Gardoon (Iranian magazine), 139
Garzon, Jaime, 126
Gatabaki, Njehu, 148
Gazprom (Russia), 32
Ghana, 73
Ghanaian Chronicle (Ghanaian periodical), 73

Gheishan, Yousef, 154–55
Ghezali, Salima, 90–94, 204
Gidada, Negasso, 119
Giwa, Dele, 48
glasnost, 31, 32
Glasnost Defense Foundation, 95, 206
Goh Chok Tong, 110
Gokongwei, John, 149
Goldsmith, Michael, 135–37
Golembiovsky, Igor, 32
Golos Armenii (Armenian newspaper), 149
González, Jaime, 164
Goodale, James, 201
Gorbachev, Mikhail, 31, 32, 34
Gordon, Joshua, 193
Gore, Al, 170
Gorriti, Gustavo, 148
Grachev, Pavel, 65, 66, 68
Graham, Katharine, 198
Great Britain. *See* Britain
Guardian (Nigerian newspaper), 48, 50
Guatemala, 72
Guerin, Veronica, 58–61; attacks on, 58, 60; International Press Freedom Award for, 60; and Irish libel laws, 145–46; killing of, 3, 60–61; photograph of, *59*
Gulf War, 34

Haiti: Dominique killing, 140; Feldstein driven out by police, 153–54; journalists attacked during protests in, 99
Harmoko, 75
Harrigan, Steve, 81
Haydarsho, Khushvakht, 96
Hen Vipheak, 125
Hermianchuk, Ihar, 177
Herzog, Werner, 137
Hildebrandt, César, 155–56
HKJA (Hong Kong Journalists Association), 42, 120, 203
Holbrooke, Richard C., 198
Honduras, 139–40
Hong Kong, 220–23; and China Wide Web, 187; Chinese economic pressure on Lai Chee-ying, 149–50; Chinese government tolerating press freedom in, 221–22; Feign's satire of China, 120–21; *Ming Pao*, 42, 105, 106–7; *Mirror Monthly*, 55–56; *Next Magazine*, 149; *Overseas China Daily*, 56; police raid

newspaper office in, 210; press freedom in, 3, 4, 39, 41–43; self-censorship in, 192; *South China Morning Post*, 43, 120, 121; Taiwan election of 2000 covered in, 221; *The World of Lily Wong* comic strip, 120–21, *121*, 221; and Xi Yang case, 105, 107, 108; *Yazhou Zhoukan*, 36, 37, 43, 184
Hong Kong Journalists Association (HKJA), 42, 120, 203
Horizons (Algerian newspaper), 92
Horn (Nigerian newspaper), 140
human nature, as militating in favor of press freedom, 216–18
Human Rights Watch, 197, 208
Hungary, 3
Hussein, Saddam, 54

Ibru, Alex, 48
IFEX (International Freedom of Expression Exchange), 206–7
Iliescu, Ion, 131
Ilyushenko, Alexei, 130–31
imprisonment of journalists: of Anyanwu, 47; of Chaladze, 144; in China, 4, 82, 141; as decreasing, 220; of Doan Viet Hoat, 110–12; in Ethiopia, 141; of Gao Yu, 56; of Karimzadeh, 124–25; of Kuttab, 178, 180; of Lin Hai, 188–89, 191; in Nigeria, 48; from 1982 through 1999, 2, 218; of Omurzakov, 142–43; of Paez Nuñez, 147; of Taufik, 75; in Turkey, 82, 141, 198, 199; worst countries for, 141; of Xi Yang, 107–8; of Yurtçu, 85–86
Independen (Indonesian magazine), 74, 75
Independence Morning Post (Taiwanese newspaper), 144
independent journalists. *See* journalists
Independent Reporters and Editors (IRE), 62
Index on Censorship, 207
India: Kashmiri separatist uprising, 78–81, 88; Pakistani Web site blocked by, 183; press freedom in, 3, 80, 211; press freedom suspended with separatist uprisings, 77; as sixth most dangerous country for reporters, 81
Indonesia: Alliance of Independent Journalists, 74, 75, 206; *D&R*, 76; demonstrations bringing down government of,

104; fires of 1997, 119; *Independen*, 74, 75; journalists attacked for corruption stories in, 73–76; lack of press freedom and economic crisis in, 213–14; liberalization in, 36, 211; partly free press in, 5; separatist uprising in East Timor, 77; strong press while other democratic institutions are weak, 5; *Suara Independen*, 75; Suharto, 73, 74, 75, 76, 119, 131, 214; *Tempo*, 73–74

Indonesian Journalists' Association (PWI), 74, 131

Institutional Revolutionary Party (PRI) (Mexico), 21–22, 24

insult laws, 143, 147

International Freedom of Expression Exchange (IFEX), 206–7

International PEN, 207

International Press Freedom Award: for Blancornelas, 15; for Chan, *41*; for Guerin, 60; for Masyuk, 35; presentation of, 197, 200; for Taufik, 76; for Yurtçu, 1, 87

International Press Institute, 86

International Women's Media Foundation, 47, 98

Internet, 167–85; AMIN Web site, 178, 180, 212; and censorship, 167, 168, 183–84; Chan's use of, 1, 39, 184–85, 212; and China, 185, 186–94, 217; Digital Freedom Network, 94, 181, 207; E-Mail, 39, 188, 189, 197; Ghezali using, 94; growth of, 167; IFEX's Web site, 206–7; Indonesian journalists using, 75; journalists using, 8; radio broadcast over, 168–76; Reporters Sans Frontières tracking attempts to restrict, 205; Reporters Sans Frontières' Web site, 205–6; uncensored news on, 212

Internet Café (Shanghai), 192–93

Iran: Article 19 campaign against Rushdie death threat, 207; Karimzadeh case, 124–25; lashing of journalists in, 139; political change in, 211–12, 223; press freedom lacking in, 4

Iraq: Bazoft case, 53–54; Internet access lacking in, 167; press freedom lacking in, 4

IRE (Independent Reporters and Editors), 62

Ireland: Guerin killing, 58–61; libel laws in, 145–47; Official Secrets Act, 146

Islamic fundamentalism, 90–91, 218

Israel: journalists attacked during protests in, 101–2, *103*; Kuttab's Web site in, 177–80; press freedom in, 3

Ivancic, Viktor, 126–30, 201

Ivanov, Valery, 138

Ivcher, Baruch, 148

Ivory Coast, Neruda's satires in, 121–24

Jameel, Yusuf, 78–80

James, Kenneth, 109, 110

Japan: influence of trade with, 213, 214; press freedom in, 3, 58

Jennings, Peter, 197

Jiang Zemin, 4, 188

Johnstone, Helen, 193

Jordan: *Al-Arab al-Youm*, 154; *Al-Bilad*, *103*; Gheishan case, 154–55; insult laws in, 147; journalists attacked during protests in, 102–3

journalists: behavior of, 8, 11–62; bonding with ordinary people, 215–16; choice of backing down or standing up to attacks, 153–66; demonstrations by, *103*; economic pressures on, 148–50; in free countries, 58; guerrilla journalists in Nigeria, 51; Internet used by, 8, 167–85; legal pressures on, 142–48; in newly opened societies, 21; outlook for, 210–23; print rather than broadcast reporters as independent, 33; refusing to be censored, 1–2; in repressive countries, 53–58; responses to attacks on, 7–8, 151–209; types of attacks on, 5–6, 133–50; types of stories that trigger attacks on, 6, 63–132; watchdog role of, 215. *See also* advocacy groups for journalists; imprisonment of journalists; violence against journalists

Kabondo, Clementine Mutshingi, 114

Kanguku (Rwandan newspaper), 97

Karimzadeh, Manouchehr, 124–25

Kashmir: journalists attacked in, 3, 78–81; journalists demonstrating in, *103*; Pakistani Web site giving information on, 183; self-censorship in, 156

Kazakhstan, 156–57

Kelmendi, Aferdita, 174–76
Kemal, Yasar, 85, 87
Kenya, 148
Khabeisa, Abdel Rahman, 101
Khadzhiev, Ramzan, 81
Khamenei, Ayatollah Ali, 139
Kholodov, Dmitri, 32, 65–68
killing of journalists: of Alempour, 94–96; of Bancayrin, 140; Bazoft execution, 53–54; of Berg, 62; Blancornelas attempt, 13, 16–20; of Bolles, 62; of Buendía, 16–17, 69; of Cabezas, 203, 216; of Cano Isaza, 70–72; of Chaikova, 31; during civil wars, 89–98; Committee to Protect Journalists' statistics on, 201, 220; of Diaz, 141; of Dominique, 140; since 1812, 2; of Félix Miranda, 14–15; of Flores González, 161–65; of Garzon, 126; of Guerin, 3, 60–61; homicide as leading cause of job-related death, 218; IFEX statistics on, 207; of Kholodov, 65–68; of Lopez de la Calle, 81; in Mexico, 15; most dangerous countries in the world, 81; in Nigeria, 48; from 1982 through 1999, 2; in Russia, 31–32, 67, 68; in Tajikistan, 95, 204; as varying by region, 138
Kin-ming Liu, 42
KMT (Koumintang) (Taiwan), 36, 38, 39, 185
Knight, Alan, 43, 192, 222
Knight Foundation, 198
Komsomolskaya Pravda (Russian newspaper), 32
Koppel, Ted, 197
Korzhakov, Alexander, 130
Kosovo, 170, 172, 174–76
Kostic, Rastko, 99
Koumintang (KMT) (Taiwan), 36, 38, 39, 185
Kukly (Russian television show), 130–31
Kulikov, Anatoly, 67
Kurds, 6, 77–88, 156
Kuttab, Daoud, 177–80, 179
Kuwait, 126
Kyrgyzstan, 142–43

La Chronique du Soir (Ivory Coast newspaper), 122
La Griffe (Gabonese newspaper), 115–16
Lai Chee-ying, Jimmy, 149–50

L'Alternative (Ivory Coast newspaper), 124
La Nation (Algerian newspaper), 91, 92, 93
La Prensa (Mexican newspaper), 161, 164
lashing, 139
La Tercera (Chilean newspaper), 180
Latin America: beatings of journalists in, 139–40; Brazil, 5; Chile, 125, 180–81; democracy in, 211; Guatemala, 72; Honduras, 139–40; Panama, 145, 148; Paraguay, 72–73; threats to press freedom in, 6; Uruguay, 116–17, 210; violence against journalists in, 138. See also Argentina; Colombia; Cuba; Mexico; Peru
Latvia, 144
La Voie (Ivory Coast newspaper), 122, 123
lawsuits: as threat to journalists, 6, 38. See also criminal libel
Lebanon, 125
Le Bucheron (Gabonese newspaper), 115–16
Le Calame (Mauritanian newspaper), 118
Lee Chu-ming, Martin, 107–8
Lee Wei-shin, 40
legal pressures on journalists, 142–48; insult laws, 143, 147; sedition laws, 148. See also lawsuits
Le Matin (Algerian newspaper), 92
Le Messager (Cameroon newspaper), 117
Le Monde (French newspaper), 115, 205
Le Palmares (Zairean newspaper), 118
Le Soir d'Algérie (Algerian newspaper), 89
Let's Survive until Monday (Kazakhstan newspaper), 157
Levin, Alexander, 131
libel. See criminal libel
Libya: Al-Darrat case, 141; Internet access lacking in, 167; press freedom lacking in, 4
Li Hongkuan, 189–91, 194
Linares, Luis, 143
Lin Hai, 188–89, 191
Li Peng, 149
Liu Binyan, 158–61, 166
Liu, Kin-ming, 42
Liu Tai-ying, 37, 38, 39, 40
Li Yuet-wah, Daisy, 57
Lone, Ghulam Mohammad, 80
Lopez de la Calle, Jose Luis, 81
Lovejoy, Elijah, 21

Low Hop Bing, 148
Lukashenko, Aleksander, 177
LUKoil (Russia), 32
Lu Ping, 42
Luya, Michel, 117–18

Machuca, Abner, 201
Makabenta, Leah, 118
Malaolu, Niran, 48
Malashenko, Igor, 32, 131
Malaysia: on CPJ list of worst violators of press freedom, 202; law used to punish journalists in, 148; Makabenta's exposé of labor conditions in, 118
Manila Times (Philippine newspaper), 149
Mao Tse-tung, 158, 159, 160
Marcela, Marin, 130
Marcus, Aliza, 84–85, 195–96
Maroufi, Abbas, 139
Martinez, Jesus, 182
Marton, Kati, 198
Masyuk, Yelena, 26–35; criminal investigation of, 28; held hostage in Chechnya, 26–27; International Press Freedom Award for, 35; journalistic career of, 34; on official version of Chechen war, 30; pulled out of Chechnya, 35; reporting from Chechnya, 27, 33; right-wing papers sued by, 7; Russian establishment seeing her as an enemy, 29; as taking chances, 33; Teffi Award for, 34
Matic, Veran, 171, 172, 173
Mauritania, 118
May, Greg, 187
Mayor, Federico, 208
McCormick Tribune Foundation, 198
McCurry, Mike, 204
Medellín cocaine cartel, 71
Media-MOST (Russian media company), 219
Mekbel, Saïd, 92–93
Menem, Carlos Saúl, 8
Menon, Kavita, 5, 21, 49
Mexico: ABC, 23; American model as influence on, 215; American pressure resented in, 202; beatings of journalists in, 139; Blancornelas challenging druglords in, 13–25; Buendía killing, 15–16, 69–70; conference on self-defense for journalists, 16; corruption in

justice system, 20–21; criminal libel lawsuits in, 143–44; drug culture eroding institutions of, 16; Excelsior, 69; Flores González killing, 161–65; journalists bribed by government, 23, 149; journalists forming associations in, 7; journalists killed in, 15; La Prensa, 161, 164; PAN, 24, 161; partly free press in, 5; political and social change in, 21–22, 211, 223; potential for free press not fully realized in, 218, 220; press liberation in, 22; PRI, 21–22, 24; Reforma, 139; as second deadliest country for reporters in Latin America, 15–16; self-censorship in, 156, 161; separatist uprising in Chiapas, 77; Sociedad de Periodistas, 202–3; strong press while other democratic institutions are weak, 21; threats to press freedom in, 6; Zeta, 14, 17–20, 18, 19, 23–24, 220
Mickiewicz, Ellen, 30
Middle East: imprisonment of journalists in, 141; Internet use in, 167; Kuwait, 126; lashing of journalists in, 139; Lebanon, 125; self-censorship in, 155; Syria, 4, 167. See also Egypt; Iran; Iraq; Israel; Jordan; Palestinian Authority; Saudi Arabia; Turkey
Middleton, Mark E., 37, 40
Milosevic, Slobodan, 168–74, 198
Ming Pao (Hong Kong newspaper), 42, 105, 106–7
Mirror Monthly (Hong Kong magazine), 55–56
M'membe, Fred, 114–15
Mobutu Sese Seko, 117–18
Moeller, Susan D., 100
Monetary Authority of Singapore (MAS), 109, 112
money, exposés about, 116
Monroy, Jorge Luis, 139–40
Moriarty, Francis, 222
Morozov, Vladimir, 68
Morton, David, 96
Moscow Union of Journalists, 34
Mubarak, Hosni, 144
Mukmusoni, Jeanne d'Arc, 97
Muladjanov, Shod, 67
murders of journalists. See killing of journalists

Mwape, Bright, 183
Mwila, Stewart, 73
Myanmar (Burma), 4, 141

Nacional (Croatian newspaper), 117
Nation (U.S. weekly), 215
National Action Party (PAN) (Mexico), 24, 161
NBC, 153–54
Neel Sagar (Bangladeshi weekly), 99
Neeson, Eoin, 61
Nelson, Anne, 138, 197
Neruda, Freedom (Tieti Roch d'Assomption), 1, 122–24
Nesin, Aziz, 165–66
Netherlands, the: influence of, 215; Yugoslav Internet broadcasts aided by, 169, 175, 176
Neumann, A. Lin, 42, 43, 222
New Breed (Sierra Leone newspaper), 116
New China News Agency, 187
News (Nigerian magazine), 48, 50, 140, 149, 177
Newseum (interactive museum), 208
New York Times, 143–44, 193
New Zealand, 3
Next Magazine (Hong Kong magazine), 149
Niazi, Zamir, 166
Nigeria: Adams arrested in, 104; African Concord, 50; Ajibade case, 51, 216; AM News, 51; Anyanwu case, 44–47, 199; Babangida, 45, 50, 51; broadcast media controlled by government in, 49; counterfeit periodicals distributed by government, 149; Guardian, 48, 50; guerrilla journalism in, 51; Horn, 140; IFEX alerts for, 207; journalists appealing to IFEX, 206; journalists beaten in, 140; journalists' computers destroyed by police, 8; journalists imprisoned in, 48; journalists killed in, 48; News, 48, 50, 140, 149, 177; Olorunyomi case, 48, 49, 52, 200–201; partly free press in, 5, 44–52; PM News, 51; political change in, 211; state terrorism against journalists in, 166; strong press while other democratic institutions are weak, 5, 21; Sunday Magazine, 44, 45, 47, 149; Tell, 48, 49, 149, 166; Tempo, 48, 51, 149; tradition of inde-

pendent reporting in, 45, 49–50. See also Abacha, Sani
Nikulin, Viktor, 96
Nixon, Richard, 38
Njawe, Pius, 117
Nolan, Webster, 194
North Africa: Tunisia, 183, 202. See also Algeria; Libya
North America: Canada, 3, 58; Internet use in, 167. See also United States
North Korea: longtime dictatorship in, 218; press freedom lacking in, 4, 217
Noureddin, Fayez, 119
Nshimiryo, Eudès, 97
NTV (Russian television network), 26, 27, 28–29, 32, 130–31, 219

Obi, Comfort, 45, 47
Observer (British newspaper), 53
Official Secrets Act (Ireland), 146
Ojudu, Babafemi, 50–52, 177
Oladepo, Tunde, 48
Olorunyomi, Dapo, 48, 49, 52, 200–201
Olshanskaya, Julia, 138–39
Omurzakov, Yryspek, 142–43
Open Society Institute, 198
Organization for Security and Cooperation in Europe, 204
Organization of American States, 204
Orinya, Sunday, 140
Orme, William, Jr.: on Abacha regime in Nigeria, 48–49; on Argentine protest of Cabezas murder, 216; on Chan's story, 41; on corruption as cause of attacks, 70; on CPJ riding the political currents, 199; on Cronkite in Marcus case, 196; on homicide as cause of journalists' deaths, 218; on Hong Kong as most important press freedom story, 221; on increase in attacks on journalists, 7; on a journalist killed nearly every week, 2; on journalists during civil wars, 90; on journalists killed during Rwandan civil war, 96–97; on Kurdish uprising in Turkey, 88; on Mexican government paying journalists, 22; on murder of journalists in Asia, 138; and Yurtçu case, 86
Ortiz Franco, Francisco, 20, 22, 24, 156, 161
Osuna Jaime, Héctor, 24
Ovechkin, Valentin, 159

Overseas China Daily (Hong Kong newspaper), 56
Oxford University Center for Socio-Legal Studies, 8–9, 209
Özgür Gündem (Turkish newspaper), 83
Özgür Ülke (Turkish newspaper), 84–85

Paez Nuñez, Lorenzo, 147
Pakistan: *Dawn* Web site blocked by India, 183; exposé of labor conditions in, 119; journalists demonstrating in, 103; and Kashmiri separatist uprising, 78, 88; Niazi on press freedom in, 166; partly free press in, 5; strong press while other democratic institutions are weak, 5, 21
Palestinian Authority: journalists attacked during protests in, 101; Kuttab's Web site criticizing, 178, 180; Noureddin beating, 119
PAN (National Action Party) (Mexico), 24, 161
Panama, 145
Paneco, Vinicio, 72
Pantic, Drazen, 169
Paraguay, 72–73
Parekh, Vikram, 80
People's Literature (Chinese periodical), 160
perestroika, 34
Pérez Balladares, Ernesto, 145
Peru: on CPJ list of worst violators of press freedom, 202; druglords attacking journalists in, 72; IFEX alerts for, 207; journalist's citizenship revoked in, 148; potential for free press not fully realized in, 220; self-censorship in, 155–56; *Sí*, 72; strong press while other democratic institutions are weak, 5, 21; *Without Censorship* television show, 155
Philippines: Bancayrin killing, 140; economic pressures on publishers in, 149; press freedom in, 3
Phiri, Masautso, 114
photographers, attacked during protests, 100
Pinochet, Augusto, 125
PKK (Kurdistan Workers' Party), 83, 85
PM News (Nigerian newspaper), 51
Poland: journalists attacked during protests in, 100–101; press freedom in, 3
political change, 211–12

Popovskikh, Pavel, 68
Post (Zambian newspaper), 113–14, 182–83
Powell, Adam, 183–84
press freedom: battleground countries, *xii*, 4–5; countries falling into three groups regarding, *xii–xiii*, 3–5, 217–18; countries lacking, *xiii*, 3–4; countries with, *xii*, 3; CPJ annual list of ten worst violators of, 202; factors militating against, 218–20; and free-market economy, 3, 213, 214; human nature as militating in favor of, 216–18; IFEX archive on violations of, 207; as increasing in the world, 2–3; independent journalists fighting for, 1–2, 21; outlook for, 210–23; Reporters Sans Frontières' barometer of, 205; as safeguard against instability, 214; threats to, 5–6; UNESCO/ Guillermo Cano World Press Freedom Prize, 57, 72, 208, 209; World Press Freedom Day, 208, 209. *See also* censorship; International Press Freedom Award
Press Freedom Survey 2000, 2, 3–4
PRI (Institutional Revolutionary Party) (Mexico), 21–22, 24
Prigione, Geronimo, 16
Progressive Networks, 169
protests, journalists attacked during, 99–105
Pukanic, Ivo, 117
Punto Final (Chilean weekly), 125
Putin, Vladimir, 219
PWI (Indonesian Journalists' Association), 74, 131

Qi Yanchen, 191
Quamruzzaman, Mohammad, 99

radio, Internet broadcasting of, 168–76
Radio Free Asia, 217
Radio Free Europe/Radio Liberty, 169, 177, 219
Radio Netherlands, 175, 176
Radio Sonora (Guatemalan radio station), 72
Radio 21 (Yugoslav radio station), 174–76
Rakhmonaliev, Daviatali, 96
Rakhmonov, Emomali, 95
Randal, Jonathan C., 137
Rather, Dan, 197, 198

Rawlings, Jerry, 73
RealAudio, 169
Reforma (Mexican newspaper), 139
Reporters Sans Frontières (Reporters Without Borders; RSF), 204–6; Anyanwu given award by, 47; barometer of press freedom of, 205; on beating of journalists in Nigeria, 48; Dazibao section of Web site of, 94, 205; Digital Freedom Network posting information from, 207; Ghezali contributing to Web site of, 94; as press-advocacy group, 7; Radio 21 in Yugoslavia aided by, 176; Web site of, 205–6; in Yurtçu case, 86
Res Publika (Kyrgyzstan weekly), 142, 143
Reuter News Agency, 79, 84, 187, 193, 195, 214
Reyes, Herasto, 145
riots, journalists attacked during, 99–105
Riva Palacio, Raymundo, 20–21, 23
Rohde, David, 198
Romania, 131
Ross, John, 16
RSF. *See* Reporters Sans Frontières (Reporters Without Borders)
Rudnev, Viatcheslav, 68
Ruffo Appel, Ernesto, 24, 161
Rugman, Jonathan, 95
Rukondo, Emmanuel-Damien, 97
Rushdie, Salman, 165, 207
Russia: Babitsky case, 219; censorship struggle in, 31–33; Chechen war coverage restricted by, 29, 210, 217; criminal gangs in, 67; Glasnost Defense Foundation, 95, 206; journalists killed in, 31–32, 67, 68; journalists killed in Chechen uprising, 81; Kholodov killing, 65–68; and killing of journalists in Tajikistan, 95; *Komsomolskaya Pravda*, 32; *Kukly* television show, 130–31; Masyuk's coverage of Chechen war, 26–35; NTV, 26, 27, 28–29, 32, 130–31, 219; partly free press in, 5; political change in, 211, 223; potential for free press not fully realized in, 218–19; Putin, 219; satires of leaders, 130–31; as third most dangerous country for reporters, 81; "Vzglyad" television show, 34; Yeltsin, 28, 32, 35, 67, 130, 131; *Zavtra*, 28; Zhirinovsky's attack on television crew, 138–39

Rwabukwizi, Vincent, 96, 97
Rwanda, journalists killed during civil war in, 96–98
Rwandan Patriotic Front, 97

Safire, William, 214
Saihi, Horria, 98
Sakharov Prize, 93
Salah, Zineddine Aliou, 89
Salinas Pliego, Ricardo, 143
Salisbury, Harrison, 34
samizdat, 217
Samoa, 144–45
Samoa Observer (Samoan periodical), 145
Satanic Verses, The (Rushdie), 165
satire, journalists attacked for, 120–32
Saudi Arabia: longtime dictatorship in, 218; press freedom lacking in, 4; self-censorship in, 155
SBS radio (Australia), 175
Schizophrenia (film), 68
sedition laws, 148
self-censorship, 155–57, 161, 192
Senegal, 211
separatist movements. *See* ethnic separatist movements
Serbia. *See* Yugoslavia
sex, exposés about, 113–16
Sfeir, Nasrallah Boutros, 125
Shanmugaratnam, Tharman, 109–10
Sheikh, Ghulam Rasool, 80
Shenderovich, Viktor, 131, 132
Shieh Chung-liang, 37, 38, 39, 40, *41*
Shiner, Cindy, 49
Shumack, Andrew, 31
Sí (Peruvian newsweekly), 72
Sierra Leone: continuing warfare in, 218; Deen case, 201; journalists attacked during civil war in, 89–90; Strasser accused of becoming rich, 116; Strasser accused of smoking pot, 119
Simon, Joel, 22
Simpson, Alan, 34
Singapore: *Business Times*, 109–10; criminal libel laws in, 39, 157; Internet flooded with government propaganda in, 183; press freedom lacking in, 3, 4, 39, 213, 214; Shanmugaratnam case, 109–10, 112; threats to press freedom in, 6

Slobodna Dalmacij (Croatian newspaper), 126–27
Slovakia, 3
Smalto, Francesco, 115, 116
soccer, in satire, 124–25
Sociedad de Periodistas (Mexico), 202–3
Solidarity movement, 100
Soltis, Yuri, 68
Soros, George, 198
Soros Foundation, 170, 175
Soskovets, Oleg, 29
South Africa, 3, 211
South China Morning Post (Hong Kong newspaper), 43, 120, *121*
South Korea: economic problems of, 214; liberalization in, 36; press freedom in, 3
Soviet Union: Gorbachev, 31, 32, 34; *samizdat*, 217. *See also* former Soviet Union
Soyinka, Wole, 47
Spain, Lopez de la Calle killing in, 81
Spiegel, Mickey, 208–9
Spring (film), 54
Stahl, Lesley, 60
Strasser, Valentine, 116, 119
Suara Independen (Indonesian magazine), 75
Sudan, 119
Suharto, 73, 74, 75, 76, 119, 131, 214
Sunday Independent (Irish newspaper), 58, 145
Sunday Magazine (Nigerian magazine), 44, 45, 47, 149
Surbakti, Ramlan, 73
Svaboda (Belarussian newspaper), 177
Syria, 4, 167

Taiwan: Chan libel trial, 36–43; criminal libel lawsuits in, 144; Democratic Progressive Party, 38; election of 2000 covered in Hong Kong, 221; *Independence Morning Post*, 144; international status of, 38; Koumintang, 36, 38, 39, 185; liberalization in, 36, 38; press freedom in, 3, 41; threats to press freedom in, 6
Tajikistan: Alempour murder, 94–96; editor terrorized for criticizing government policies, 112; as fourth most dangerous place for journalists, 81, 95; journalists murdered in, 95, 204
Taliban, 218
Taufik, Ahmad, 73–76

Teffi Award, 34
Tegen, Tesfaye, 124
television: governments often controlling, 33; Nigerian government control of, 49; NTV in Russia, 26, 27, 28–29, 32, 130–31, 219
Tell (Nigerian magazine), 48, 49, 149, 166
Tempo (Indonesian newsmagazine), 73–74
Tempo (Nigerian magazine), 48, 51, 149
Terlitsky, Eduard, 104
Thailand, 3
Thompson, Lea, 153
Tiananmen Square protests, 42, 55, 158, 161, 191
Tian Ye, 107, 108
Tonga, 148
Trizno, Oleg, 104
Tudjman, Franjo, 117, 126–30, *129*, 201
Tully, Mark, 88
Tung Chee-hwa, 43
Tunisia, 183, 202
Tunnel (electronic newsletter), 191, 194
Turkey: Article 312 prosecutions in, 85, 195; censorship laws in, 87, 88; Committee to Protect Journalists' efforts in, 198–99; Erkanli satire case, 125–26; IFEX alerts for, 207; journalists imprisoned in, 82, 141, 198, 199; Kurdish separatism in, 77, 82–88; Marcus case, 84–85, 195–96; Nesin publishing *Satanic Verses*, 165–66; *Özgür Gündem*, 83; *Özgür Ülke*, 84–85; relaxing press controls to gain favorable trade, 214; self-censorship in, 156; types of stories that trigger attacks on journalists in, 6; Yurtçu case, 82–88

Ukraine, 202
UNESCO/Guillermo Cano World Press Freedom Prize, 57, 72, 208, 209
Uneximbank (Russia), 32
Unicom Sparkice, 193
United Nations: as source of support for journalists, 208–9; UNESCO/Guillermo Cano World Press Freedom Prize, 57, 72, 208, 209
United States: Berg killing, 62; Bolles killing, 62; influence of, 215; press freedom in, 3, 58, 215, 217; Radio Free Asia, 217; Radio Free Europe/Radio Liberty, 169, 177, 219; war coverage restricted in,

United States *(continued)*
6; Yugoslav Internet broadcasts aided by, 169, 175, 176
Universal Declaration of Human Rights, 207
Uruguay, 116–17, 210

Valdes, Nelson, 182
Valenzuela, Cecilia, 155
Valero Elizaldi, Luis Lauro, 13, 17, 25
Viera Gonzalez, Mario, 181
Vietnam: Doan Viet Hoat case, 110–12; press freedom lacking in, 4
Vietnam War, 6, 34
violence against journalists, 135–41; beatings, 139–40; lashing, 139; as varying by region, 138. *See also* killing of journalists
VIP Reference (electronic newsletter), 188, 189–91, 194
Voirel, Lorescu, 99
"Vzglyad" (Russian television show), 34

Wang Juntao, 57
war coverage: attacks on journalists over, 6; censorship of, 6, 223; during civil wars, 89–98; Gulf War, 34; Masyuk's coverage of Chechen war, 26–35; Russia restricting coverage of Chechen war, 29, 210, 217; in separatist uprisings, 77–88; Vietnam War, 6, 34
Wasmosy, Juan Carlos, 116
Web, the. *See* Internet
Wei Jingsheng, 43
Wessat, Atta, 101–2
West, the: Canada, 3, 58; influence of, 215; influence of trade with, 213, 214. *See also* United States; Western Europe
Western Europe: press freedom in, 3, 58; Spain, 81. *See also* Britain; France; Ireland; Netherlands, the
Windhoek Declaration, 209
Without Censorship (Peruvian television show), 155
Wolosky, Lee, 219
World Association of Newspapers (WAN), 57, 201
World of Lily Wong, The (comic strip), 120–21, *121*, 221
World Press Freedom Day, 208, 209
world trade, 212–15

World Wide Web. *See* Internet
Wu Jichuan, 188

Xi Yang, 105–8, *106*
Xu Simin, 55

Yau, L. P., 43
Yazhou Zhoukan (Hong Kong newsmagazine), 36, 37, 43, 184
Yeltsin, Boris, 28, 32, 35, 67, 130, 131
Yemen: insult laws in, 147; lashing of journalists in, 139; reporter standing up to government in, 166
Yilmaz, Mesut, 87
Yugoslavia: B92 radio station, 168–74, 176; on CPJ list of worst violators of press freedom, 202; ethnic cleansing in, 174; ethnic separatist movements in former, 77; IFEX alerts for, 207; journalists attacked during protests in, 99; Kosovo, 170, 172, 174–76; NATO bombing of, 172, 175; Radio 21 radio station, 174–76; Rohde case, 198. *See also* Croatia
Yurtçu, Ocak Isik, 82–88; charges against, 85; Committee to Protect Journalists supporting, 86, 199, 200; as dissident journalist, 83; imprisonment of, 85–86; international campaign for, 86–87; International Press Freedom Award for, 1, 87; *Özgür Gündem* founded by, 83; photograph behind bars, *xiv*, 1; presidential pardon refused by, 86; released from prison, 87; self-censorship of, 156

Zaire, 117–18
Zambia: Chiluba accused of having a mistress, 113–15; Chilubas accused of drug trafficking, 73; *Post,* 113–14, 182–83
Zavtra (Russian newspaper), 28
Zedillo Ponce de León, Ernesto, 20
Zeng, Edward, 193
Zenger, John Peter, 21
Zepada, Jorge, 22, 203
Zeta (Mexican newspaper), 14, 17–20, *18,* *19,* 23–24, 220
Zhirinovsky, Vladimir, 138–39
Zhu Rongji, 57, 107
Ziater, Djamel, 89
Zorrilla Pérez, José Antonio, 69–70
Zouabri, Antar, 90

About the Author

ANTHONY COLLINGS served for more than thirty years as a national and foreign correspondent. He reported for the *Wall Street Journal* in New York, served as Associated Press correspondent in Moscow, London, and Bonn, and was *Newsweek* bureau chief in Bonn and London. In 1981 he joined CNN as Rome bureau chief and roving correspondent, covering such stories as the assassination of Egyptian President Anwar Sadat, martial law in Poland, and armed clashes in Lebanon. While in Lebanon he and a CNN crew were captured and held at gunpoint by Syrian and Palestinian forces. Collings also has been detained by police in Rome, Athens, and Damascus while covering the news.

In 1986 he became a national affairs correspondent for CNN in Washington. He shared a National Headliner Award with CNN colleagues for coverage of the Iran-Contra affair in 1987, and was among a team of CNN reporters honored with an Emmy award for coverage of the Oklahoma City bombing in 1995. He joined the faculty of the Department of Communication Studies at the University of Michigan in 1997 as the Howard R. Marsh Visiting Professor in Journalism, and he is currently a lecturer in Communication Studies at the university. His Web site about this book is at www.umich.edu/~collings.